MICROFINANCE REVOLUTION IN INDIA

Success and Sustainability

MICROFINANCE REVOLUTION IN INDIA

Success and Sustainability

J. U. Ahmed
D. Bhagat
G. Singaiah

New Central Book Agency (P) Ltd
LONDON
HYDERABAD ERNAKULAM BHUBANESWAR
DELHI KOLKATA PUNE

REGD OFFICE
8/1 Chintamoni Das Lane, Kolkata 700 009, India
email: ncbapvtltd@eth.net

OVERSEAS
NCBA (UK) Ltd, 149 Park Avenue North, Northampton, NN3 2HY, UK

EXPORT
NCBA Exports Pvt. Ltd, 212 Shahpur Jat, New Delhi 110 049
email: ncbaexp@ncbapvtltd.com

BRANCHES

208B Peacock Lane, Shahpur Jat
New Delhi 110 049
email: ncbadel@ncbapvtltd.com

House No. 3-1-315, 1st Floor
Nimboliadda, Kachiguda, **Hyderabad** 500 027
email: ncbahydb@ncbapvtltd.com

Shop Nos. 3 & 4, Vinayak Towers
681/B Budhwar Peth, Appa Balwant Chowk
Pune 411 002
email: ncbapune@ncbapvtltd.com

GSS Shopping Complex, 1st Floor
Opposite College Post Office, Convent Road
Ernakulam 682 035
email: ncbaernk@ncbapvtltd.com

Shop No. 15, Bharati Towers, Ground Floor
Forest Park, **Bhubaneswar** 751 001
email: ncbabub@ncbapvtltd.com

MICROFINANCE REVOLUTION IN INDIA

First Published: July 2011

PUBLISHER AND TYPESETTER
New Central Book Agency (P) Ltd
8/1 Chintamoni Das Lane, Kolkata 700 009

PRINTER
New Central Book Agency (P) Ltd
Web-Offset Division, Dhulagarh, Sankrail, Howrah

COVER DESIGNER
Soumen Paul

COVER PRINTER
Biswanath Studio, Kolkata

PROOF CHECKING
Subas Maitra

PROJECT TEAM
Sarab Chatterjee, Swapan Sarkar and Prabhat Jas

ISBN: 978-81-7381-671-0

Price: ₹ 495.00

Dedicated

To

ALL THE PEOPLE WHO ARE WORKING DEVOTEDLY
FOR THE SUCCESS OF MICROFINANCE
REVOLUTION IN INDIA

Contents

FOREWORD

Few terms have been discussed and debated so much in recent times world-over as much as microfinance (mF). The reason is not difficult to seek. If inclusive growth has been the major developmental plank, mF has been an effective instrument of financial inclusion and inclusive growth cannot be thought of without financial inclusion. The concept and practice of mF—since its evolution way back in 1976 by its father Professor Muhammad Yunus of Bangladesh Grameen Bank—has by now become a worldwide development phenomenon. Realizing the need for and significance of mF for meeting the financial requirements of tiny- and micro-enterprises in the country, the Government of India has already enacted 'Micro Small and Medium Enterprises (MSMEs) Act 2006 and also set up a separate 'Ministry of Micro Small and Medium Enterprises' to exclusively develop micro-enterprises in the country. The fact remain that both mF and micro-enterprise by now have become buzzwords in development terminology and hardly miss mention in any development forum, debate, and discussion.

mF being the evolutionary and relatively new concept worldover, in general, and in India, in particular, not much research work has so far been done in the subject. No doubt, limited is the development of mF in India, but much more limited is the availability of data on whatever mF exists there. Whatever information is available is scanty and highly scattered in some newspapers and research articles. As such, our knowledge and understanding about mF has so far been far from adequate and satisfactory. Thus, the absence of reliable and required data hampers the formulation of realistic plans and policies in this regard. The present compendium entitled "Microfinance Revolution in India: Success and Sustainability" edited by J. U. Ahmed, D. Bhagat and G. Singaiah, fills this hiatus, to a great extent.

The compendium includes 24 research papers which are very thoughtfully and logically presented under five sections relating to mF. Section I includes five research papers and presents the mF background in the country. mF—both philosophically and practically—is meant for poverty alleviation in rural areas of the country. The four papers under Section II exemplify with empirical evidences how mF helps alleviate poverty stalking the land, especially in rural India. mF generally implies finance for rural development. Therefore, Section III has accordingly been devoted to establish interrelation between mF and rural development. mF being the developmental intervention inevitably involves institutional interface, on the one hand, and its impact assessment on rural development and poverty alleviation in the country, on the other. Five empirical research evidences highlight the same in Section IV. Finally, Section V running into five research papers highlights the role of mF in micro-enterprise development in the country.

I find the present volume very timely addition to our existing knowledge about mF in India.

I sincerely congratulate the editors of this volume, J. U. Ahmed, D. Bhagat and G. Singaiah, for undertaking such a painstaking but academically highly meaningful activity. I am sure the compendium will be found very useful and rewarding by the planners, policymakers, research scholars and the general public having interest in mF.

I enjoyed the compendium with great academic interest and delight. The discernible readers, I am sure, will feel likewise.

S. S. Khanka
15th June 2010
Faridabad, India

Professor and Coordinator
Fellow, Programme in Management
National Institute of Financial Management
Ministry of Finance, Government of India
Sector 48, Pali Road, Faridabad 121 001
(Haryana), India

Contributors

Arup Roy, Assistant Professor, Department of Business Administration, Tezpur University, Assam 784 028, India

B. K. Barooah, Professor and Head, Dept. of Agricultural Economics and F.M., Assam Agricultural University, Jorhat, Assam, India

Baharul Islam Laskar, Associate Professor, Department of Economics, Government Aizawl West College, Aizawl, Mizoram 7900, India

Balin Hazarika, Senior Lecturer, Department of Commerce, Kaliabor College, Nagoan, Assam, India

Bhabananda Deb Nath, Research Scholar, North Eastern Hill University, Shillong, 22, Meghalaya, India

Chandana Goswami, Professor and Head, Department of Business Administration, Tezpur University, Naapam 784 028, Assam, India

D. K. Dey, Senior Lecturer, Department of Economics, Srikrishna College, Bagula, Nadia, W.B, India

Deba Prasad Sharma, Centre for Rural Development (CRD), Guwahati, Assam, India

Deepak Bhagat, Assistant Professor, Dept. of Management, North Eastern Hill University, Tura Campus, Tura, Meghalaya 794 002, India

Dipanwita Deb, Department of Management, North Eastern Hill University, Tura Campus, Meghalaya, India

G. Singaiah, Professor, Department of Management, North Eastern Hill University, Tura Campus, Meghalaya, India

Gino A. Sangma, Research Scholar, Department of Management, North Eastern Hill University, Tura Campus, Meghalaya, India

Jagadish Nath, Department of Marketing, INC, Guwahati, Assam, India

Jaynal U. Ahmed, Associate Professor of Finance, Department of Management, North Eastern Hill University, Tura Campus, Tura 794 002, Meghalaya, India

K. Lalromawia, Research Scholar, School of Management Studies, University of Hyderabad, Hyderabad, India

K. C. Kabra, Associate Professor, Department of Commerce, North Eastern Hill University, Shillong, Meghalaya, India

K. Hriyia Kayina, Research Scholar, Department of Management, North Eastern Hill University, Tura Campus, Meghalaya, India

Komol Singha, Department of Economics, Royal University of Bhutan, GCBS, Gedu, Bhutan

M. Chakraborty, Lecturer, Department of Commerce, Don Bosco College, Tura, West Garo Hills, Meghalaya, India

M. K. Awasthi, Indian Institute of Management, Lucknow 226 013, UP, India

Mohammad Awais, Research Scholar, Department of Agricultural Economics and Business Management, Aligarh Muslim University, Aligarh, India

Mohd. Mohsin Khan, Professor, Department of Commerce, Aligarh Muslim University, Aligarh, UP, India

Mohd. Shamim, Senior Lecturer, Department of Commerce, Aligarh Muslim University, Aligarh, UP, India

Nazimuddin Khadem, Assistant Professor, Department of Economics, N. C. College, Badarpur, Karimganj, Assam, India

Nilotpal Saha, Faculty Member, ICFAI University, Tura Bazar, Tura, Meghalaya, India

Pranay Jyoti Goswami, Associate Professor, Department of Commerce, Assam University, Silchar, Assam, India

Raihan Uddin Ahmed Bora, Department of Management, North Eastern Hill University, Tura Campus, Meghalaya, India

Rais Ahmad, Chairman, Department of Agricultural Economics and Business Management, Aligarh Muslim University, Aligarh, India

S. Rajbongshi, Lecturer, Department of Commerce, Don Bosco College, Tura, West Garo Hills, Meghalaya, India

Sitaram Prasad Sah, West Garo Hills Community Resource Management Society (WGHCRMS), IFAD, Tura, Meghalaya, India

Sujit Sikidar, Professor, Department of Commerce, Gauhati University, Guwahati, Assam, India

EDITORIAL

Conventionally, efforts to deliver formal credit and financial services to the rural poor in developing countries have not been successful. Banks generally do not serve the needs of the rural poor because of the perceived high risk and the high transaction costs associated with small loans and savings deposits. Many governments have tried to deliver formal credit to rural areas by setting up special agricultural banks or directing commercial banks to loan to rural borrowers. However, these programs have almost all failed because of the political difficulty for governments to enforce loan repayment, and because the relatively wealthy and powerful, rather than the poor, received most of the loans.

The recent proliferation of innovative microfinance programs, often based on a group-lending methodology, has been largely inspired by the belief that such programs reach the poor and have a positive impact on various measures of their welfare, including economic measures, social measures, and less tangible measures such as 'empowerment'. The popular press has waved the banner of microfinance as perhaps the most important recent tool to reduce poverty. The 1997 Micro credit Summit called for the mobilization of $20 billion over a 10-year period to support microfinance. Much of this faith in microfinance is based on the highly selective anecdotal evidence of individuals who are reported to have pulled themselves and their families out of poverty with the benefit of micro-credit. Yet, despite the proliferation of these programs and the outpouring of support by donors, there has been precious little sound empirical research that tests the hypotheses that they are reaching and benefiting the poor. To form the basis of such a significant investment to reduce poverty compared to alternative investments in other poverty alleviation programs, the proposition that microfinance reaches the poor and positively affects their welfare should be established and not just understood.

The issues relating to the sustainability of microfinance is a much needed academic exercise—particularly in Indian context—which would help to develop tailor-made models considering cultural diversity of the country.

The papers compiled in this book were presented in a National Seminar on *Microfinance Revolution: Understanding Its Success and Sustainability* held during 19-20th June 2009, organized by the Department of Management, North Eastern Hill University, Tura Campus, Meghalaya. The papers would offer a vital podium for choosing the real pathway for success and sustainability of micro- finance revolution.

A glimpse of these papers are presented below:

Section I deals with ***Issues Relating to Microfinance in India***. In this section, Sikidar in his keynote paper decorated the evolution and working of microfinance in India. The paper highlighted the concepts of microfinance. Microfinance refers to the provision of financial services to low income clients, including consumers and the self employed. Micro-credit should not be confused with microfinance, which addresses a full range of banking needs for poor people. Largely, it refers to a movement that envisages a world in which as many poor and near poor households as possible have permanent access to an appropriate range of high quality financial services, including not just credit but also savings, insurance and fund transfer to those who promote microfinance poor people out of poverty.

Laskar, in an attempt, has made an analytical study in North Eastern Region with special reference to Mizoram. He observed that Mizoram, though it has joined the programme lately, has shown a noticeable progress. There is a need to review the performance of Self Help Groups Bank Linkage programme in the NER, identify factors that retard its progress and take corrective measures to improve its performance throughout the entire region. Success of Microfinance in the region required is a multi-prolonged strategy to overcome the assorted challenges it poses. Banks, policymakers and NGOs must come together to think through suitable modifications in policy.

Microfinance has emerged worldover as an effective tool for poverty alleviation, equitable and inclusive growth, and women empowerment. In this line Ahmad and Awais in a study scrutinized that microfinance does not directly address some structural problems facing Indian society and the economy, and it is not yet as efficient as it will be when economies of scale are realized and a more supportive policy environment is created. However, during last two decades, India has achieved remarkable success. NABARD started this programme in 1992 and presently it is the world's largest programme and about 35 lakh SHGs have linked with the banks and, side by side, MFIs also have achieved good results by disbursing loans to the poor women in urban and rural areas without any collateral.

Barooah gave an account of microfinance situation in Assam. He observed that the state has a network of banks, cooperatives and other financial institutions which are responsible for providing credit support to customers who belong to different sectors of the economy. The state—being predominantly agrarian—depends primarily on agriculture and allied activities. The progress that has taken place during post nationalization fails to bring significant changes to the large scale developmental disparities which prevailed in the economy of the state.

Bora in his treatise painted that banking system in India—although the largest network in the world—did not meet the credit requirements of the poor. It is observed that microfinance is the provision of a broad range of financial services such as deposits, loans, payment services, money transfers and insurance to poor and low income households and their micro-enterprises. The study supported that microfinance is identical to rural finance as practiced in India.

Section II examines ***Microfinance and Poverty Alleviation.*** In this section, Khan and Shamim viewed microfinance is revolutionary in the sense that it aims at servicing the poorest of the poor, who were hitherto considered unfit for anything except charity. Through group lending, many factors contributing to difficulties in extending credit to rural areas were successfully dealt with. The banking industry discovered to its delight that recovery rates for loans were 90 per cent and non-performing assets were very low as compared to the industries.

Realizing the necessity of microfinance for socio-economic transformation, Ahmed attempted to examine microfinance as an instrument for poverty reduction in North-east India. He observed that Microfinance is acclaimed as a gracious alternate for informal credit and a successful instrument for poverty reduction among people who are economically active but financially constrained. The microfinance demonstration in Western and Southern India have received greater attention in academic field. North-east India has not experienced the benefits of its revolution because of insignificant presence of any large micro-finance institution.

Nath and Singha, in a study in the Gedu town of Bhutan, tried to seek some basic factors which determine the choice between joint liabilities or individual liabilities among micro-credit customers. Among others, factors like age, gender, educational qualification, income levels, skill level are some which have been considered in the study. The study confirms that micro-credit is preferred more by womenfolk than the males.

Kayina reviewed the existing literature on microfinance. The paper tried to find out the study gap on this specified area. Based on information gathered from literature, a set of recommendations that could increase MFIs' efficacy is also offered. The reasons for the growth in importance of microfinance have been discussed and how far microfinance has actually helped in reducing poverty. The issues such as high interest rates and group lending practices of microfinance institutions are discussed in his paper.

The ***Role of Microfinance for Rural Empowerment,*** the title of **Section III,** highlighted microfinance and rural transformation. In this section, Dey, in a study on the experience of SGSY, examined that the Swarnajayanti Gram Swarajgar Yajona (SGSY) as a self-employment programme has been implemented in rural areas in order to eradicate poverty. The paper highlighted the relevance of such programme in respect of economically and socially backward areas including empirical evidences from the district of Purulia, West Bengal. It is observed that the success of any micro-credit programme can be evaluated in both quantitative and qualitative ways. The study indicated that even in extremely deprived rural areas women SHGs would have considerable impacts upon the lives of the members.

Saha and Sharma studied on microfinancing in Centre for Rural Development at Guwahati. The paper viewed that microfinance is considered as providing financial services like saving, credit, insurance, money transfer to the so far un-served strata of population—those who earn low income, own a few assets and are constrained in voicing out their interest. However, it may include a wider range of services and it represents something more than microcredit. The Centre for Rural Development, Guwahati—popularly known as "Rickshaw Bank" to the local people—is serving the so called non-bankable population by providing a different type of credit.

The Non Government Organizations (NGOs) in the field of Microfinance processing, utilization and its monitoring have a major role by different ways. Realizing these, Nath, in a case study, emphasized that the NGOs' movements towards social upliftment, especially for the poor people, are well-working and the government of India takes these organizations as their helping hands. Because, many government departments assume that a step with NGOs will bring more success due to their local informational awareness in which the government departments may lack. The study has been confined mainly on the role of NGOs in microfinance.

Bhagat, in a study, explored the women empowerment and leadership through microfinance. He observed that microfinance acts as a forum which unites and organizes the people to learn from the peers and help the peers. By taking the evidence from grassroot level, he established that the SHG is also an opportunity for unity and empowerment of women, providing them the space and voice to negotiate and participate as equals both within the family and in the society in general.

Deb, in her exploration, highlighted that the microfinance is an alternative source of credit to the rural poor which include financial services to them in small amount which enables them to sustain in different dimensions. The microfinance for women empowerment came into limelight when the concept of Grameen Bank was started by Mohammad Yunus. Subsequently many NGOs and other financial institutions started the programme of micro-credit. It is observed that the microfinance is of immense benefit to women as it helped poor women and has resulted in the development of their entire household.

Section IV entitled ***Institutional Innovations and Impact Assessment***, deals with microfinance institutions and impact assessment of microfinance. In this section, Awasthi highlighted that the conventional approach for studying impact of microfinance initiatives has largely overlooked the effects of group dynamics on microfinance processes even though it is critical to study the process through which group members interact with each other and collaborate. The paper conceptualizes an alternative framework which can be used to study group dynamics and plan new channels of impact effects on the individuals participating in microfinance schemes.

Roy, Goswami and Sikidar opined that microfinance has raised the standard of living of the poor and brought significant increased productivity among the rural poor. With the changes of microfinance phenomenon, regulation etc., performance management and inbuilt accountability has become critical because MFIs operate in deviate forms in different places with entirely different operational mechanism. Hence, the paper proposed to examine the micro-credit delivery system of the Micro Financial Institutions (MFIs) in a district of Assam which will help to understand the operational mechanism and tried to find out the micro-credit assessment and micro-credit monitoring system that is practiced in Assam.

Sangma found that the lack of access to credit for the poor is attributed to practical difficulties arising from the discrepancy between the mode of operation followed by financial institutions and the economic characteristics and financing needs of low-income households. The income of many self-employed households is not stable, regardless of its size. A large number of small loans are needed to serve the poor, but lenders prefer dealing with large loans in small numbers to minimize administration costs. Hence, the paper is an exploration on micro-finance institutions.

Common Pool Resources (CPRs) significantly contribute to livelihood of people, despite their rapid depletion and decline in the physical productivity. In this light, Kabra opined that the institutional measures play an important role in the management of natural resources in general and CPRs in particular, under any property right regime. His paper analysed the activities of WGHCRMS including microfinance mechanism in Garo Hills of Meghalaya.

Sah studied a Women's MFI in Garo Hills of Meghalaya—BILCHAM. He observed that in the West Garo Hills district, SHG movement has been accelerated by West Garo Hills Community Resource Management Society. The WGHCRMS—IFAD is an established apex confederation of SHGs, NaRM-Gs, Cluster associations and SHG federation. The BILCHAM is being registered under the Meghalaya Society Act. Currently, they are running their office with two permanent staff and two temporary staff.

In the concluding **Section V *Microfinance and Micro-enterprises,*** Goswami viewed that the co-operative societies in India are playing multi-functional roles—both in rural and urban areas. The paper discussed the needs and importance of linkages of SHGs with cooperatives for providing microfinance in order to improve the socio-economic condition of the poor and underprivileged group of population of the country. It highlighted the performance of cooperatives for the country as a whole as well as NER, Assam and Cachar district in particular.

Khadem scanned the impact of microfinance on enterprise performance and job creation in Aizawl city of Mizoram. The enterprise performance has been captured in terms of sales revenue of the micro-enterprises. The cross-sectional data for the financial year 2007-08 have been fitted to the regression models and the results have been judged by statistical techniques for the purpose of impact assessment. The study found that microfinance efforts have significant potential to contribute the revenue generation and job creation of the micro-enterprises.

Hazarika and Singaiah, in a study on microfinance for micro-enterprises found that of all the problems faced by the micro-enterprise in Nagaon district of Assam, non-availability of sufficient finance seems to be one of the major hurdles. The flow of institutional finance in Assam is still at very low ebb. The micro-credit facilities which consist of a series of schemes have not been able to create much spurt in the growth of industries. In recent years, there is a marked increase in the amount of financial assistance flowing to the district from the banks and financial institutions, but yet the district is not able to get full support from the financial institutions.

Rajbongshi and Chakraborty studied the sustainability of micro-enterprises (MEs) under the microfinance programme. The analysis revealed that sustainability of business units of different types of MEs is insufficient. But in order to become self-sufficient, it is prudent to understand how much income has been earned by entrepreneur to support his business as well as the family background. The study indicated that the business activities of different MEs are not positively significant for long time sustainability in the state.

Microfinance is considered as a viable tool for reaching the unreached. In this connection, Lalromawia studied the role of microfinance in developing micro-enterprise in North East India. It has access to all societies in developmental activities which are overlooked because of various reasons. The paper also critically analyzed the lacunas of microfinance in nurturing micro-enterprise in North East India and the needs for further development.

14th June 2010
NEHU, Tura Campus

JAYNAL U. AHMED
DEEPAK BHAGAT
GANDU SINGAIAH

SECTION I

ISSUES RELATING TO MICROFINANCE IN INDIA

1

Microfinance: Evolution and Working

Sujit Sikidar

ABSTRACT: *Microfinance refers to the provision of financial services to low income clients, including consumers and the self-employed. The term also refers to the practice of sustainable delivering of those services. Micro-credit (or loans to poor micro-enterprises) should not be confused which microfinance, which addresses a full range of banking needs for poor people. More broadly, it refers to a movement that envisions a world in which as many poor and near-poor households as possible have permanent access to an appropriate range of high quality financial services, including not just credit but also savings, insurance and fund transfer to those who promote microfinance to pull poor people out of poverty. The paper is an attempt to examine the evolution and working of microfinance.*

Introduction

Microfinance broadly refers to a movement that envisions a world in which low-income households have permanent access to a range of financial services to finance income-producing activities, build assets and stabilize consumption. These services are not limited to credit, but include savings, insurance and money transfers. Microfinance entails providing loans—generally less than Rs. 10,000—to individuals, usually women, to establish or expand a small, self-sustaining business. Microfinance institutions (MFIs) offer business advice and counselling, while clients provide peer support to each other through solidarity circles. An equally important part of microfinance is recycling of funds. Loans are repaid usually in six months to a new year. This continual reinvestment multiplies the import of each amount loaned. The methods include group lending and liability, pre-loan savings requirements, gradually increasing loan sizes and an implicit guarantee of ready access to future loans if present are repaid fully and promptly.

Most jobs in MFIs involve either granting or processing of loans or training and development. Loans managers usually decide who receives money and then track repayment. Non-loan positions involve educating entrepreneurs on how to run their companies, business planning and strategy. However, loan and non-loan positions can overlap.

Several MFIs start as not-for-profit organizations like NGOs, credit unions and other financial cooperatives and state-owned development and postal savings banks. An increasing number of MFIs are now organized as for-profit entities, often because it is necessary to obtain license from banking authorities to offer savings services. For-profit MFIs may be organized as NBIs or commercial banks that specialize in microfinance.

Some MFIs provide nonfinancial products such as business development and health services. Commercials and government-owned banks that offer microfinance services are frequently referred to as MFIs even though only a portion of their assets may be committed to rendering financial services to the poor.

A vast majority of loans go to women because studies have shown that women are more likely to reinvest their earnings in the business and in their families. As families cross the poverty line and micro-business expand, their communities benefit. Jobs are created, knowledge shared, civic participation increases and women are recognized as valuable members of their families and communities.

According to a Mckinsey Survey, rural India has the potential to become a 500 billion dollar market by 2020. The number of MFIs in India is more than 200 and increasing at a fast pace. There are about 52,000 branches of commercial banks, 14,522 branches of PBRs and 1, 00,000 Cooperative bank branches.

MFIs such as financial Cooperatives, financial NGOs and rural banks provide credit to the poor at reasonable interest rates. A loan as little as Rs. 2,500 can give the poor a chance to set up a small business, and possibly create more jobs (The Telegraph dated 21st May, 2009).

Evolution of Microfinance

The concept of microfinance (MF) has been evolved for economic low-income groups. The term refers to the provision of financial services to low income groups, including the self-employed. The declaration of the Microcredit summit held in Washington DC in 1997 defined micro-credit programmes as those 'extending small loans to poor people for self employment projects that generate income allowing them to care for themselves and their families' ('Declaration and Plan of Action', Micro-credit Summit, Washington DC, 1997).

According to the Task Force on supportive policy and Regulatory framework for MF constituted by the NABARD in 1999, MF is the 'Provision of thrift, credit and other financial services and products of very small amounts to the poor in the rural, semi urban and urban areas for enabling them to raise their income levels and improve living standards'. It crosses not only consumption and production loans, but also include other credit needs such as housing and shelter improvements and other financial services like savings and insurance. (Report of the Task Force on Supportive Policy and Regulatory Framework for Microfinance, NABARD, 1999).

Some MF organizations also provide insurance and payment services. By helping the poor to accumulate usably sufficient sum of money, MF expands their choices and reduces the risks they face.

MF Models

There are various MF models. Microfinance in India is dominated by self help groups (SHGs)-Bank linkage programme. It tries to create/build financial relationship informal groups of people that are the SHGs and formal agencies like banks that are the SHGs and financial service requirements of the poor, especially women. Apart from the banks, government agencies, and non-government organizations (NGOs) play an important role in promoting, nurturing and establishing linkage between the SHGs and the banks. Those models are described hereunder (Report on Trend and Progress of Banking in India, 2006-07, RBI, Mumbai).

Model I: Bank SHG with active support of SHPI

The most common linkage model in India is where the banks deal directly with individual SHGs. In case of most of these SHGs the Self Help Promoting Institutions (SHPIs), like NGOs, government agencies DRDA etc provide the initial training and, guidance to rural poor in organizing themselves into thrift and credit groups. In many cases, the SHPIs also provide some initial support to these SHGs to segment their resources. The SHPIs also keep a watch and ensures satisfactory functioning of the SHGs ever after the linkage. While linkage of the banks is direct with the SHGs, the SHPI has an important role in pre- as well as post-linkage stages. But these SHPIs do not involve themselves in the financial interaction process. The financial interaction takes place in the following channels:

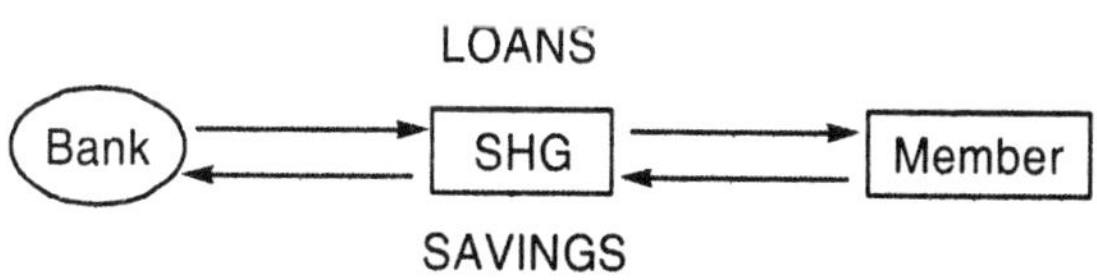

Model II: Bank-SHG

A slight variant to Model I is where Banks have provided financial support to SHGs, which had almost spontaneously without any intervention of any SHPI. The SHGs were initially on the basis of a common activity, problem and took up thrift and credit activities. The cases of such linkage are, of course, not very common.

Model III: Bank-SHPI-SHG

In this model the SHPIs have taken the role of a financial intermediary between the banks and a member of SHGs. Again, the SHPIs take up such responsibilities only in respect of the groups promoted and nurtured by them and not for other groups. The SHPI accepts the contractual responsibilities for repayment of the loan to the bank. In this respect it is indirect linkage support to the SHGs. This model is quite common:

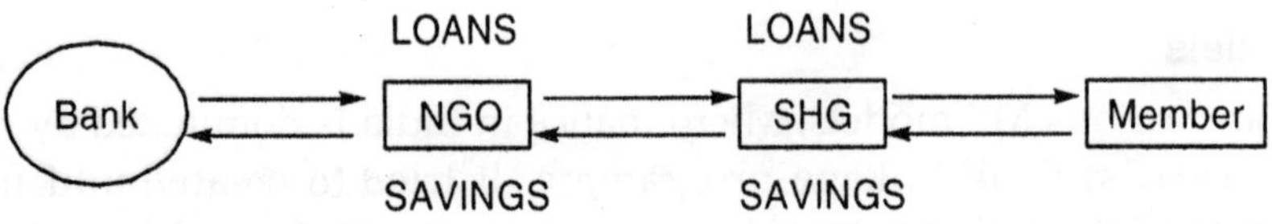

According to the RBI, out of the three models which have emerged under the SHG-Bank linkage programme over the years, about 74 percent of total SHGs have been formed and 81.1 percent of the total amount of bank loans have been provided to SHGs under Model I.

In Model I, the lending takes place directly from the bank to SHG. Banks themselves assume the work of forming and nurturing the groups, opening their savings accounts and providing the bank loan.

In Model II, SHPI or NGOs as facilitator of the SHGs to link with the bank, SHPI form groups and nourish them to get loan from the bank. However, NGOs or SHPI are not directly involved in financial transactions. They simply introduce the SHG to the bank, NGOs; formal agencies like SHPI act only as facilitators. They facilitate organizing, forming and nurturing of groups; and train them in thrift and credit management. Banks give loan directly to those SHGs.

In Model III, SHPI and NGOs or MFIs act as financial intermediary between bank and SHGs. Banks lend money to MFIs for on lending to the SHGs. Under this model, where banks face constraints in lending, the NGOs and other formal agencies like SHG Federation, NBFCs are encouraged to approach a suitable bank for bulk loan assistance. This, in turn, is used by these agencies for on-lending to the SHGs.

Microfinance interventions have been recognized as an effective instrument for poverty alleviation and empowering the poor; in improving the socio-economic conditions of the poor, and, specially, empowering women. The impact of microfinance programme through SHGs has been effective in making positive social change to all members, irrespective of the direct borrowers of the micro-credit, the SHGs provide social protection and income opportunities to the members, redistribution of income and opportunities in the community.

Need for Microfinance

Mainstream financial institutions which constitute the core financial infrastructure of the country are reluctant to finance the poor on the ground that these are neither economic nor commercial. In that case, SHGs emerge as an intermediary and SHG-Bank linkage model has become workable. Having accepted the model, NABARD had launched a pilot project for linking 500 SHGs with banks in 1992. Under the SHGs-Bank linkage programme the concerned bank under whose service area the SHG operates together with NABARD identify the group. After that the micro-credit requirements of the group is taken up with the bank on behalf of the bank.

As per the NABARD's circular No. DPD/104 dated 26th February 1992 a group is selected on the basis of the following criteria:

- The group should have been in active existence for at least a period of six months.
- The group should have successfully undertaken savings and credit operations from its own resources.
- The group operates in a democratic manner.
- The group maintains proper accounts and records.
- The banker should be convinced that the group has not come into existence only for the sake of participation in the project and availing benefits there—under. There should be genuine need to help each other and work together among the members.
- The SHG's members should preferably have homogeneous background and interest.
- The interest of the NGO, or the Self Help Promoting Institution (SHPI) concerned, if any, in the group is evident and the agency is helping the SHG by way of training and other support for skill upgradation and proper functioning.

There has been a longstanding debate over the sharpness of the trade off between outreach (the ability of microfinance institution to reach poorer and more remote people) and its sustainability (its ability to cover its operating costs and possibly also its cost of serving new clients from its operating revenues). Although it is generally agreed that microfinance practitioners should seek to balance these goal to some extent, there is a wide variety of strategies ranging from the minimalist profit orientation of Bancosot in Bolivia to the highly integrated no-profit orientation of BRAC in Bangladesh. This is true not only for individual institutions, but also for governments engaged in developing national microfinance systems.

Microfinance experts generally agree that women should be the primary focus of service delivery. Evidence shows that they are less like to default on their loans than men. Industry data from 2006 for 704 MFIs reaching 52 million borrowers includes MFIs using the solidarity lending was 0.9 pc after 30 days (individual lending 3.1 pc) while 0.3 pc of loan was written off (individual lending 0.9 pc). However a recent study of micro-entrepreneurs from Sri Lanka published by the World Bank, find that the return on capital for male owned businesses (half of the sample) overage 11 pc, whereas the return for women-owned businesses was 0% or slightly negative.

Microfinance services are needed everywhere, including developed world. However, in developed economics intense competitions within the financial sector, combined with a diverse mix of different types of financial institutions with different missions, ensure that most people have access to some financial services. Efforts to transfer microfinance innovations such as solidarity lending from developing countries to developed ones have met with little success.

Financial Need of Poor People

Most people are met through mix of saving and credit. A benchmark impact assessment of Grameen Bank and two other large microfinance institutions in Bangladesh found that for every dollar 1 they were lending to client to finance rural non-farm micro-enterprise about dollar 2.50 came from other sources, mostly their clients' savings. This parallels the experience in the West in which family businesses are funded mostly from saving, especially during start up.

The work of Rutherford, Wright and others has focused on a key aspect of micro-credit paradigm; that poor people get out of poverty by borrowing, building micro-enterprises and increasing their income. The new paradigm places more attention on the efforts of poor people to reduce their much vulnerability by keeping more of what they earn and building up their assets. While they need loans, they may find it as useful to borrow for consumption as for micro-enterprise. A safe, flexible place to save money and withdraw it when needed is also essential in managing household and family risk.

Scale of Microfinance Operation

An 'alternative financial institutions' in the developing world were set up in 2004. Regionally, the highest concentration of the client accounts was in India (188 million accounts representing 18 pc of the total national population). The lowest concentrations were in Latin America and the Caribbean (14 millions accounts representing 3 pc of the total population) and Africa (27 million accounts representing 4 pc of the total population). That most bank clients in the developed world need several active accounts to keep their affairs in order, these figures indicate that the task the microfinance movement has set for itself is still very far from finished. By type of service, 'savings accounts in alternative finance institutions outnumber loans by about four to one. This is worldwide pattern that does not vary much by region.

An important source of detailed data for selected microfinance institutions is the Micro Banking Bulletin. At the end of 2006, it was tracking 704 MFIs that were serving 52 million borrowers (23.3 billion dollars in outstanding loans) and 56 million savers (15.4 dollar in deposits). Of these clients, 70 pc were in Asia, 20 pc in Latin America and the balance in the rest of the world.

Inclusive Financial Systems

The micro-credit era that began in the 1970s has lost its momentum to be replaced by a 'financial systems' approach. While micro-credit achieved a great deal, especially in urban and near urban areas and with entrepreneurial families, its progress in delivering financial services in less densely populated rural areas has been slow. Another major goal of the micro-credit movement was to put the traditional moneylender, who typically charges at least 10 pc a monthly and often much more, out of business. There is little evidence of progress towards this goal.

The new financial systems approach pragmatically acknowledges the richness of countries of microfinance history and the immense diversity of institutions serving poor people in the developing world today. It is also rooted in an increasing awareness of diversity of the financial service needs of the world's poorest people, and the diverse settings in which they live and work.

Brigit Helms, in her book 'Access for All: Building Inclusive financial Systems,' distinguishes between four general categories of microfinance providers, and argues for a pro-active strategy of engagement with all of them to help them achieve the goals of the microfinance movement:

1. **Informal Financial Service Providers:** These include money lenders, pawnbrokers, savings collectors, money guards, ROSCAs, ASCAs, and input supply shops. Because they know each other well and live in the same community, they understand each other's financial circumstances and can offer very flexible, convenient fast services. These services can also be costly and the choice of financial products are limited and very short-term. Informal services that involve saving are also risky—many people lose their money.

2. **Member Owned Organizations:** These include self help groups (SHGs), credit unions, and a variety of hybrid organizations like financial service associations and CVECAs. Like their informal cousins they are generally small and local, which means they have good access to knowledge about each others' financial circumstances and can offer convenient flexibility. Since they are managed by poor people, their costs of operation are at reasonable. However, these providers may have little financial skill and can run into trouble when the economy turns down or their operations become too complex. Unless they are effectively regulated and supervised,

they can be captured by one or two influential leaders, and the members can lose their money.

3. **NGOs:** The Micro Credit Summit Campaign counted 3,316 of these MFIs NGOs leading to about 1,33 million clients by the end of 2006. Led by Grameen Bank and BRAC in Bangladesh, Prodem in Bolivia; and FINCA International, head quartered in Washington DC, these NGOs have spread around the developing world in the past three decades; others like the Gamelan Council, address larger regions. They have proven very innovative, pioneering banking techniques like solidarity lending, village banking and mobile banking that have overcome barriers to serving poor populations. However, they do not necessarily represent either their capital or their customers, their governance structure can be fragile and they are overly dependent on external donors.
4. **Formal Financial Institution:** In addition to commercial banks, these include state banks, agricultural development bank, saving bank, rural bank and non-bank financial institution (NBFIs). They are regulated and supervised, offer a wider range of financial services and control a branch network that can extend across the country and internationally. However, they have proved reluctant to adopt social missions, and, due to their high costs of operation, often cannot deliver services to the poor or remote populations. The increasing use of alternative data in credit scoring such as trade credit is increasing commercial banks' interest in microfinance.

With appropriate regulations and supervision, each of these institution types can bring leverage to solving the microfinance problem. For example, efforts are being made to link SHGs to commercial banks, to network member owned organizations together to achieve economics of scale and scope, and to support by commercial bank to downscale by integrating mobile banking and e-payment technologies into their extensive branch networks.

Microfinance and Social Interventions

These are currently a few social inventions that have been combined with micro-financing to increase awareness of HIV/AIDS. Such innervations like the 'Intervention with Microfinance for AIDS and Gender Equity' (IMAGE) which incorporates microfinancing with the 'Sister for Life' programme—a participatory programme that educates on different gender roles, gender based violence, and HIV/AIDS infections to strengthen the communication skill and leadership of women. The 'Sister for Life' programme has two phase where phase 1 consist of ten one hour training programs with a facilitator with phase 2 consisting of identifying a leader amongst the group, train them further, and allow them to implement an 'action plan' to their respective centres.

REFERENCES

1. B. Chhatoi, A. Shanti and K. K. Nayak, Financing the Poor through SHG-Bank Linkage Programme, *The Indian Journal of Commerce*, Vol. 62, No. 1, January-March, 2009, pp. 10-11
2. The Telegraph dated 21st May, 2009
3. Declaration and Plan of Action', Microcredit Summit, Washington DC, 1997
4. Report on Trend and Progress of Banking in India, 2006-07, RBI, Mumbai
5. Report of the Task Force on Supportive Policy and Regulatory Framework for Microfinance, NABARD, 1999

2

Microfinance in North East India: An Analytical Study with Reference to Mizoram

Baharul Islam Laskar

Abstract: *Microfinance as a major financial service emerged in the 1970s, notably after Muhammad Yunus of Nobel Prize fame started the Grameen Bank in Bangladesh. The new generation microfinance was slow in coming to India. The first breakthrough emerged from policy support to enable informal self help groups of 5-20 members to transact with commercial banks. These groups build up and rotate savings amongst themselves, open bank accounts and take responsibility for lending and recovering money financed by banks. With the missionary zeal of the National Bank for Agriculture and Rural Development (NABARD), insights gained by NGOs, the increasing enthusiasm of bankers and emerging successes in repayment and social impacts, this national movement now encompasses over 20 million members in such groups. The present paper is an analytical study based on the secondary data on the progress in the field of Microfinance in the North Eastern Region with special reference to Mizoram.*

Introduction

Microfinance is a new reality in the world of development discourse and financial intermediation. Broadly speaking, microfinance means providing financial services to the poor long excluded by mainstream banking and finance market. Neo-liberals support it as it does not disturb the *status quo*. Commercial banks see in it a new profitable area of credit with a high repayment rate in a world of mounting non-performing assets and sub-prime hazards. Many governments welcome it as a less burdensome manner of fighting poverty. The most important economic rationale in bringing financial services to the door-steps of the poor households is the economy in the transaction costs. For formal banks, it will be costly to mobilize the small savings of the poor families lying widely scattered. Equally prohibitive is the cost to the conventional banks in financing a large number of these families who require credit frequently and in small volume and that too not backed by collateral securities.

The definition of microfinance as provided by Robinson is, '*Microfinance refers to small-scale financial services for both credits and deposits — that are provided to people who farm or fish or herd; operate small or micro-enterprises where goods are produced, recycled, repaired, or traded; provide services; work for wages or commissions; gain income from renting out small amounts of land, vehicles, draft animals, or machinery and tools; and to other individuals and local groups in developing countries, in both rural and urban areas.*' Microfinance is thus "the provision of financial services to low-income poor and very poor self-employed people". These financial services generally include savings and credit but can also include other financial services such as insurance and payment services. It is "*the attempt to improve access to small deposits and small loans for poor households neglected by banks.*" Therefore, microfinance involves the provision of financial services such as savings, loans and insurance to poor people living in both urban and rural settings who are unable to obtain such services from the formal financial sector.

Microfinance and Micro-credit

In the pertinent literature, the terms micro-credit and microfinance are often used interchangeably, but it is important to highlight the difference between them because both terms are often confused. Micro-credit refers to small loans, whereas microfinance is appropriate where NGOs and MFIs supplement the loans with other financial services like savings, insurance, etc. Therefore micro-credit is a component of microfinance in that it involves providing credit to the poor, but microfinance also involves additional non-credit financial services such as savings, insurance, pensions and payment services.

Select Literature Review

Nobel Laureate Milton Friedman holds that the poor stay poor, not because they are lazy but because they have no access to capital. Micro-credit and microfinance are relatively new terms in the field of development, first coming to prominence in the 1970s (Robinson, 1998). Prior to then, from the 1950s through to the 1970s, the provision of financial services by donors or governments was mainly in the form of subsidized rural credit programmes. These often resulted in high loan default, high losses and an inability to reach poor rural households (Robinson, 2001). Robinson states that the 1980s represented a turning point in the history of microfinance in that MFIs such as Grameen Bank of Bangladesh and Bank Raykat Indonesia (BRI) began to show that they could provide small loans and savings services profitably on a large scale. They received no continuing subsidies, were commercially funded and fully sustainable, and could attain wide outreach to clients (Robinson, 2001). It was also at this time that the term "micro-credit" came to prominence in development. The difference between micro-credit and the subsidized rural credit programmes of the 1950s and 1960s was that micro-credit insisted on repayment, on charging interest rates that covered the cost of credit delivery and by focusing on clients who were dependent on the informal sector for credit and it was clear for the first time that microcredit could provide large-scale outreach profitably.

The 1990s "saw accelerated growth in the number of microfinance institutions created and an increased emphasis on reaching scale" (Robinson, 2001). Dichter (1999) refers to the 1990s as "the microfinance decade". Microfinance had now turned into an industry according to Robinson (2001). Along with the growth in microcredit institutions, attention changed from just the provision of credit to the poor, to the provision of other financial services such as savings and pensions when it became clear that the poor had a demand for these other services.

Microfinance as a major financial service emerged in the 1970s, notably after Muhammad Yunus—now of Nobel Prize fame—started the Grameen Bank in Bangladesh. The Bank began to offer financial services to the poor once excluded from formal banking—primarily because they lacked collateral. Today, microfinance has emerged as an industry in which even big multi-national and national banks are interested because they are sure of repayment and fetches profit.

Amartya Sen (1999) elaborated that there is a great need to consider the quality of human resources, their capabilities and functionings in any poverty conceptualization. For him, poverty is capability deprivation. Capability refers to the freedom one has to choose from a range of functionings, which means achieving what one wants to do or be. Poverty in this perspective would mean absence of elementary capabilities. The basic question in poverty reduction is one of expansion of elementary capabilities, namely, education, health care, employment, gender equity and women empowerment and provisioning of social and economic security. Of course, we affirm that the elementary capability of being adequately nourished in the official PL implicitly recognized an important aspect of the conceptual foundations of poverty. Second, the PL takes no notice of the fact that when the income of one individual or group of individuals close to a PL falls down, she becomes poorer. It thus violates the axiom that a reduction of income of any one below the PL given everything else must increase the poverty measures.

Throughout the developing countries, innovative lending programmes have emerged that specializes in supplying small capital loans to low-income entrepreneurs. In many of these programmes it is common to find that a large percentage of borrowers are women. For example, based on a 1996 survey of microfinance institution around the world, the World Bank estimated that 61% of all clients were women (World Bank, 1997). In two rather well documented lending programs, the Grameen Bank in Bangladesh and Bancosol in Bolivia, the percentages are 95% and 72%, respectively. These high female participation rates have raised a number of research questions and have, in turn, inspired a growing number of empirical investigations.

The Commercial Banks and Regional Rural Banks played a crucial role in the formation of groups in the SHGs Bank Linkage Programmes in Andra Pradesh while the Cooperative Banks in West Bengal. Among women who had taken loans for income-generating activities, only 5% reported having total autonomous control over the money 56% reported that they share control over the loan money with their husbands, and 38% reported that their husbands have sole control over the proceeds of the loan. The above conclusion shows that microfinance program does not explain the strong form of Women empowerment—rather it is a weak form of women empowerment (Basu, 2006).

Microfinance programmes do provide the poor with access to credit, enable them to undertake income generation programmes and contribute to higher recovery rates. Considering that the formal banks have not had much success in improving the access to credit for the poor, the strategy of supporting the formation and nurturing of micro-finance groups for poverty alleviation is worth pursuing. However, responsibilities such as development of economic infrastructure and providing additional funds to micro-finance groups must be undertaken by the government as the micro-finance programmes alone cannot alleviate poverty (Rajasekhar, 1999).

Microfinance has shown a slow start in the north east region, but the programme has recorded rapid growth—particularly in Assam, Tripura and Manipur—in terms of SHGs financed and loan disbursed. However, in Meghalaya, the progress of the programme has been very slow in spite of the spurt in the implementation of the programme in the late 1990s. There is a need to review the performance of Self Help Groups Bank Linkage programme in the NER to find out the factors that retard its progress and take corrective measures to improve the performance of Microfinance in the region (Umdor, 2007).

The success of Microfinance programmes in North East required is a multi-dimensional approach to overcome the many issues of the region. Banks, policymakers and NGOs in particular and the common people of the region in general must come forward to think through suitable and positive adjustments in policy. Banks may have to change their system of reviewing risks. There is need for capacity building and expansion of infrastructure. The existing policy may be modified, in certain special cases to suit the local needs and culture (Deshpande, 2008).

Major Development in Microfinance in India

The new generation microfinance was slow in coming to India. Low levels of grants to microfinance institutions, an unfavourable policy environment, substantial traditional banking infrastructure and a search for context—specific solutions has constrained rapid scale-up. The first breakthrough emerged from policy support to enable informal self-help groups of 15-20 members to transact with commercial banks. These groups build up and rotate savings amongst themselves, open bank accounts and take responsibility for lending and recovering money financed by banks. With the missionary zeal of the National Bank for Agriculture and Rural Development (NABARD), insights gained by NGOs, the increasing enthusiasm of bankers and emerging successes in repayment and social impacts, this national movement now encompasses 1.4 million such groups (over 20 million members). The major milestone in Microfinance in India is given in Table 1.

TABLE 1

Major Milestone in Microfinance

Year	Achievements
1969	Nationalization of banks
1971	Establishment of priority sector lending norms
1975	Establishment of regional rural banks
1982	Establishment of NABARD
1992	Launching of the SHG-bank linkage programme
1993	Establishment of Rashtriya Mahila Kosh
1998	NABARD sets a goal for linking one million SHGs by 2008
2000	Establishment of SIDBI foundation for micro-credit
2005	One million SHG linkage target achieved
2006	Committee of financial inclusion
2007	Microfinance Regulation Bill intoduced

Source: *Presented in the NAC on Microfinance in India by M.S.Sriram, IIM, Ahmedabad, May 2007*

Microfinance in North East India

The North Eastern Region comprises Arunachal Pradesh, Assam, Nagaland, Manipur, Meghalaya, Mizoram, Tripura and Sikkim. Each of these eight states differs widely in terms of political and socio-economic environment. Almost 98% of the land area in the Region runs along international borders with Bhutan, Bangladesh, Myanmar and China. Almost 70 % of the region is hilly. Population, except in the valleys and in Assam, is sparsely distributed.

The entire region has roughly a population of 3.88 crore, of which 3 crore is concentrated in Assam. The rail network is poor and also concentrated in Assam. Compared to the national average of 73 km of road per 100 square km, the average road length in the region is low, at 53 km, with Arunachal Pradesh having the least length of roads—12.20 km per 100 sq km. Access to markets with the rest of India is difficult due to the poor infrastructure. Almost 75 % of the workforce in this region is engaged in the primary sector and agriculture is the mainstay of the economy. Most other economic activity is small scale and heavily dependent on traditional skills of weaving and handicraft.

The Self Help Group and Bank Linkage Programme in India (SHG-BLP) is one of the key factors in the success of Microfinance Programme and have emerged as the largest Microfinance programme in the world. Under the programme a cumulative amount of Rs. 113.98 billion has been disbursed by banks to as many as 22,38,565 SHGs till March 2006. The southern states, especially Andhra Pradesh, shows the largest number of SHGs and also the amount of bank credit disbursed.

The North Eastern States which had started the programme during the late nineties shows a relatively high growth rate. In the initial years the programme had slow start and till the end of March 1999, the cumulative number of SHGs credit linked in the entire region was only 93, which was less than half a per cent of the cumulative number of SHG credit linked in the country under the programme. During March 1999 to March 2001, the cumulative number of SHGs in NER increased from 93 to 477, i.e. a little more than five times while at the India level it was increased by seven times.

Within the North Eastern Region, Assam and Meghalaya, in 2001, accounted for majority share of the SHGs credit links (at about 58 and 34 per cent, respectively), and also that of the cumulative credit disbursed in the region (about 45 and 46 per cent, respectively) as against the very low share of states like Manipur (7 per cent), Sikkim (1 per cent) and Tripura (1 per cent) in the total cumulative number of SHG credit linked. The remaining states of Arunachal Pradesh, Nagaland and Mizoram did not have any SHGs credit linked under this programme by 2001. Until 2001, more than 90 per cent of the SHGs credit linked in the North Eastern Region was from the two states of Assam and Meghalaya.

It is seen that the performance of banks in providing credit to the SHGs has been good in the State of Assam and Tripura (Table 2), while it is poor in other States of the region. It is quite interesting that Mizoram has experienced a very poor movement of SHGs (only 251 number of credit linked SHGs); however, the highest amount per group was lent in this State. SHG movement in Assam has gained momentum during the last two years. So far, 49,237 SHGs has been credit linked to the extent of Rs.197.29 crore as on March 31, 2005. The RRBs particularly Pragjyotish Gaonlia Bank, has been playing a lead role in the SHG movement. Presently, 47 Self Help Promoting Institutions (SHPIs) including 5 RRBs and 11 Farmers' Clubs were involved in the SHG-Bank linkaged programme in the State. During 2004-05, the Joint Liability Group (JLG) concept was introduced to all the 5 RRBs in the State and 98 JLGs had been financed to the tune of Rs. 53.22 lakh by three RRBs viz. Subansiri Gaonlia Bank, Pragjyotish Gaonlia Bank and Langpi Dehangi Rural Bank.

In the district of West Tripura, each Gram Panchayat was to form one SHG in a month and 12 SHGs in a year under SGSY. The SHG movement received such equally enthusiastic response from other districts also and some Panchayat exceeded the target. It is expected that all the villages in the State will have around 20,000 new SHGs by the end of the year. As per reports, 4,000 SHGs have already passed first gradation stage, 10,000 were eligible for such tests and 16,000 had passed second gradation. The Bharat Gyan Vigyan Samiti, Tripura micro-study, found that while group formation had a significant impact on social indicators and led to accumulation of handsome savings by SHGs, the impact on poverty alleviation was minimal, since SHGs concentrated more on thrift and credit activities in first few months and economic activities are taken up only later after Group stabilization. As reported, the subsidy was adjusted and no matching was sanctioned by some banks.

TABLE 2

Status of Microfinance in North Eastern Region (Up to March 2005)

States	Amount in Rs. Lakhs		Average lending in Rs.
	Cumulative no. of credit linked SHGs	Cumulative total amount of loan sanctioned	
Assam	49,237	19,729.42	40,070
Arunachal Pradesh	229	58.01	25,330
Manipur	1,885	457.33	24,260
Meghalaya	1,315	475.62	36,170
Mizoram	251	188.61	75,140
Nagaland	442	259.97	58,820
Tripura	6,921	2,797.07	40,410
TOTAL	**60,280**	**23,966.03**	**39,757**

Source: *Office of the State Coordinator, Self Help Groups, Meghalaya, Shillong*

Within the NER States, banks have emerged as important self-help promoting agencies. In Assam, in 2006, 79 per cent of the SHGs were promoted and financed by the banks themselves; while in Tripura and Sikkim more than half of the SHGs credit linked (51 and 75 per cent, respectively) have been promoted by banks. In the remaining States, such as Meghalaya (77 per cent), Manipur (68 per cent), Arunachal Pradesh (100 per cent) and Nagaland (93 per cent), majority of the SHGs credit linked have been formed by NGOs.

The poor performance in the progress of microfinance is mainly due to the sparse population in this region, lack of experienced NGOs for formation and nurturing of SHGs and lack of homogeneity in Groups in the respective States. The local institutions like Marup in Manipur, Village Development Boards (VDBs) in Nagaland, Village Darbar in Meghalaya, Kebang in Arunachal Pradesh and Young Mizo Association in Mizoram could be activated to further the SHG movement in the respective States.

Banking Scenario in Mizoram

The State of Mizoram under the Indian Union is situated on the North-Eastern corner of India. The erstwhile Lusai Hill district became Union Territory on 21st January 1972 and got statehood on 20th February 1987. The Mizo district was not only upgraded but also got its present name Mizoram. The developmental programmes initiated by the State Government and the policies of the Central Government to provide full financial support has acted as a catalyst in helping a predominantly tribal populace to realize a better living standard. Consequently, behavioural and structural changes took place which has been manifested in the fast changing consumption pattern, social values and decreasing importance of traditional institutions. The economy of the State is mainly agrarian and solely depends on nature. Due to the unique topography of the State, there is a scarcity of plain and irrigable areas of land; a hill-type of shifting cultivation called jhumming is practiced by most of the cultivators. At present about 70% of the population are engaged in agriculture. According to the 2001 census, 60.66% (cultivators and agricultural labourers) of the total work force are engaged in the primary sector of the economy (Table 3) whereas only 1.5 percent and 37.9 per cent of the total work force is engaged in the secondary and tertiary sectors respectively.

TABLE 3

Occupational Structure of Mizoram (2001)

Sl. No.	Category	Number	Percentage
1	Total population	8,88,573	–
2	Number of workers (Total work force)	4,67,159	52.6
3	Cultivators	2,56,332	54.9
4	Agricultural labourer	26,783	5.7
5	Household industrial workers	7,100	1.5
6	Other workers	1,76,944	37.9

Source: *Directorate of Census Operations, Government of India, Aizawal, Mizoram*

Banking has always served as one of the most important instrument for economic development. In Mizoram, public sector banks have widened the horizon of banking activities, especially during the last two decades in tune with the socio-economic needs of the State. By March 2008, there were 107 branches of financial institutions in Mizoram consisting 36 nationalized commercial banks, 61 branches of Mizoram Rural Bank and 11 branches of Mizoram Cooperative Apex Bank.

TABLE 4

District-wise Number of Banks in Mizoram (2008)

Banks 1	Districts	Mamit	Kolasib	Aizawal	Cham-phai	Serchhip	Lunglei	Lawng	Saiha	Total
SBI		3	3	8	1	2	6	2	1	**26**
UCO		0	0	1	0	0	0	0	0	**1**
Vijaya		0	0	1	0	0	0	0	0	**1**
IDBI		0	0	1	0	0	0	0	0	**1**
UBI		0	0	1	0	0	0	0	0	**1**
Axis		0	0	1	0	0	0	0	0	**1**
Syndicate		0	0	1	0	0	0	0	0	**1**
CBI		0	0	1	0	0	0	0	0	**1**
BOB		0	0	1	0	0	0	0	0	**1**
PNB		0	0	1	0	0	0	0	0	**1**
MCAB		0	1	5	1	1	1	1	1	**11**
MRB		6	6	23	8	6	8	1	3	**61**
MUCO		0	0	1	0	0	0	0	0	**1**
Total		**9**	**10**	**46**	**10**	**9**	**15**	**4**	**5**	**108**

Source: *Statistical Handbook, Mizoram 2008, Directorate of Economics and Statistics, Aizawl*

Commercial banks and MRBs together account for about 90 percent of the total bank coverage in the State while Cooperative banks accounts for only 10 percent (Table 4). As far as the Banking and Financial sector is concerned, the State shows a satisfactory progress, out of the 108 branches of banks functioning in the State, it too includes new generation banks like The Axis Bank and IDBI. Financial institutions like NABARD, SIDBI and NEDFi also have their presence in the State. The total deposits with the Banks in 2007 was 1,345.12 crore rupees and the total advance is 760.24 crore rupees. The Credit Deposit (CD) ratio is 56.52 percent.

The total number of population served by each bank branch in the State is around 8,500 which is much lower as compared to the national average of 15,000 —indeed a positive sign. The locational aspects of the bank branches are skewed towards cities and urban centres. The State capital Aizawl and the second largest city Lunglei together accounts for about 56 percent (61 out of 108) of the total bank branches in the State. There are many villages which are deprived of banking services even within the radius of 80-100 kilometers. This is mainly due to the poor number of households in these areas, slow economic activities etc. which make the branch banking unviable.

Microfinance in Mizoram

The Indian state put stress on providing financial services to the poor and underprivileged since independence. The commercial banks were nationalized in 1969 and were directed to lend 40% of their loanable funds, at a concessional rate, to the priority sector. The priority sector included agriculture and other rural activities and the weaker strata of society in general. The aim was to provide resources to help the poor to attain self-sufficiency.

To supplement these efforts, the credit scheme Integrated Rural Development Programme (IRDP) was launched in 1980. But these supply side programmes (ignoring the demand side of the economy) aided by corruption and leakages, achieved little. Further, the share of the formal financial sector in total rural credit was 56.6%, compared to informal finance at 39.6% and unspecified sources at 3.8%. Not only had formal credit flow been less but also uneven. The collateral and paperwork based system shied away from the poor. The vacuum continued to be filled by the village moneylender who charged interest rates of 2% to 30% per month.

It was in this cheerless background that the Microfinance Revolution occurred worldwide. In India it began in the 1980s with the formation of pockets of informal Self Help Groups (SHGs) engaging in micro-activities financed by Microfinance. The first official effort materialized under the direction of National Bank for Agriculture and Rural Development (NABARD) when the Mysore Resettlement and Development Agency (MYRADA) sponsored project on "Savings and Credit Management of SHGs" was partially financed by NABARD during 1986-87.

In Mizoram, the Microfinance programme started lately with the setting up of Mizoram Rural Bank in 1983 with its head office at Aizawl, the State capital of Mizoram. Since its inception the bank is serving hard to achieve its objectives. In view of the emphasis given by the central government on promotion of micro-enterprises in rural areas through the mechanism of self-help groups, the bank branches are advised to form self-help groups and was intended that SHG linkage as a part of banks' mainstream credit operation. In its endeavour, till March 2008, MRB has formed 1,165 SHGs out of which 1,080 groups have been credit linked.

The Swarnajayanti Gram Swarojgar Yojana (SGSY) is a major ongoing programme which promotes Microfinance programme by forming self help groups in the State. The programme was started in 1999 with the objective of bringing the poor families above the poverty line by ensuring appreciable income over a period of time. The programme tries to organize the rural poor into self-help groups through a process of social mobilizing, training, capacity building and provision of income generating assets through a mix of bank credit and government subsidy.

Self-help groups (SHGs) are a group of rural poor who volunteer to organize themselves in a group which may consist of 10 to 20 members. The lowest numbers of members are 5 in case of minor irrigation projects, disabled persons and in difficult areas like desert and hilly areas with scattered and sparsely distributed population which is applicable in case of Mizoram.

A total of 1,805 SHGs was formed under SGSY from 2000 to 2007 in the State (Table 5) out of which 1,058 groups were given financial assistance with a total expenditure of Rs.9.89 crore. During 2000-01, total 225 SHGs were formed but only 97 groups got financial help. The number of SHGs has increased considerably during the successive years; simultaneously the number of financially assisted groups has also increased considerably. Aizawl district has shown the highest number of SHGs formation during the year 2006-07, out of which 15 groups has been assisted under the SGSY scheme with an expenditure of Rs. 32.40 lakh. Serchhip district shows the lowest amount of expenditure (Rs. 6.00 lakh only), having 7 SHGs with an average financial assistance of Rs.0.85 lakh per group.

TABLE 5

Progress under SGSY in Mizoram (2000-2007)

Year	Number of SHGs formed	No. of SHGs assisted	Total Expenditure (in Rs. Lakh)
2000-01	225	97	141.57
2001-02	379	230	101.71
2002-03	294	156	84.31
2003-04	216	128	138.02
2004-05	290	153	183.58
2005-06	255	192	200.82
2006-07	146	102	139.57
TOTAL	**1,805**	**1,058**	**989.58**

Source: *Statistical Abstract of Mizoram 2007, Directorate of Economics and Statistics, Aizawl*

The average financial assistance given to each SHGs in the State during 2006-07 was Rs. 1.37 lakh (Table 6). The highest amount of financial assistance was received by the groups in Champhai district, each SHGs in the district was given Rs. 2.82 lakh during the year 2006-07.

National Bank for Agriculture and Rural Development (NABARD), which is pioneering the Microfinance programme in the country, appears in the banking scenario of the state in 1995 as a sub-office of its Guwahati Regional Office. This sub-office has been upgraded to Regional Office in 2000. NABARD initiates

TABLE 6

District-wise Progress of SGSY in Mizoram (2006-07)

District	Number of SHGs formed	Number of SHGs assisted	Total expenditure (in Rs. Lakh)
Mamit	23	23	9.85
Kolasib	5	7	11.69
Aizawl	57	15	32.40
Champhai	24	10	28.29
Serchhip	7	7	6.00
Lunglei	13	13	24.59
Lawngtlai	10	9	16.19
Saiha	7	18	10.69
TOTAL	**146**	**102**	**139.57**

Source: *Economic Survey of Mizoram, 2007-08, Planning and Programme Implementation Department, Government of Mizoram, Aizawl*

Microfinance programme in the State and is doing well in this field. To make the Microfinance programme popular among the tribes of the State, NABARD prescribes the formation of SHGs with at least 20 members. Suitable modifications have been made in the policies to suit the region which leads to dramatic changes in the programme. The number of SHGs linked to banks in the State was just 28 in March 2005. By March 2006 their number had jumped to 974, which means 946 new SHGs had opened accounts with banks. In SHGs, the emphasis is on savings, and credit is given later, after the banks have made their own assessment of risks involved. In Mizoram, the NABARD chief made it possible for SHGs to open accounts only when assured of a loan. That encouraged the formation of SHGs and their linkages with banks.

TABLE 7

Annual Progress of NABARD under Microfinance (2007-08)

Name of the SCB/DCCBs	No. of SHGs	Amount of loan disbursed *(Rs. in lakhs)*
Commercial Banks	64	222.31
Regional Rural Banks	626	852.47
Cooperative Banks	13	5.68
TOTAL	**703**	**1,080.46**

Source: *NABARD, Regional Office, Aizawl*

During the year 2007-08 NABARD has disbursed Rs. 1,080.46 lakh to 703 SHGs (Table 7) under its Microfinance programme. The highest amount has been disbursed through Rural Banks i.e. Rs.852.47 lakh to 626 SHGs. Up to March, 2008, there were 4,681 SHGs who had opened account with various banks with a total savings of Rs.790.38 lakh. Commercial banks have the largest number of SHGs account holders (2,754) while Rural banks has the highest amount of savings (Rs.752.03 lakh) (Table 8).

TABLE 8

SHG Savings with Banks (as on 31st March 2008)

Name of the SCB/DCCBs	No. of SHGs	Amount (Rs. in lakh)
Commercial Banks	2,754	33.46
Regional Rural Banks	1,506	752.03
Cooperative Banks	421	4.89
TOTAL	**4,681**	**790.38**

Source: *NABARD, Regional Office, Aizawl*

Aizawl district shows the highest number of SHGs which succeeded in getting financial assistance under Microfinance programme of NABARD during the year 2007-08. Aizawl district alone accounts for about 40 percent of the total SHGs in the State which received financial assistance in 2007-08.

The average bank loan disbursed to the SHGs in Aizawl district was Rs. 2.96 lakhs which is the highest in the State, while the SHGs in Serchhip district has disbursed, in an average, only Rs. 36 thousand of bank loan (Table 9). The main reason behind the uneven growth of SHGs and the progress of Microfinance

TABLE 9

District-wise Progress under Microfinance Programme (2007-08)

District	No. of SHGS	Amount of loan disbursed (in Rs. lakh)
Aizawl	267	790.41
Kolasib	75	36.32
Champhai	97	48.80
Mamit	66	34.25
Serchhip	43	15.53
Lunglei	79	111.47
Lawngtlai	42	23.26
Saiha	34	20.42
TOTAL	**703**	**1,080.46**

Source: *NABARD, Regional Office, Aizawl*

among the districts in the State may be due to the sparse distribution of population, poor awareness among the people, lack of banking and other financial services etc. However, Aizawl district shows a comparatively satisfactory progress which may be due to the better provisions of infrastructural facilities which are available as compared to other parts of the State such as power, transport, banking, and marketing etc. Moreover, there exists the economies of scale—both internal and external—in the State capital.

Conclusion

The analysis of the progress of Microfinance in the North Eastern region shows that despite a slow start in the programme in the region, the programme has recorded rapid growth—particularly in Assam, Tripura and Manipur in terms of SHGs financed and loan disbursed. Mizoram, though it has joined the programme lately, has shown a noticeable progress. However, in Meghalaya, the progress of the programme has been very slow in spite of the spurt in the implementation of the programme in the late 1990s. There is a need to review the performance of Self Help Groups Bank Linkage programme in the NER, identify factors that retard its progress and take corrective measures to improve its performance throughout the entire region.

Success of Microfinance in the region required is a multi-prolonged strategy to overcome the assorted challenges it poses. Banks, policymakers and NGOs—the major actors in the field of Microfinance—must come together to think through suitable modifications in policy. Banks may have to change their system of assessing risks.

There is an urgent need for capacity building and expansion of infrastructure. People of the region must be made aware of the programme. In some areas, the SHG model may have to be replaced by other models to suit the local needs and culture.

References

1. Annual Progress under Microfinance, 2007-08, NABARD Regional Office, Aizawl, Mizoram.
2. Basu, J. P. (2006): Microfinance and Women Empowerment—An Empirical Study with special reference to West Bengal. http://www.papers.ssrn.com
3. Deshpande, A. (2008): The challenges of micro-finance in the north east, www.infochangeindia.org
4. Dichter, T. W. (1999):Pakistan, Aga Khan Rural Support Program 1982-1994—Case studies in microfinance, Amazon Books.
5. Economic Survey of Mizoram 2007-08, Planning and Programme Implementation Department, Govt. of Mizoram, Aizawl.
6. Friedmann, J. (1992): Empowerment: The Politics of Alternative Development, Cambridge, Blackwell Publishers.

7. http://www.bankingindiaupdate.com
8. http://www.csesindia.org
9. http://www.databank.nedfi.com
10. http://www.nedfi.com
11. http://www.nerdatabank.nic.in
12. http://www.northeast.nic.in
13. Karmakar, K. G (1999): Rural Credit and Self Help Groups—Microfinance needs and Concepts in India, Sage Publications, New Delhi.
14. Laskar, B. I. (2007): 'Small Scale Industries in Mizoram—A study' in Ahmed, J.U. (ed.), Industrialisation in North-Eastern Region, Mittal Publications, New Delhi.
15. Laskar, B. I. (2009): Small Scale and Cottage Industries in Mizoram; Problems and Employment Prospects, (Unpublished Ph.D Thesis). SEMIS, Mizoram University, Aizawl.
16. Ledgerwood, J. (1998): Microfinance Handbook: An Institutional and Financial Perspective, World Bank Publications.
17. Microfinance in India, 2007-08, NABARD, http://www.nabard.org
18. Mizoram Rural Bank, 25th Annual Report 2007-08, Aizawl, Mizoram.
19. Rajasekhar, D. (1999): Microfinance, Poverty Alleviation and Empowerment of Women, ISEC Publications, Bangalore.
20. Robinson, M. (2001): The Microfinance Revolution: Sustainable Finance for the Poor, World Bank Publications.
21. Robinson, M. (1998): Strategic Issues in Microfinance, Ashgate Publishing, Aldershot.
22. Satish P. (2005): Mainstreaming Indian Microfinance, Economic and Political Weekly, Vol. 40 No. 17 April 23 - April 29.
23. Schreiner, M., Colombet, H. H. (2001): Building or Repairing Institutions: Microcredits in Argentina, Vol. 48, Springer Netherlands.
24. Sen, Amartya (1999): Development as Freedom, Oxford University Press.
25. Statistical Abstract of Mizoram 2007, Directorate of Economics and Statistics, Aizawl.
26. Statistical Handbook Mizoram 2006 & 2008, Directorate of Economics and Statistics, Govt. of Mizoram, Aizawl.
27. Umdor, S. (2007): Microfinance in North East India, http://www.northeasterner.in.
28. World Bank, (1997): Sustainable Banking with the Poor: An Inventory of Microfinance Institutions in Latin America and the Caribbean. World Bank Publication, Washington, DC.

3

Growth and Development of Microfinance—A New Paradigm for Poverty Alleviation

Rais Ahmad and Mohammad Awais

ABSTRACT: *Microfinance has emerged worldover as an effective tool for poverty alleviation, equitable and inclusive growth, and women empowerment. Microfinance in India has gathered momentum to become a major force. Microfinance does not directly address some structural problems facing Indian society and the economy, and it is not yet as efficient as it will be when economies of scale are realised and a more supportive policy environment is created. During last two decades India has achieved remarkable success under NABARD's SHGs Bank Linkage Programme. NABARD started this programme in 1992 and today it is the world's largest programme and about 35 lakhs SHGs have linked with the banks; and, side by side, MFIs also have achieved good results by disbursing loans to the poor women in urban and rural areas without any collateral. With this end in view, the present paper highlights the growth and development of microfinance as a prototype of poverty eradication in India.*

Introduction

Today in most of the developing countries, there is a national agenda in poverty alleviation by supporting rural folks through developing their skills to make them an entrepreneur; however, this can happen only by providing financial support to start their own cottage industries in their respective areas. Word Bank grant or government subsidies may provide temporary solution to the problem and it may not succeed in removing the grassroots level poverty.

To solve this problem the most successful tool that has emerged is known as "Microfinance" (Rastogi, 2008). Microfinance has become the buzz world all over the world to improve the access of credit to the unreached/under-served poor (Agrawal, 2008). Microfinance has emerged world over as an effective tool for poverty alleviation, equitable and inclusive growth, and women empowerment. (Manoj, P. K., 2009). Microfinance in India has gathered momentum to become a major force.

Microfinance does not directly address some structural problems facing Indian society and the economy, and it is not yet as efficient as it will be when economies of scale are realised and a more supportive policy environment is created (Pandey, Bharat et al, 2009). During the last two decades India has achieved remarkable success under NABARD's SHGs Bank Linkage Programme. NABARD started this programme in 1992 and today it is the world's largest programme, and about 35 lakh SHGs have linked with the banks, and, side by side, MFIs also have achieved good results by disbursing loans to the poor women in urban and rural areas without any collateral. SHG members who had taken this programme seriously are enjoying improving their economic and social status in the society but, at the same time, it is seen that non-serious people are not in position to improve their economic conditions and loan under this programme has become a burden for them.

Conceptual Framework of Microfinance

The concept of Microfinance has come into India very recently. Microfinance is a human right and way to end poverty though socio-empowerment has been considered as best alternative for empowerment of rural poor and social change. Microfinance movement is broadly defined on group based institution. In group lending programmes, the function of screening, monitoring, and enforcement of repayment are to a large extent transferred from the bank to the borrower-the group members themselves (Sharma et al, 1997). These perceived advantages of collective actions are seen during the time of screening of loan application and monitoring of borrowers. Even in the area of 'social banking 'banks were highly unapproachable for the rural poor. Due to worldwide wave of economic reforms, the access to credit has fallen further. In this regard microfinance explores new avenue of credit for the rural poor.

In India the model of microfinance delivery can be broadly classified as the Self Help Groups (SHGs) model which is actually a Grameen Bank replication model (Mukherjee and Kundu, 2009). It has been observed that Microfinance often gets equated merely as credit for micro-enterprises while the poor also need savings, consumption loans, housings loans and insurance services. Microfinance is, in fact, a much broader topic and can be defined as the "provision of thrift, credit and other financial services and products of very small amounts to the poor in rural, semi-urban or urban areas for enabling them to raise their income levels and improve living standards. (Sharma, Megna, 2009).

A good definition of microfinance as provided by Robinson is " Microfinance refers to small-scale financial services for both credits and deposits—that are provided to people who farm or fish or herd ; operate small or micro-enterprises where goods are produced, recycled, repaired, or traded; provide services; work for wages or commission; gain income from renting out small amount of land, vehicles, draft animals, or machinery and tools; and to other individuals and local groups in developing countries, in both rural and urban areas"(Robinson 1998).Three different approaches could be identified in the evolution of micro-finance in the world: the Latin American model, the Grameen Bank model and the SHG-based model.

Latin American model is a commercial model. Emphasis on social and community development of poor women is totally missing in such a model. The Grameen model, on the other hand, is basically centred on women and poverty. The self-help group (SHG)-based model is the Indian variant of micro-finance popularized and institutionalized by NABARD, largely through the commercial banking system (Oommen M. A. 2008). The term microfinance sometimes is used interchangeably with the term micro-credit. However, while micro-credit refers to purveyance of loans in small quantities, the term microfinance has a broader meaning covering in its ambit other financial services like saving, insurance as well.

Objectives of Microfinance

The main objectives of microfinance can be summarized as:

1. Providing credit to the deprived and small scale groups and units.
2. Financing the expansion and diversification of such groups' business.
3. Achieving a balanced geographical growth.
4. Promoting and encouraging self-employment for low-skilled and semi-skilled entrepreneurs, especially rural based and backward area groups.
5. Improving the quality of life in education, health sector and on overall basis of weaker sections of the society and eradication of poverty.
6. Enhancing the credit growth in the economy, removal of hurdles to growth in village industries and providing avenues of growth to low priority and general priority sectors.

Microfinance Movement in India

In India, institutional credit agencies (banks) made an entry in rural areas initially to provide an alternative to the rural money lenders who provided credit support, but not without exploiting the rural poor. The first of these pivotal events was India's bank nationalization drive launched in 1969 which required commercial banks to open rural branches resulting in a 15.2% increase in rural bank branches in India between 1973 and 1985 (Wanchoo, Rajat 2007). Today, India has over 33,000 rural branches of commercial banks, about 15,000 branches of regional rural banks, and about 100,000 branches of PACs. On the basis of a research study the NABARD found that even after having multi-agency approach in spreading banking facility in rural areas, the poorest of the poor is not in a position to access the banking facilities due to the meagre requirement of loans. Therefore, in 1992, the NABRD introduced SHG Bank Linkage

Programme to extend the banking facilities to the poorest of poor through informal banking system of SHGs.

Actually, microfinance system was initially started in Bangladesh by Prof. Muhammed Yunus in 1976. The experiment of Prof. M. Yunus delivered very successful results under microfinancing programme through SHGs. Soon the success stories of Bangladesh spread throughout the world and this has been recognised as an effective tool for eradication of poverty.

Poverty Alleviation

According to Adam Smith "Man is rich or poor according to degree in which he can afford to enjoy the necessities, the conveniences and the amusement of the human life." Poverty indicates the condition in which a person is not able to access basic needs of minimum living standards adequate for his physical and mental development. According to the Planning Commission of India, around Rs. 40,000 crores have been spent on poverty alleviation programmes (PAPs). However, a large section of Indian population is still living below poverty line. The Indian economy has prospered rapidly in the last few decades. However, there has been a limited impact from the rising GDP on the 750 million people living in the rural areas of the country. In spite of major developments in the industrial and service sectors, most of the rural population is still occupied in agriculture, which is heavily dependent on seasonal monsoons. Today, about 300 million Indians live on less than $1/day (Kalpana, 2007).

Alleviation of poverty, the core of all development efforts, has remained a very complex and critical concern among developing countries. Poverty is more deep rooted covering several interlocked aspects such as assetlessness, under-employment, uncertain and relatively unproductive employment, low remuneration, lack of bargaining power, economic vulnerability, literacy, proneness to disease, social disadvantage and political powerlessness. Also, poverty has its various manifestations like malnutrition, overcrowding, squalor, slum housing conditions, and infant mortality, drought, flood, and cyclone and resource- poor areas (Nair K and B Girija, 2005). The spread of microfinancing programme is contributing some successful results in improving economic and social status of women in Indian society.

A foremost impact discernible is the reduced dependence of SHG household on informal sources of credit. The members of the SHGs have been able to reduce their dependence on moneylenders very significantly. A study on SHGs reported a decline in the share of moneylender's loan from 66 to 15 percent for the members. In another study, nearly 51 percent of the members closed their old debt with the moneylenders using SHG loans. The members, at the same time, have been able to generate a substantial surplus for themselves due to good performance of their business (Shylendra, H.S, 2008).

Women Empowerment Paradigm

The term 'empowerment' is frequently used in general terms, often synonymous with a multi-dimensional definition of poverty alleviation, the term 'women's empowerment' is often considered best avoided as being too controversial and political. The concept of empowerment has been the subject of much intellectual discourse and analysis. For the purpose of this discussion, the conceptual framework expounded by United Nations is a useful starting point (United Nations 2001). Empowerment is defined as the process by which women takes control and ownership of their lives through expansion of their choices. Thus, it is the process of acquiring the ability to make strategic life choices in a context where this ability has previously been denied. The core element of empowerment have been defined as agency (the ability to define one's goals and act upon them), awareness of gendered power structures, self-esteem and self-confidence (Kabeer, 2001). Empowerment can take place at a hierarchy of different levels—individual, household, community and societal—and is facilitated by providing encouraging factors (e.g. exposure to new activities, which can build capacities) and removing inhibiting factors (e.g. lack of resources and skills) (Chen 1996, and Johnson, 1997).

Here the underlying concerns are gender equality and women's human rights. Women's empowerment is seen as an integral and inseparable part of a wider process of social transformation. The main target group is poor women and women capable of providing alternative female role models for change. Increasing attention has also been paid to men's role in challenging gender inequality.

Microfinance is promoted as an entry point in the context of a wider strategy for women's economic and socio-political empowerment which focuses on gender awareness and feminist organization. As developed by Chen in her proposals for a sub-sector approach to micro-credit, based partly on SEWA's strategy and promoted by UNIFEM, microfinance must be:

Part of a *sectoral strategy* for change which identifies opportunities, constraints and bottlenecks within industries which, if addressed, can raise returns and prospects for large numbers of women. Possible strategies include linking women to existing services and infrastructure, developing new technology such as labour-saving food processing, building information networks, and shifting to new markets, policy level changes to overcome legislative barriers and unionization based on *participatory* principles to build up incremental knowledge of industries and enable women to develop their strategies for change (Chen, 1996).

Economic empowerment is, however, defined in more than individualist terms to include issues such as property rights, changes in intra-household relations and transformation of the macroeconomic context. Many organizations go further than interventions at the industry level to include gender-specific strategies for social and political empowerment. Some programmes have developed very effective means for integrating gender awareness into programmes and for organizing women and men to challenge and change gender discrimination. (Mayoux, Lindai, 2006). The gender inequality is recognized as an issue, the focus is on assistance to households and there is a tendency to see gender issues as cultural and, hence, not subject to outside intervention. The assumption is that increasing women's access to microfinance will enable women to make a greater contribution to household income and this—together with other interventions to increase household—well-being, will translate into improved well-being for women and enable women to bring about wider changes in gender inequality (Mayoux, Lindai, 2006).

Women empowerment and poverty alleviation are two areas which attracted concern of the people worldwide from all the walks of the society like economists, statesmen, politician, saints, poets and who not. Albeit their efforts had brought a gradual change in eradication of poverty and improving the status of women against male chauvinism, they could not contribute significantly on these lines. One proven concept that had universal acceptance in empowering women and eradication of poverty is Micro-credit. People, especially women, who were offered this facility, grabbed the opportunity since they were looking for a medicine that would cure the cancer of poverty and vulnerability (Palanichamy P and P. S. Velmurugan, 2009). Microfinance programmes are currently being promoted as a key strategy for simultaneously addressing both poverty alleviation and women's empowerment (Ahirrao, Jitendra, 2009):

- Increasing women's income levels and control over income leading to greater levels of economic independence.
- Access to networks and markets giving wider experience of the world outside the home, access to information and possibilities for development of other social and political roles.
- Enhancing perceptions of women's contribution to household income and family welfare, increasing women's participation in household decisions about expenditure and other issues and leading to greater expenditure on women's welfare.
- More general improvement in attitudes to women's role in the household and community.

It is found that microfinance programmes have provided opportunities to poor women in urban and rural areas to improve their economic, social and political status in the society. If this programme is tailor-made and adequate amount of loan is provided easily to the poor women in different region it can deliver remarkable results for empowering women.

Growth and Development

Microfinance is a form of financial development that has as its primary aim poverty alleviation. The development paradigm, microfinance, has evolved as a need based policy and programmes to cater to the so far neglected target groups such as women—poor, rural, deprived, etc. Its evolution is based on the concern of all developing countries for empowerment of the poor and the alleviation of poverty. Development organizations and policy-makers have included access to credit for poor people as a major aspect of many poverty alleviation programmes. Microfinance programmes have, in the recent past, become one of the more promising ways to use scarce development funds to achieve the objectives of poverty alleviation. Furthermore, certain microfinance programmes have gained prominence in the development field and beyond.

The basic idea of microfinance is simple: if poor people are provided access to financial services, including credit, they may very well be able to start or expand a micro-enterprise that will allow them to break out of poverty (Patra, 2009). The microfinance sector is characterised by a variety of microfinance service providers. These include various apex financial institutions like SIDBI and NABARD, Government owned societies like Rashtriya Mahila Kosh, formal sector financial institutions, commercial banks, RRBs, in addition to member based institutions like cooperatives, mutually aided cooperative societies, SHG federations, private sector companies, like specialized NBFCs, societies, trusts etc. Besides the existence of such a large number of players in the organized/ semi-organized sector, the rural credit market in India was largely dominated by the all pervading network of indigenous moneylenders.

There are a multitude of NGOs who can be virtually found in all villages and blocks in India. Most of these NGOs have similar origin in that they started off as social service and welfare organization with a focus on helping the poor and needy in times of disaster, famine or epidemic. The emphasis, therefore, was mainly on social and welfare activities like housing, health, education, safe drinking water, sanitation etc. However, with the growing popularity of Microfinance in India, these NGOs have also taken up Microfinance activity as a part of their overall service strategy. While some have adopted Microfinance as their core activity, large number of such institution have adopted multiple operations with a limited investment in Microfinance. These organizations include fully government to semi-government as well as private entities (Pandey P. 2009).

Today, when the majority of the world's population is living below subsistence level, more than 3,000 organizations are providing microfinance services to millions of the world's poor. In India, the NABARD is playing an important role in alleviating poverty by increasing the SHGs-Bank linkage programme through its partner agencies. The promotion of SHGs in India began more formally in 1992 with the launch of the SHG-Bank Linkage Programme by National Bank for Agriculture and Rural Development (NABARD). The programme's main aim was to improve the rural poor's access to formal credit system in a cost-effective and sustainable manner by making use of SHGs (Shylendra H.S., 2008).

The present status of microfinance sector appears to be good and satisfactory with repayment rates as high as 98 percent. But this does not mean that all is smooth selling. The sub-prime market collapse has made many microfinance institutions nervous. And rightly so: like banks in developed nations,

Table 1

Largest Microfinance Institutions

Institution	Country	No. of Borrowers (mn)
Grameen Bank	Bangladesh	5.1
ASA	Bangladesh	4.2
Brac	Bangadesh	4.2
BRI	Indonesia	3.3
Proshika	Bangladesh	1.6
Share	India	0.8
Spandana	India	0.8
Caja Popular Maxicana	Mexico	0.6
Compartamos	Mexico	0.5
Bantara	Peru	0.5

Source: *Microcapital Monitor, Microfinance Information Exchange*

microfinance organizations were incentivised to expand rapidly in recent years, transforming the sector from an industry dominated by NGOs, like Grameen Bank in Bangladesh , to one led by for profit companies including compartamos in Mexico and SKS Microfinance in India(Vassiliou and Oliver 2009). Table 1 shows the name of different popular MFIs with number of borrowers.

SHGs-Bank Linkage Programme

NABARD (2005) explains that the Self Help Group is a group with "an average size of about 15 people from a homogeneous class. They come together for addressing their common problems. They are encouraged to make voluntary thrift on a regular basis. They use this pooled resource to make small interest bearing loans to their members. The process helps them imbibe the essentials of financial intermediation including prioritization of needs, setting terms and conditions and accounts keeping. This gradually builds financial discipline in all of them. They also learn to handle resources of a size that is much beyond the individual capacities of any of them. The SHG members begin to appreciate that resources are limited and have a cost.

Once the groups show this mature financial behavior, banks are encouraged to make loans to the SHG in certain multiples of the accumulated savings of the

SHG. The bank loans are given without any collateral and at market interest rates. The groups continue to decide the terms of loans to their own members. Since the groups' own accumulated savings are part and parcel of the aggregate loans made by the groups to their members, peer pressure ensures timely repayments."

The SHG bank linkage programme links a SHG group to banks, where the banks provide a loan to a mature group. The group places its savings in the group deposit account in the bank (at about 12% per annum), using its group savings and group guarantee as a collateral. NABARD provides subsidized refinancing support to banks to encourage such lending. India has 37% of the world's population earning less than $1 a day, of which 60% are women (Human Development Report, 2003). The Government of India, National Policy for the Empowerment of Women (2001), declared various measures aimed towards achieving greater equality between men and women.

In India, a number of self-help groups (SHGs) were created in the 1980s for providing credit facilities to the poor, especially women, in both urban and rural areas. A self-help group has been defined as a small and informal association of poor having preferably similar socio-economic background and who have come together to realize some common goals based on the principles of self-help and collective responsibility.

SHGs become relevant because of the following reasons: First, a SHG working on the principle of solidarity helps the poor for their savings and access credit facilities. A SHG, by tapping social capital like trust and reciprocation, helps in replacing physical collateral, a major hurdle faced by the poor in obtaining formal credit. Then, through the principles of joint liability and peer pressure, a SHG

TABLE 2

Showing the SHG-Bank Linkage Cumulative Progress (1992-2008)

Up to End March	SHGs	Growth in Percentage	Bank Loan (Rs.) Million	Growth in Percentage
1992-99	32,995		571	
1999-00	1,14,775		1,930	
2000-01	2,63,825	129.95	4,809	149.17
2001-02	4,61,478	74.92	10,263	113.41
2002-03	7,17,360	55.44	20,487	99.62
2003-04	10,79,091	50.42	39,042	90.56
2004-05	16,18,456	49.98	68,985	76.69
2005-06	22,38,565	38.31	1,13,975	65.22
2006-07	29,24,973	30.66	1,80,407	58.29
2007-08	34,77,965	18.90	2,54,198	40.90

Source: *NABARD, Mumbai (www.nabard.org)*

ensures prompt loan recovery from the members. In the process, a SHG helps the poor, especially women, to establish their creditworthiness (Shylendra H.S., 2008). The SHGs-Bank Linkage Program in India is the largest microfinance programme in the world. NABARD has been playing supportive role by way of refinancing banks, organizing training programmes for NGOs, bank officers and SHG members for upgrading skills for smooth operation of SHGs Bank Linkage. The launching of the Pilot Project initiating the SHG-bank Linkage in Feb. 1992 is indeed a landmark in development banking with the poor as it has been covering the poorest of the poor who were so far neglected by the formal financial sector (Lokhande A. and Murlidhar, 2009).

Table 2 shows the growth of SHGs under the NABARD's SHG Bank Linkage Programme. The SHG-Bank Linkage Programme of NABARD has emerged as the primary model for providing Microfinance (MF) services in the country. It is a proven tool of extending to the un-banked rural clientele access to formal financial services. Encouraged by the success of the programme, NABARD promoted the linkage of Microfinance Institutions (MFIs) with the banking sector. The MFI–bank linkage model too has assumed importance on account of credit support extended by banks for lending to clients by MFIs. During the year 2008-09 5,52,992 new SHGs (excluding SGSY) were credit linked with banks and bank loan of Rs.2,541.98 crore disbursed, taking the cumulative number of SHGs credit linked to 34,77,965 as on 31 March, 2008. In addition 1,86,883 existing SHGs were provided repeat loan of Rs.1,685.60 crore. The programme has covered more than 5.8 crore poor households, making it the largest MF programme in the world. During 2006-07, bank credit of Rs.6, 570.39 crore and Rs.1,151.56 crore was disbursed to 11.05 lakh SHGs (including 1.88 lakh under SGSY) and 334 MFIs, respectively (NABARD, 2007-08).

Issues and Challenges

Important challenge facing the banking sector is to extend financial services to all sections of society. Like others, the poor need a range of financial services that are convenient, flexible, and affordable; and not just loans. The concept of "financial inclusion" has come up at right time and it is beneficial for society as well as banking institutions. The microfinancing system and financial inclusion may work effectively for alleviation of poverty from the country and the micro-financing system in India is playing a very significant role in providing credit through the informal banking system to the poorest of the poor who so far have been neglected.

The SHG Bank Linkage Programme has shown a much skewed growth pattern in the country. The programme is largely concentrated in the southern region of the country. It is necessary that the microfinance programme must spread more evenly so that the benefits are available equally to all sections of the society in all regions of the country. The challenge for NGOs and MFIs is to achieve their own financial self-sufficiency without transferring all the overhead costs to their poor clients. They need to ensure sufficient investment to provide diversified livelihood options and employment creation by optimizing existing resources through timely credit, technical inputs, skill training and knowledge transfer. It is crucial to arrive at the right trade off between the needs of the poor and the sustainability of the MFIs. Now the economy is facing a new challenge of financial inclusion with an inclusive growth. The banking sector can play a lead and proactive role in ensuring financial inclusion through SHG-Bank Linkage Programme. It is necessary that SHG quality must be improved, and all stakeholders should work together towards it.

A few impediments in efficient working of microfinance system are—the information gap, lake of use of KYC (know your client) data, illiterate populace, lack of infrastructure etc. Steps should be taken up to remove these impediments. It is necessary to develop an IT platform where knowledge can be shared with all the stakeholders. Government institutions like NABARD, SIDBI etc. should take necessary steps to allow the MFIs to raise funds by issuing bonds and debenture to the public. In this way adequate funds will be available and loans can be disbursed to the poor at lower rate of interest. Government should ensure that the rate of interest on micro-loans should not be more than the primary lending rate and this can be done by taking the microfinancing business by the banking sector under the category of prime lending.

Conclusion

The microfinance system has shown very fast growth across the country in terms of geographical coverage, increased clientele, portfolio, institutional involvement etc. since it was taken up by the NABARD in 1992 under its SHG-Bank Linkage Programme. Increasingly more and more promoting organizations, financial institutions, donors and clients are getting associated with this programme because it has the aim for alleviation of poverty and empowering women. It is said that this programme is quite useful in empowering women. This idea is based on the view that women are more likely to be credit constrained, have restricted access to wage labour market and have limited decision-making and bargaining power within the household. If women empowerment is to be pursued as a serious objective by SHG programmes in particular and the larger microfinance community in general, greater emphasis needs to be placed on training, education and creating awareness in order to achieve a larger and more lasting empowerment. Women should be encouraged to work in groups and produce goods of standard quality to achieve growing and sustainable business. An individual cannot produce goods of standard quality under the microfinancing system—specially in rural area. These women do not know the need and choice of the urban area consumers. Therefore, they should work in focused manner by taking up one item for production and distribution and its business by converting SHG into a cooperative enterprise after reaching a certain level of business. In this way the membership of women and branches of cooperative enterprise will increase rapidly in different regions of the country. They should work on the pattern of SEWA and Lijjat Papad.

References

1. Agarwal, G. K. (2008), "In the Credit Microcosm", *The Economic Times*, New Delhi, January 1.
2. Ahirrao, Jitendra (2009), "Rural Women Empowerment through Microfinance", *Kurukshetra*, Vol.57, No. 4, February, pp. 23-25.
3. Attali, Jaques (2008), "Linking Microfinance with Poorest of Poor", *The Economic Times*, New Delhi, June 10.
4. Basu, P. and Srivastava, P. (2005), "Scaling up Microfinance for India's Rural Poor", World Bank Policy Research Working Paper 3646, Washington DC.
5. Chen, M (1996), "Beyond Credit: A Subsector Approach to Promoting Women's Enterprise", Agha Khan Foundation, Canada.
6. Harris-Daley, Sam (2009), "Microfinance most cost-effective, efficient way of reducing poverty', The Economic Times, New Delhi, April 21.
7. Johnson, S. (1997), Gender and Microfinance: Guidelines for best Practices, *Action Aid*, London, U.K.
8. Kabeer, N. (2001), "Resources, Agency, Achievements: Reflection on the Measurement of Women's Empowerment", in *Discussing Women's Empowerment—Theory and Practices*, SIDA Studies No. 3.
9. Kalpana, Sarkar(2007), "Microfinance Institutions: Challenges for Start Up", *Microfinance Focus*, August.
10. Lokhande, Murlidhar A. (2009), "Microfinance Initiatives in India", *Kurukshetra*, Vol. 57, No. 4, February, pp. 16-18.
11. Manoj, P. K. (2009), "Microfinance in India—the Way Ahead", *Microfinance and Women Empowerment*, Part 2, (ed.) Dr. Rais Ahmad, Mittal Publications, New Delhi, pp. 621-638.
12. Mayoux, Lindai (2006), "Women's Empowerment through Sustainable Microfinance: Rethinking Best Practices", *Gender and Microfinance*, http://www.genfinance.net
13. Mukherjee, Arghya Kusum and Amit Kundu (2009), "Accessibility of Credit to Rural Poor—Reduction of Transaction Cost", Proceeding *Micro Finance – Performance Evaluation and Enterprise Development*, (eds.) Dr. Daniel Lazar and Prof. Malabika Deo, Allied Publishers Pvt. Ltd., New Delhi, pp. 59-74.
14. NABARD (2005), "Progress of SHG-Bank Linkage in India"; Micro-credit Innovations Department, Mumbai.
15. NABARD Annual Report 2007-2008, Mumbai.
16. Nair, K. Manoharan, (2005), "Microfinance: The New Development Paradigm for Poverty Eradication and Women's Empowerment", *Kurukshetra*, Vol.53, No. 6, April, pp. 18-20.

17. Oommen, M.A. (2008), Microfinance and Poverty Alleviation: The Cases of Kerala Kudumbashree, Working Paper No. 7, URL www.cseindia.org

18. Palanichamy, P. and P. S. Velmurugan(2009), "The Role of Micro Credit in Empowering Women in the Coastal Areas of Pondicherry", Proceeding *Micro Finance – Performance Evaluation and Enterprise Development* , (eds.) Dr. Daniel Lazar and Prof. Malabika Deo, Allied Publishers Pvt. Ltd., New Delhi, pp. 288-303.

19. Pandey, Priyanka(2009), "Microfinance in India – Emerging Perspectives and Trends", *Microfinance and Women Empowerment,* Part 2,(ed.) Dr. Rais Ahmad, Mittal Publications, New Delhi, pp. 483-502.

20. Pandey, Bharat (2009), "Growth of Microfinance in India: Opportunities and Challenges", Proceeding *Micro Finance – Performance Evaluation and Enterprise Development* , (eds.) Dr. Daniel Lazar and Prof. Malabika Deo, Allied Publishers Pvt. Ltd., New Delhi, pp. 83-95.

21. Patra, Sudhir Ch.(2009), "Microfinance and Alleviation of Poverty", *Microfinance and Women Empowerment,* Part 2, (ed.) Dr.Rais Ahmad, Mittal Publications, New Delhi, pp. 645-652.

22. Rastogi, Tripathi (2008), "Microfinance And Poverty Prevention", Abstract Published in Souvenir of Seminar *Environment, Agriculture and Poverty* held on 10-11 February, at GSH College, Amroha, p. 64.

23. Robinson, Marguerite, (1998), "Microfinance: the Paradigm Shift from Credit Delivery to Sustainable Financial Intermediation", (eds.) Mwangi *et al, Strategic Issues in Microfinance,* Ashgate Publishing, Aldershot.

24. Sharma, Megna (2009), "Microfinance: A Comparative Analysis of Different Delivery Models in India", Proceeding *Microfinance—Performance Evaluation and Enterprise Development,* (eds.) Dr. Daniel Lazar and Prof. Malabika Deo, Allied Publishers Pvt. Ltd., New Delhi, pp. 18-30.

25. Sharma, M. and M. Zeller (1997), Repayment Performance in Group Based Credit Programs in Bangladesh: An Empirical Analysis, *World Development,* Vol. 25, No. 10, pp. 1731-1742.

26. Shylendra, H. S. (2008), "Microfinance: Roles of Self Help Groups", *Yojana,* Vol. 52, January, pp. 25-28.

27. United Nations (2001), "Empowerment of Women throughout the Life cycle as a Transformative Strategy for Poverty Eradication", Report.

28. Vassiliou, Philip and Oliver Justin (2009), "Microfinancers must stay clear of credit risks" *The Economic Times,* New Delhi, July 22.

29. Wanchoo, Rajat (2007), "Microfinance in India: The Changing Face of Microcredit Schemes", MPRA paper No. 3675.

4

An Account of Macro- and Microfinance Situation in Assam

B. K. Barooah

Abstract: *Credit is one among those facilities which—in different forms and structures—originate from the existing financial institutions with the objectives of bringing overall economic development of the State. The State has a network of banks, cooperatives and other financial institutions which are responsible for providing credit support to customers who belong to different sectors of the economy. The State, being predominantly agrarian, depends primarily on agriculture and allied activities. The progress that has taken place in institutional financing in the State over the years during post-nationalization, post-reform period fails to bring significant changes to the large scale developmental disparities which prevailed in the economy of the State. At this juncture, the present article gives an account of Macro- and microfinance situation in Assam.*

Assam—like any other seven North Eastern states of India has—many inequalities. Credit is one among them which, in different forms and structures, originate from the existing financial institutions with the objectives of bringing overall economic development of the State. The Ståte has a network of banks, cooperatives and other financial institutions which are responsible for providing credit support to customers who belong to different sectors of the economy. The State, being predominantly agrarian, has 53 per cent population depend primarily on agriculture and allied activities for their livelihood. There is 26.83 lakh farm families out of which 62.2 per cent are marginal farmers (having less than 1 ha. of land) and 20.9% are small farmers (having 1-2 ha of land). The large farmers (with holding of 10 ha or more) concentration in the State is only 0.2% recording an average land holding of 1.17 hectares only. The large farmers with holding of 10 ha or more) concentration in the State is only 0.2% recording an average land holding of 1.17 hectares only. Assam for being the largest worth Eastern State accounted 68.7 per cent of the North East population. In Assam 36 per cent of the population live below poverty line and 88.9 per cent of the population lives in rural areas.

The progress that has taken place in institutional financing in the State over the years during post-nationalization, post-liberalization and post-reform period failed to bring significant changes to the large scale developmental disparities prevailed in the economy of the State. The quarterly statistics of deposits and credit of scheduled commercial banks of Reserve Bank of India in March 2010 indicate that Assam has 1,517 branches of Schedule commercial banks out of which 403 were Regional Rural Banks. Each bank branch office served on an average 17,600 population (based on 2001 census) in the state in March 2010 which is, however, quite unsatisfactory in comparison to the all India average of 12,500 population during the same period.

The banking services in the rural areas are far more inadequate with one branch office for every 29,000 people in Assam against one branch for 23,000 people in the country. The credit-deposit ratio of the banking institutions were also far from satisfactory in the State, being 41.2 in March 2008 against 74.2 for the country—reflecting a poor performance of banking activities. Credit outstanding per capita in rural areas as on March 2008 also depicts a dismay picture with Rs. 1,365 in Assam against as many as 22 other states with higher rural credit outstanding per capita ranging from Rs. 1,444 to Rs. 10,266 in case of Kerela and Goa respectively. Only five States of the country—namely Jharkhand, Chattisgarh, Manipur, Bihar and Nagaland—recorded to have rural credit outstanding per capita less than Assam during this period. This phenomenon is also noticed from the fact that the percentage share of priority sector lending to agriculture and allied activities in the State remained far below being 8.37 in 2003-04 and 13.42% in 2007-08 against the stipulated all India benchmark of 18 per cent.

The Reserve Bank of India has taken several initiatives to provide smooth and efficient banking services to the vast sections of the dis-advanced and low incomes without discrimination. With the said objective, the Reserve Bank of India, in consultation with State Government, has adopted a new credit policy "Financial Sector Plan for N.E. Region" for quicker financial inclusion of all people in the region including Assam. This new policy was launched in October 2006. A High Power Committee has also been set up with the Chief Secretary as Chairman to monitor the implementation of the Plan which emphasized—among other things—a rapid improvement of microfinance delivery system in Assam and the North Eastern region. Since launching of the financial sector plan, overall credit flow in the State has improved significantly over the 2 year period from 2006 to 2008, deposits grew by 47% while credit grew by 63% in March 2008—registering a CD ratio of 50.48 which includes the loan issued by NEDFI and NABARD also.

In the focus paper of 2010-11 financial year, National Bank for Agriculture and Rural Development (NABARD) stated that the bank would aim at providing services to the weaker sections and thereby attain 100 per cent financial inclusion by 2015 in the State. The bank identified agriculture, financial inclusions, development of rural infrastructure and food security as the thrust areas in the next fiscal in Assam. NABARD, under its Rural Infrastructure Development Fund (RIDF), had sanctioned till December 2009 to the extent of Rs. 1,523.68 crore for rural bridge projects, major and minor irrigation projects, rural road projects among other infrastructure projects.

Under the above background of financial intermediation, the NABARD has assessed a total credit potential of Rs. 3,255.96 crore for the financial year 2010-11 for the State of Assam. The top priority has been accorded to the agriculture sector for which the credit plan size has been projected to be Rs. 1,315.77 crore, followed by Rs. 514.24 crore for non-farm sector, and Rs. 47.77 crore for the food processing sector.

In the presence of different banking and other financial institutions, the financial performance however, could not be picked up as expected over the years due to some reasons that are peculiar to the State like any other parts of the North Eastern Region. Microfinance programme also had a late start in the State and, under this, SHG Bank Linkage Strategy has gathered momentum from 2001-02 year onwards only. By the end of March 2008, a total of 2, 57,863 SHGs have been bank linked in the State out of which 1,15,716 SHGs were credit linked. In the subsequent years, although SHG movement was gaining further momentum in the State, only 1.56 lakh out of 2.20 lakh have been credit linked by the end of March 2010.

Microfinance through self-help group has been recognised as one of the most useful and productive tools of poverty alleviation in most of the developing countries of the world. Microfinance can do miracle in an economically backward State like Assam where as high as 36 per cent of the population is living below the poverty line and where more than 21 lakh people are chronically unemployed. It is justified to plan and design a new set of financial institutions to look after the credit needs of a huge section of the State population who are till today un-reached, un-served and un-explored under the great mission of social building process.

Keeping in view the importance of microfinance on poverty alleviation, the Government of Assam, on December 6, 2009, formally launched the Chief Minister's microfinance scheme "Khudra Reen" for providing low cost fund to the Self-Help-Groups (SHGs) / Joint Liability Groups (JLGs) through MFI / NGOs for livelihood promotion and economic empowerment of the poorer section of the society. Under this scheme, the Government of Assam has made available a fund of Rs. 10 crore to Assam Financial Corporation (AFC) which is the implementing agency for the scheme. The scheme advocates an innovative credit delivery system unlike the formal collateral-oriented lending institutions and formal structures.

Swarnajayanti Gram Swarojgar Yojana (SGSY) is another popular poverty alleviation programme which aims at raising economic status of rural people through providing sustainable economic activities to the people living below the poverty line with bank loan and government subsidy. Reports of State Level Bankers Committee, Assam, indicates that, up to the year 2007-08, 1.52 lakh SHGs have been formed out of which 54,790 SHGs were given small loans amounting to a total of Rs. 31,006.57 crores by banks and SGSY.

North Eastern Development Finance Corporation Ltd (NEDFi)—which was incorporated on August 9, 1995 with its registered office at Guwahati—has been giving reasonable thrust in rural finance and microfinance and disbursed an amount of Rs. 12.39 crore during the period 1999-2000 to 2006-07. NEDFI would continue to focus on identifying microfinance institutions (MFI) as long term partners and providing credit support for their micro-credit initiatives. The MFIs may be well organized non-government organizations with good networks or other microfinance organizations. Including NEDFi, more than 119 non-banking financial companies (NBFCs) are at present functioning in the State. Most of these companies are involved with hire-purchase and leasing activities of the small social entrepreneurs.

Of late, Assam's emerging microfinance sector has received a boost, with a foreign company picking up a stake in Asomi Finance Private Ltd - an institution which undertakes microfinance, income generation and development activities in the State. Asomi got its non-banking financial company (NBFC) license from the Reserve Bank of India on October 30-2009. A Belgium microfinance company-Incofin—which operates in 23 countries in the world has contributed 34 per cent stake (Rs. 8 crore) recently in Assam. The Telegraph quoted as saying by Subhra Jyoti Bharali, the chairman-cum-managing director of AFPL, that the non-banking financial company—Asomi—was formed to raise capital to lend the rural poor in the State since 2002. But initially the company faced difficulty to raise capital to canalize to the rural mass through a non-government organization. Hence the company was formed to raise capital from the market and provide it to the people who want to engage in income generating activities to enhance their living standards. With a target of reaching two lakh families in the State, the company has been able to help 33,000 families scattered in 16 districts through finance, skill upgrades and capacity development. Asomi has nurtured dreams to initiate big microfinance project in the State. Already it has started a dairy plant where the farmers supply milk and get one of the best remunerations. The milk, in turn, is sold to customers at a competitive price. Encouraged by its good response, it now plans to set up another dairy plant in Guwahati to supply milk to the people living in Assam's capital city. It is also known that AFPL has been experimenting with a pilot project of contract farming for rice in the state.

Microfinance can play a significant role in an economically backward state like Assam, where more than one-third of the population is still living below the poverty line and where a huge section of the population are unemployed. Moreover, this programme may serve better the most potential and viable component of the Assamese society—the womenfolk—to give them the much needed self-confidence to venture into different kinds of entrepreneurial abilities. The State needs to take up more and more ambitious projects and implement them with a firm commitment of social justice and financial inclusion.

References

1. Economic Survey Assam, 2008-09, Directorate of Economics and Statistics Assam, Guwahati.
2. Roopak Goswami, Belgian Stake in Assam firm. The Telegraph, June 15, 2009.
3. Shantanu Nandan Sharma, Asomi's loans: A boon for Assam people. The Economic Times, 30th May, 2010.
4. NEDFi, Microfinance Scheme: Microfinance Scheme—News and Features Development News, India, June 19, 2010.
5. The Assam Tribune. CM asks banks to step up rural credit. June 15, 2010.
6. Department of Agriculture, Government of Assam. Scheme and Projects: Agricultural Credit, June 21, 2010.
7. Namita Devi, CM's microfinance scheme. The Assam Tribune, January 26, 2010.

5

Microfinance in India: The Task Ahead

Raihan Uddin Ahmed Bora

ABSTRACT: *Indian banking system—although the largest banking network in the world—did not meet the credit requirements of the poor. Microfinance services are financial services that poor people desire and are ready to pay for. The term also refers to the practice of sustainable delivering those services. Broadly, it refers to a movement that envisions a world in which as many poor and near-poor households as possible have permanent access to an appropriate range of high quality financial services, including not only credit but also savings, insurance, and fund transfers. Microfinance is the provision of a broad range of financial services such as deposits, loans, payment services, money transfers, and insurance to poor and low income households and their micro-enterprises. Thus, it is identical to rural finance as practiced in India. Realizing this, the present paper is an attempt to highlight the problems and prospects of microfinance in India.*

Introduction

Indian banking system, which is among the largest banking networks in the world, did not contact most of the rural poor in India. About 70 per cent of the Indian population from rural areas accounted for only 30 per cent of bank deposits. The banks did not meet the credit requirements of the poor and they were forced to fall back on moneylenders for credit. Though the banks were nationalized, they perceived rural credit to be a high risk and high cost proposition. The rural borrowers were bogged down by elaborate procedures that were required to obtain loans. The central bank in India, RBI, on its part, tried to cater to the needs of the rural poor by establishing regional rural banks and cooperative banks, but did not meet with success. In the early 1990s, to provide credit and savings services to the poor, microfinance was envisaged. It received further boost with involvement of several non-governmental organizations and microfinance institutions.

Microfinance services are financial services that poor people want and are ready to pay for. The term also refers to the practice of sustainable delivering those services. Broadly, it refers to a movement that envisions a world in which as many poor and near-poor households as possible have permanent access to an appropriate range of high quality financial services, including not only credit but also savings, insurance, and fund transfers. Microfinance is the provision of a broad range of financial services such as deposits, loans, payment services, money transfers, and insurance to poor and low income households and their micro-enterprises. Thus, it is synonymous to rural finance as practiced in India. Of late, semi-formal institutions such as non-governmental organizations and non-banking financial companies have entered the rural credit business, bringing in a new approach of lending to groups of people popularly known as Self-Help Groups. It is this nature of lending involving SHGs which is referred to as microfinance in the present parlance.

Precincts of Microfinance

Hypothetically, microfinance included financial service used by deprived people including those they access in the informal economy, such as loans from a village moneylender. In practice however, the term is usually only used to refer to institutions and enterprises whose goals include both profitability and reducing the poverty of their clients. Microfinance services are needed everywhere, including the developed world. However, in developed economies, extreme competition within the financial sector, combined with a diverse merge of different financial institutions with different missions, ensures that most people have access to some financial services. Efforts to transfer microfinance innovations such as solidarity lending from developing countries to developed ones have met with little success. Microfinance can also be distinguished from charity. It is better to provide grants to families who are destitute, or so poor they are unlikely to be able to generate the cash flow required to pay back a loan.

Need for Microfinance

The conventional rural credit system in India has not been successful, notwithstanding its long existence and various interventions, in reaching the needy sections of the society. Till 1991, it was exposed by All India Debt and Investment Survey (GOI 1998), dependence of rural households on informal sources of finance for cash debt was to the tune of 37.4 per cent. Paradoxically, the level of confidence on informal agencies continued at the same level and has seen impressive expansion of network of credit institutions. Further, most of the credit institutions are in continuous loss or insignificant profits so that their sustainability in the rural credit business is at chance. Thus, there seems to be a big vacuum so far as flow of credit to small borrowers—comprising marginal and small farmers, as also artisans and village craftsmen—are concerned. The women and agricultural laborers have already been barred from the beginning from the purview of institutional credit system, as they cannot offer the necessary collateral the banks demand for extending the credit. These deprived sections are either excluded or oppressed through. Thus, there are certain categories of rural inhabitants having only aspirations to prosper without the necessary access to credit. In fact, an efficient and viable credit delivery system catering to a large section of the poor is still a distant dream. This situation has led to the introduction of SHGs in the country by some NGOs in the mid-1980s. The movement received institutional back-up with the linking of SHGs with banks.

Growth of Microfinance in India

A multiplicity of microfinance schemes and various approaches have been practiced by both governmental and non-governmental organizations in India. Leading national financial institutions like the National Bank for Agriculture and Rural Development (NABARD), the Small Industries Development Bank of India (SIDBI) and the Rashtriya Mahila Kosh (RMK) have played a significant role in making micro-credit a real movement in India. Professional Assistance for Development Action (PRADAN), International Centre for Entrepreneurship and Career Development (ICECD), Mysore Resettlement and Development Agency (MYRADA), Self Employed Women's Association (SEWA); act as resource organizations and have been successful in replicating their experiences in other parts of the country without restricting to one area.

There are three models being followed in the area of Microfinance in India: In Model 1, banks themselves take up the work of forming and nurturing the self-help groups, opening their accounts and providing them with bank loans. Up to March 2008, about 22 per cent of SHGs financed were from this category. In Model 2, where SHGs are formed by formal agencies other than banks, NGOs and others, but directly financed by banks, have occupied the major share with 73 per cent of the total number of SHGs as on 31th March 2008. Model 3 consists of SHGs financed by banks using NGOs and other agencies as financial intermediaries. The share of cumulative number of SHGs linked to this model is relatively small i.e., 6 per cent. There is an increase in the number of SHGs financed through banks from 32,995 in the year 1992-99 to 22,38,565 in the year 2005-06. The amount of loans disbursed through the banks have increased from Rs.571 million in the year 1992-99 to Rs.1,13,975 million in the year 2005-06. The refinance support made available were Rs. 4,15,978 million. As per the information available, 90 per cent of the SHGs linked to banks were women SHGs. For the purpose of providing microfinance, not only the SHGs were linked to bank, but also they link to RRBs and cooperative banks.

Up to the year 2005-06, nearly 44,362 branches of 547 banks have participated in the SHG-Bank Linkage Programme. All the 27 public sector banks and 20 private sector banks and the cooperative banks had participated in this linkage programme. SBI credit linked the highest number of SHGs followed by the Indian Bank and Canara Bank. During that year, IOB, PNB, Andhra Bank, Bank of India, Bank of Baroda registered impressive growth in SHG-Bank Linkage.

Constraints Attributed to Microfinance Services

1. ***Restriction in access to financial services:*** Women in particular have found it difficult to access financial services provided by the mainstream banking systems. Banking laws may contain discriminatory provisions, and inheritance laws, property rights provisions and matrimonial property rules may also discriminate against women and prevent them from concluding loan contracts or provide conventional collateral. As a consequence, many women use microfinance services. Access to microfinance services may, however, also be difficult. Women may lack the time and money required to undertake repeated journeys to the nearest microfinance institutions. High formal and informal loan application fees can also restrict access, as can bias attitudes by (male) microfinance institution staff. Women's low levels of literacy and numeracy skills may also constitute an obstacle to access. At the same time, women do enjoy easier assess to financial services than men where microfinance institutions specifically target women.
2. ***Lack of control over microfinance loans:*** Commentators have observed that women do not always control the use of the loans they have obtained, and that male family members strongly influence loan use. In some cases, women are intermediaries between male members of the household and microfinance institution staff. This has been particularly well documented in Bangladesh among the large microfinance institutions. Where microfinance institutions target women users exclusively, the incentive for men to use women as intermediaries is further accentuated. Moreover, men's resentment towards women in their household who have obtained loans has led to cases of domestic violence. On the other hand, the most economically successful families among the poor were those in which both husband and wife were economic factors in their own right working in partnership. These experiences are indicative of existing intra-household power relations. Lack of empowerment of women is thus an area requiring further attention.
3. ***Lack of sustainability of microfinance institutions:*** Microfinance institutions must be financially self-sustainable if they are to provide long-term reliable services to users. Most literature refers to the viability of microfinance institutions as their ability to cover costs from earned revenue. Three levels of viability are identified: (a) subsidy dependent, (b) operationally self-sufficient, and (c) fully financially self-sufficient.

4. ***Lack of sustainability of micro-enterprise projects:*** *Micro*-enterprise projects must be viable and sustainable if they are to reduce poverty. A major concern in this respect is the size of projects supported by microfinance loans. Loans obtained by women tend to be small compared to those obtained by men, because poorer women tend to be more risk-averse, prefer to draw on own savings, or may have limited access to credit because of their credit history or compulsory savings requirements of a microfinance institution. Thus, their project activities remain on a small scale or, at best, grow very slowly.
5. ***Shortcomings in analysis of poverty:*** The definitions, measurement and analysis of poverty mostly focus on income and consumption patterns. However, it is difficult to determine the exact depth and extent of poverty among women. Sex-disaggregated income statistics on women's participation in the formal labour market rarely exist. Income and consumption patterns are expressed in standard of living measurements based on household surveys that do not reflect the intra-household distribution of income and assets, and intra-household consumption patterns. Factors such as household diversity with regard to size and structure, resource allocation within the household (pooling of resources for common welfare or allocation for individual welfare and the associated decision-making process), and responsibilities among household members for meeting daily consumption needs are important aspects in determining women's poverty.
6. ***Limitation in measuring women's empowerment:*** The empowerment of women has recently been described as the process by which women take control over their lives, acquiring the ability to make strategic choices. Empowerment is thus the process of acquiring the ability to make strategic life choices in a context where this ability was previously denied. Empowerment is both a goal and a process. While empowerment is a process of change that can only be driven by women themselves, it can be facilitated by others. Empowerment involves changes on several levels that are mutually reinforcing: individual level, group/community level, as well as at the level of society and its institutions.

The Road Ahead

Commercial banks have usually not served poor clients as they must incur substantial costs to manage a client's account. However, there has been significant advancement relating to the concept and practice of SHG-based microfinance. It has now developed deep heredity in many parts of the country. Impact assessment being rather limited so far, it is hard to measure and quantify the effect that this Indian micro-credit experience so far has had on the poverty situation in India. However, more needs to be accomplished in terms of outreach to make a serious dent on poverty. This apart, the reason and rationale of SHG-based microfinance have been established firmly enough.

Micro-credit has effectively graduated from an experiment to a widely-accepted paradigm of rural and developmental financing in India. In fact, to the extent that people's mindsets are the biggest roadblock in the success of an innovation, it may be one of the most important steps in the history of microfinance. The path ahead is obviously strewn with challenges. The expansionary zeal of micro-credit practitioners should be unbiased with the quality of loans and is certainly an important challenge. The government involvement in SHG-based microfinance is a development but it is not free from its limitations. Government aid almost always brings in its wake political corruption. It is important to ensure that the government microfinance initiatives do not go the way of their several well-intentioned predecessors.

The biggest challenge in development, however, is the simultaneous development of investment potential and improvement of skill levels of the borrowers. Since microcredit lighten the credit availability problem, the need for micro-consulting, business planning and services like marketing are being felt with larger intensity. Micro-credit cannot be expected to be a panacea to rural developmental problems. The empowerment of women and the inculcation of financial training and discipline amongst the poor will undoubtedly have long-term socioeconomic benefits. The principles of self-help and micro-credit thus hold the key to economic and socio-cultural autonomy for India's poor.

The Ideology of Microfinance

Key philosophy of microfinance are summarized as:

1. Microfinance can pay for itself, and must do so if it is to reach very large numbers of poor people.
2. The poor people need a diversity of financial services, not just loans.
3. Microfinance is about building permanent local financial institutions.
4. The job of government is to enable financial services, not to provide them.
5. The key bottleneck is the shortage of strong institutions and managers.

Conclusion

The success of microfinance will not only improve the economic status of the poor but there will also be a drastic change in their social status. SHGs have developed human dignity among the poor women. In the context of rural development, SHGs certainly have a potential task to play. In the absence of proper follow-up, the main purpose will crush. The SHGs over time may see some setback due to internal rivalries, domination of self-interested people, corrupt leadership etc. It is true that quality of SHGs is diluting. Moneylenders' activities are done by SHGs dominating members. Therefore NABARD, Banks,

NGOs and voluntary organizations have to be careful about these issues and mainly educate the people to prevent such unhealthy situations. There is need for capacity building and expansion of infrastructure. In some cases, the SHG model may have to be replaced by other models.

References

1. Harper, Malcolm, 2000. Why are commercial banks not entering the microfinance market? In *Microfinance: emerging challenges*. Kishanjit Basu and Krishan Jindal (eds). New Delhi: Tata McGraw-Hill Publishing Company.
2. NABARD. 1995. *Study of credit management groups.* Mumbai: National Bank for Agriculture and Rural Development.
3. NABARD. 1999. *Task force on supportive policy and regulatory framework for microfinance.* Mumbai: National Bank for Agriculture and Rural Development.
4. Nair, T. S. 2000. Rural financial intermediation and commercial banks: review of recent trends. *Economic and Political Weekly* 36: pp. 299-305.
5. Nanda, Y. C. 1998. Linking banks and self-help groups in India and the role of NGOs: lessons learned and future perspectives. *Asia-Pacific Rural Finance*: pp. 23-31.
6. Puhazhendhi, V. 1995. *Transaction costs of lending to rural poor: nongovernmental organizations and self-help groups of the poor as intermediaries for banks in India.* Australia: The Foundation for Development Cooperation.

Section II

MICROFINANCE AND POVERTY ALLEVIATION

6

Microfinance as a Tool for Poverty Alleviation in Rural India

Mohd. Mohsin Khan and Mohd. Shamim

Abstract: *Microfinance is an emerging discipline in the financial world today. It is gaining importance by leaps and bounds not only in India but also in the global scene. It was born in the East. The idea of Microfinance arose in Asia as a reaction to the rural poverty in various countries such as India and Bangladesh. It aims at servicing the poorest of the poor, who were hitherto considered unfit for anything except charity. The Microfinance concept is based on group lending. Microfinance has been showing tremendous growth qualitatively as well as quantitatively. If this growth is minutely analyzed then it is observed that the growth is not balanced and there is a lot of disparity among different regions of India. A growth of around 75% is in southern region of India. The region showing poorest growth is North-East region of India. The growth and development should be balanced and without much regional disparity. The paper is a modest attempt to highlight microfinance as a means of poverty reduction in India.*

Introduction

Microfinance is an emerging discipline in the field of global financial system. It has gained global acceptance and now it is getting acknowledgment from Indian small entrepreneur and government agencies like NABARD, IDBI, NGOs etc. Its genesis can be traced from the economic history of east national economies. These economies are fundamentally different from those of the developed countries. Hence, these economical problems are also unique in nature. As a result, economists, planners and political thinkers of these countries have designed such, a financing system in order to cater to the needs of the rural population. This new phenomenon is called Microfinance.

Group lending helps in removing many difficulties faced by the government, banks and other agencies in extending the credit facilities to the poorest in rural areas of India. After financial reforms in banking sector, it successfully brought down NPAs and increased recovery rate to more than 90% due to the group lending.

Around 70 percent of our people live in the villages. "India is poor because the villagers of India are poor. India will be rich if people living in the villages of India are rich" (*Pt. Jawaharlal Nehru*). Therefore, the basic problem is to remove the poverty from the Indian villages. Many steps have been taken by the Government of India and RBI for the smooth flow of finance to the rural areas and how to establish credit institutions in India like cooperative banks, RRBs and SHGs. How can SHGs get finance and penetrate into the rural areas? All such problems can be solved through microfinance.

Microfinance is gathering momentum to become a major force in India. The Self Help Group (SHG) model with bank lending to groups of (often)-poor women without collateral has become an accepted part of rural finance. The typical microfinance clients are low-income persons that do not have access to formal financial institutions. Microfinance clients are typically self-employed, often household-based entrepreneurs. In rural areas, they are usually small farmers and others who are engaged in small income generating activities such as food processing and petty trades. In urban areas, microfinance activities are more diverse and include shopkeepers, service providers, artisans, street vendors, etc. Microfinance clients are poor and vulnerable who have a relatively unstable income and does not have permanent source of income.

India has about 24.5 million hectares of wasteland and 16.6 million hectare of fallow land. Sizeable parts of these could be converted into cultivable land through appropriate crop selection, improved water-use efficiency, adoption of watershed approach and development of irrigation potential. However, this requires substantial investments in the form of extending financial support to farmers in the form of cheap credit and subsidies. This is imperative to ensure that the farmers are able to adopt modern methods of farming such as using high yielding varieties of seeds, fertilizers, insecticides, modern tools and implements. Investment in such resources may be treated as an integral part of agriculture lending.

However, even today, the rural credit markets are dominated by money-lenders and indigenous bankers. There are yet some reported instances of bonded labours in some parts of the country. Farmers are often required of much needed funds for the adoption of modern agricultural practices, tools, fertilizers, insecticides etc. It is the duty of the Government of India to address the main problems of shortfall of finance. So the Union Budgets of last many years have stressed the need for increasing agriculture credit in future. Over the past few years, Microfinance, through the formation of Self Help Groups – SHGs, has proved to be an effective channel for disbursement of credit in rural areas.

Self Help Groups (SHGs)

A Self Help Group can be defined as "Small economically homogeneous and affinity group for rural poor voluntarily coming together."

The salient features of a SHG are:

1. Group members save small amounts regularly and voluntarily agree to contribute to a common group fund.
2. Within the group they have simple and responsive rules.
3. Decision-making is collective and is based on consensus, if any are resolved democratically.
4. Loans are provided for production as well as consumption purposes.
5. Loans are provided without collateral and interest rates charged are comparable to those of the market, i.e. banks, cooperative etc. However, these interest rates are lower than those charged by the moneylenders.

The villages in India hold unique place both in the social and economic spheres. In the past, villages were homogeneous, closely-knit and self-sufficient units. According to Census 2001, there are 6,38,365 villages in India. The average population of a village in India is around 1,000. The average varies from state to state. The highest average population per village is 16,978 in Kerala, while the lowest average population per village is 181 in Arunachal Pradesh.

The Government of India has taken several steps to strengthen the area of Microfinance. These initiatives are:

1969	Nationalization of Banks
1971	Establishment of Priority Sector lending norms
1975	Establishment of Regional Rural Banks
1982	Establishment of NABARD
1992	Launching of the SHG-Bank Linkage programme
1993	Establishment of Rashtriya Mahila Kosh—1993
1995	Working group on credit to the poor through SHG, NGO, NABARD
1998	NABARD sets a goal for linking one million SHGs by 2008
1999	National microfinance task force
2000	Establishment of SIDBI Foundation for Micro-credit
2005	Microfinance development and equity fund (MFDEF) doubled to Rs 200 crores 2005
2005	One million SHG linkage target achieved 3 years ahead of date
2006	Committee on Financial Inclusion 2006
2007	Proposed bill on microfinance regulation introduced in Parliament

Growth of SHGs in 13 Priority States

For last many years, the growth of linked SHGs in 13 Priority States have been showing the increasing trends which are shown in the Table 1:

TABLE 1

Growth of linked SHGs in 13 Priority States

State	2003	2004	2005	2006	2007	2008
Assam	3,477	10,706	31,234	36,449	81,454	92,343
Bihar	8,161	16,246	28,015	46,221	72,339	83,776
Chhattisgarh	6,763	9,796	18,569	31,291	41,703	49,887
Gujarat	13,875	15,974	24,712	34,160	43,572	51,340
Himachal Pradesh	8,875	13,228	17,798	22,920	27,799	34,087
Jharkhand	7,765	12,647	21,531	30,819	37,317	41,889
Maharashtra	28,665	38,535	71,146	1,31,470	2,25,856	2,49,541
Madhya Pradesh	15,271	27,095	45,105	57,125	70,912	80,136
Orissa	42,272	77,588	1,23,256	1,80,896	2,34,451	2,60,656
Rajasthan	22,742	33,846	60,006	98,171	1,37,837	1,58,690
Uttar Pradesh	33,696	79,210	1,19,648	1,61,911	1,98,587	2,14,578
Uttaranchal	5,854	10,908	14,043	17,588	21,527	23,089
West Bengal	32,647	51,685	92,698	1,36,251	1,81,563	2,10,689
Total	**2,49,462**	**3,97,464**	**6,67,761**	**10,05,272**	**13,74,917**	**15,50,701**
Precent increase		**59**	**68**	**51**	**37**	**13**

Source: *Microfinance in India, 2008, by Prabhu Ghate*

From Table 1, is observed the growth of SHGs in 13 priority states. Form the year 2003, there has been a continuous growth in terms of percentage. The growth has been highest in the year 2005 which was 68%. But the growth rate is being saturated to 13% in 2008. These SHGs are having number of members from 10 to 15 and over 90 percent of them are women. The total numbers of SHG members who have ever benefited from the programme are about 51 million. About half of them are people below the poverty line.

Table 2 is clearly showing the credit facilities given by different financial and non-financial agencies. For the last many years, the role of the commercial banks has been tremendous as compared to other agencies. Its micro-credit financing was 52,441 crores in the year 2003-04 which rose to 1,56,850 in the year 2007-08. The financing of cooperative banks in terms of percent have declined in the same period. The contribution of other agencies has been quite negligible.

TABLE 2

Agency-wise Credit Flow

(Rs. Crores)

Agency	2003-04	2004-05	2005-06	2006-07	2007-08P
Cooperative Bank	26,875 (31)	31,231 (24.9)	39,404 (21.8)	42,480 (18.5)	43,684 (19.4)
RRBs	7,581 (8.9)	12,404 (10)	15,223 (8.5)	20,435 (8.9)	24,814 (11)
Commercial Banks	52,441 (60)	81,481 (65)	1,25,477 (69.5)	1,66,485 (72.6)	1,56,850 (69.6)
Other Agencies	84 (0.1)	193 (0.1)	382 (0.2)	NA	NA
Total	**86,981 (100)**	**1,25,309 (100)**	**1,80,486 (100)**	**2,29,400 (100)**	**2,25,348 (100)**

Source: *Kurukshetra—A Journal on Rural Development, February 2009, p.5* P= Provisional

The Role of Different Agencies and Institutions in Microfinance

Self-Help Groups are formed normally with the help of outsiders. Developmental NGOs often work for projects like literacy, sanitation, take to organizing SHGs, bringing people together, explaining the concept to them, attending, helping and coordinating a few of the initial group meetings, helping them in maintaining accounts and linking them with the banks. Of late, some of the rural banks themselves are being designated as Self-Help Promoting Institutions (SHPIs) and they help in the formation and 'nursing' of SHGs. In recent years, government developmental programmes have also sought to target the poor through the SHGs. Starting with the Rashtriya Mahila Kosh and the Indira Mahila Yojana, the government has used the SHG approach in many of its anti-poverty projects. The most important of the government programmes using the SHG approach is the Swarnajayanti Gram Swarojgar Yojana (SGSY) which was launched in 1999.

TABLE 3

Distribution of SHGs among different bank financing models

SHGs Formed and Financed	Percent
SHGs formed and financed by banks	16
SHGs formed by NGOs and formal agencies but directly financed by banks	75
SHGs financed by banks using NGOs and other agencies as intermediaries	9

Source: *Kropp and Suran (2002)*

Table 3 reflects SHGs formed and financed by banks and other agencies. It is shown that 75% SHGs are formed and financed by banks directly. The SHGs financed by banks using NGOs and other agencies as intermediaries is only 9%.

The SHGs financed by banks, Non-banking Financial Corporations (NBFCs) and other non-government organizations (NGOs) typically connect these SHGs to local banks or to the funds provided by wholesale credit suppliers like NABARD or SIDBI (Small Industries Development Bank of India). The SHGs develop a habit of saving among its members for a fixed period of time and then giving loans to applying members from the collective savings of the group.

The formal banking sector has played an important role in microfinance in India. Much of the microfinance initiative in India has involved Self-Help Groups (SHGs), predominantly of poor women. NABARD's Bank Linkage Programme, pilot-tested in 1991-92 and launched in full vigor in 1996, has been a major effort to connect thousands of such SHGs across the country with the formal banking system. By late 2002, it connected about half a million SHGs to the banking system with total loan disbursement of about Rs. 1,026 crores. Efforts of other organizations supplemented that of NABARD.

Problems of Microfinancing and Self-Help Groups in India

1. Majority of the members are unable to save even small amount out of their income due to uncertain income source.
2. Members are suffering due to lack of occupational training and skill. In addition to know lacuna in the operating system of microfinance, the most serious drawbacks against the success of Microfinance emerge from political intervention.
3. In spite of quality products, demands for the products are too low due to the lack of advertisement, attractive packages and transportation facilities.
4. The rate of interest charged by the banks on the loan given to SHGs is high and unaffordable to micro-enterprises. The waiver of farm loans by the Government of India has resulted in increased defaulters.
5. The financial assistance given by the bank is not sufficient and the attitude of the bank officers is also indifferent and criticized by the micro-enterprises.
6. It has been seen that male members dominate group meetings and leadership of the group. Female members do not get much support from their family members for joining the SHGs. This indicates gender discrimination which is major hurdle in the way of women empowerment.
7. Members of self-help group are unable to observe the books of accounts and unable to comprehend the financial transactions of the group. They also lack numerical skill to comprehend the accounts.

8. In India, the Rules and Regulation of Microfinance Institutions are not regulated properly. In the absence of the rules and regulation there would be high case of credit risk and defaults.
9. India is considered as the second fastest developing country after China, with GDP over 8% from the past 5 years. But these figures are just because of few sectors of economy. India's 70% population lives in rural areas and they are not duly taken care of.

Conclusion

The role of the MFIs through SHGs in providing financial services to the agricultural sector and rural areas cannot be overemphasized. It is functioning successfully in many countries, especially in India. However, lending needs to be coupled with insurance and other services such as training, marketing support, government subsidies, etc.

Earlier the regional rural banking system (RRBS) was plagued with the problem for huge Non-Performing Assets and losses. Of the many Regional Rural Banks, many were saddled with huge losses and were on the verge of closure. Even now many banks are contemplating closing down their loss making rural branches. Against this backdrop, Microfinance has ensured up to 90% of timely repayment while the non-performing assets are almost negligible. At the same time, it has helped in the empowerment of women and poverty alleviation in rural areas.

Critics may dismiss the participation of public sector banks in microfinance as a compulsion owing to the fact that they are owned by the government. But the initiative of the private sector (through NGOs) confirms the viability and feasibility of microfinance as a legitimate and profit making business.

Doubtlessly, huge efforts are required with the initiatives of government and other agencies to remove poverty. The government and NABARD have recognized this and have emphasized the SHG approach and are working along with NGOs in its initiatives. Over half a million SHGs have been linked to banks over the years but a handful of States, mostly in South India, account for over three-fourth of this figure with Andhra Pradesh being an undisputed leader. In spite of the impressive figures, microfinance in India is still presently too small to create a massive impact on poverty alleviation. But if pursued with skill and opportunity development of the poor, it holds the promise to alter the socio-economic face of the India's poor. The path ahead is full of challenges. Bringing millions of people within the fold of microfinance to strengthen the programs of poverty alleviation of rural India is the need of the hour.

References

1. Seibel, Hans D. and H.R. Dave, 2002, "Commercial Aspects of SHG Banking in India", Paper presented at the Seminar on SHG-Bank Linkage Programme at New Delhi, November November, 2002, pp. 25-26.
2. Bansal, Hema, 2003, "SHG-Bank Linkage Program in Indian: An Overview", Journal of Microfinance, Vol. 5, Number 1.
3. Bhatt, Nitin and Y.S.P. Thorat, 2001, "India's Regional Rural Banks: The Institutional Dimension of Reforms", Journal of Microfinance, Vol. 3, Number 1.
4. Chakrabarti Rajesh, 2004, "The Indian Microfinance Experience – Accomplishments and Challenges", A working paper on www.scribd.com
5. Lokhande, Murlidhar A. (2009), "Micro Finance Initiatives in India", Kurukshetra—A Journal on Rural Development, New Delhi, pp. 16-18
6. Sundar K. AND Selvaraj V. (2009), "Rural Lending Facing Rough Weather?" Banking Finance, Vol XXII, No. 3, March, pp. 5-7.
7. Reddy Yuvaraja (2009), "Impact of Self Help Groups—Bank Linkage Programme in Andhra Pradesh", Banking Finance, Vol-XXII, No. 3, March, pp. 10-12.
8. National Bank for Agricultural and Rural Development, 2001, Kisan Credit Card Plan Booklet.
9. National Bank for Agricultural and Rural Development, 2004, Potential Linked Credit Plan for Aligarh District 2004-05.
10. www.sewainsurance.org, as accessed on 28 June 2004.
11. www.sewa.org as accessed on 24 June 2004 and 28 June 2004.
12. www.basixindia.com as accessed on 30 June 2004.
13. www.rbi.org.in as accessed on 24 June 2004 and 29 November 2004.
14. Reserve Bank of India, (1996), Rural Planning and Central Office, Circular No. PL. BC. 120/04.09.22/95-96.

7

Microfinance as a Mechanism For Poverty Reduction with Reference to North-East India

Jaynal Ud-din Ahmed

ABSTRACT: *Microfinance is acclaimed as a gracious alternate for informal credit and a successful instrument for poverty reduction among people who are economically active but financially constrained. It covers a broad range of financial services including loans, deposits and payment services, and insurance to the poor and low-income households and their micro-enterprises. The microfinance demonstrations in Western and Southern India have received greater attention both in the media as well as in academic field. The work carried out in this regard by the poster boys of Indian microfinance such as SHARE, BASIX, SEWA, MYRADA, PRADAN and others are praiseworthy. North-east India has not experienced the benefits of its rebellion partly because of insignificant presence of any single large microfinance institution (MFI) in these regions. Realizing the necessity of microfinance for socio-economic transformation, the proposed paper attempts to examine microfinance as an instrument for poverty reduction in North-east India.*

Introduction

Microfinance emerged as a noble substitute for informal credit and an effective and powerful instrument for poverty reduction among people who are economically active but financially constrained. It covers a broad range of financial services including loans, deposits and payment services, and insurance to the poor and low-income households and their micro-enterprises. The microfinance sector has grown significantly in the past decades. The strength of the microfinance organizations in India is in the diversity of approaches and forms that have evolved over time. In addition to the home-grown models of SHGs and mutually aided cooperative societies the country has erudite from other microfinance experiments across the world, particularly those in Bangladesh, Indonesia, Thailand, and Bolivia, in terms of delivery of microfinancial services.

Persuaded with the potential role of microfinancing in alleviating poverty, the South Asian countries have been actively pursuing the policy of setting up formal network of microfinance institutions. These institutions include NGOs and government sponsored programmes. Some leading MFIs, e.g. Grameen Bank, have created financial modes that serve increasing number of poor. They also lead to repayment rates positively comparable with the performance of many commercial banks. These approaches have helped many MFIs in achieving a reasonable level of sustainability, and have even produced profits without government subsidies and support from donor. Nonetheless, some of the MFIs especially the NGOs are facing serious sustainability problems indicating lapse in their financial procedures, organizational design and governance. Moreover, most of the MFIs do not provide deposit services to their clients. In contrast, some of the successful MFIs like Grameen Bank in Bangladesh and BancoSol in Bolivia have incorporated the provision of deposit services in their operations.

However, Self-Help Groups (SHGs), usually at the behest of certain development oriented non-government organizations (NGOs), have quietly mushroomed in most districts of Eastern India—particularly in the state of West Bengal—over the last few years. The efficacy and sustainability of such groups need to be debated at the time of transition for change.

Andhra Pradesh, in particular, has witnessed a remarkable growth in micro-finance activities and its success stories have been widely reported as well. The North-East India has not experienced the benefits of its rebellion partly because of insignificant presence of any single large microfinance institution (MFI) in these regions. The government and MFIs have emphasized the SHG approach and working along with NGOs in its initiatives. A notable number of SHGs have been linked to banks over the years. In spite of this impressive scenario, microfinance in India is still too small to create a massive impact in poverty alleviation, but if pursued with skill and opportunity development of the poor, it holds the promise to alter the socio-economic face of the India's poor. Realizing the necessity of microfinance for rural transformation, the proposed paper attempts to examine the microfinance as an instrument for poverty reduction in North-East India.

Major Development of Microfinance in India

The new generation microfinance was slow in coming to India. Low levels of grants to microfinance institutions, an unfavourable policy environment, substantial traditional banking infrastructure and a search for context specific solutions has constrained rapid scale up. The first breakthrough emerged from policy support to enable informal self-help groups of 15-20 members to transact with commercial banks. These groups build up and rotate savings amongst themselves, open bank accounts and take responsibility for lending and recovering money financed by banks. With the missionary zeal of the National Bank for Agriculture and Rural Development (NABARD), insights gained by NGOs, the increasing enthusiasm of bankers and emerging successes in repayment and social impacts, this national movement now encompasses 1.4 million such groups (over 20 million members).

The major milestone in Micro finance in India is given:

Major Milestone in Microfinance

Year	Achievements
1969	Nationalization of Banks
1971	Establishment of Priority Sector Lending Norms
1975	Establishment of Regional Rural Banks
1982	Establishment of NABARD
1992	Launching of the SHG-Bank Linkage Programme
1993	Establishment of Rashtriya Mahila Kosh
1998	NABARD Sets a Goal for Linking One Million SHGs By 2008
2000	Establishment of SIDBI Foundation for Micro-credit
2005	One Million SHG Linkage Target Achieved
2006	Committee of Financial Inclusion
2007	Microfinance Regulation Bill introduced

Growth of Financing to Self Help Groups (SHGs)

Over a period of last few years the financing to SHGs has increased due to the efforts of the different financing agencies and initiatives taken by the Government to alleviate the poverty from the grassroot level in India. There has been a lot of pressure from the international agencies as almost 20 per cent of the world's poorest people are living in India. Even after more than 60 years of attaining independence, and numbers of programmes and schemes initiated by the Government of India, we could not succeed in solving the problem of poverty. The microfinancing schemes through SHGs has increased chance to alleviate poverty. The year-wise financial assistance and number of SHGs financing is given in Table 1.

Table 1 shows that the programme has been growing rapidly and the number of SHGs financed increased from 1.98 lakhs in 2001-02 to 6.20 lakhs in 2005-06, 6.87 lakh in 2006-07, and 7.94 lakh in 2007-2008. Again, cumulative number of SHGs financed was 4.61 lakhs in 2001-02, which has increased to 37.67 lakhs in 2007-08. It may be observed that microfinance schemes succeeded a lot despite various hurdles experienced by the agencies and beneficiaries.

TABLE 1

Year wise Increase of SHGs and Their Finance

Year	No. of SHGs financed during the year (in lakh)	Cumulative no. of SHGs'financed (in lakh)
2001-02	1.98	4.61
2002-03	2.56	7.17
2003-04	3.62	10.79
2004-05	5.39	16.18
2005-06	6.2	22.38
2006-07	6.87	29.25
2007-08	7.94	37.67

Source: *www.inblogs.com*

Microfinancing Agencies and Credit Flows

As we broaden the notion of the types of services microfinance encompasses, the potential market of microfinance clients also expanded. It depends on local conditions and political climate, activeness of cooperatives, SHGs and NGOs and support mechanism. For instance, micro-credit might have a far more limited market scope than, say, a more diversified range of financial services, which includes various types of savings products, payment and remittance services, and various insurance products. Central Government of India has established a strong and extensive link between NABARD (National Bank for Agriculture and Rural Development), State Cooperative Banks, District Cooperative Banks, Primary Agriculture and Marketing Societies at national, state, district and village levels. There are number of agencies in India to disburse the financial assistance. Their financial disbursement for the last few years is given in Table 2.

The Table 2 reflects the agency-wise credit flow to different SHGs in the name of microfinance from the year 2003-04 to 2007-08. Undoubtedly, the contribution of the commercial banks has always been as high as 60 per cent in 2003-04 which has increased to 69.6 per cent in 2008-09. The micro-credit given by cooperative banks has been increasing in terms of amount but is percent-wise decreasing. It gave credit of 31 per cent in 2003-04 and came down to 18.5 per cent in 2007-08. The micro-credits given by RRBs and other agencies have not shown any significant change during this tenure.

A perusal of Table 3 shows that in spite of having huge success and having many success stories, the spread of microfinance is not uniform in India. Most of microfinance activity is limited to the Southern region of India. Out of total SHGs linked to bank, more than half is covered by the Southern states. Even the

TABLE 2

Agency-wise Credit Flow*

(Rs. Crore)

Agency	2003-04	2004-05	2005-06	2006-07	2007-08P	Growth Rate (%)	
						2003-08P	2006-07P
Cooperative	26,875 (31)	31,231 (24.9)	39,404 (21.8)	42,480 (18.5)	43,684 (19.4)	13	8
RRBs	7,581 (8.9)	12,404 (10)	15,223 (8.5)	20,435 (8.9)	24,814 (11)	35	34
Commercial Banks	52,441 (60)	81,481 (65)	1,25,477 (69.5)	1,66,485 (72.6)	1,56,850 (69.6)	3,233	–
Other Agencies	84 (0.1)	193 (0.1)	382 (0.2)	NA	NA	–	–
Total	**86,981 (100)**	**1,25,309 (100)**	**1,80,486 (100)**	**2,29,400 (100)**	**2,25,348 (100)**	**27**	**27**

Source: *Kurukshetra—A Journal on Rural Development, February 2009, p. 5,* P= Provisional

growth of bank linked SHG in north eastern India is very slow. In 2000-01 only 0.2 percent of the bank linked SHGs are from NE which increased slightly to 2.8 percent in 2005-06. Compared to this, there is a substantial growth in northern, eastern, central and western India. Though southern region proportion is reduced to 54.3 percent from 71.2 percent, it still occupies the top position.

Microfinance in North East India

The North Eastern Region comprises Arunachal Pradesh, Assam, Nagaland, Manipur, Meghalaya, Mizoram, Tripura and Sikkim. Each of these eight states differs widely in terms of political and socio-economic environment. Almost 98 per cent of the land area in the region runs along international borders with Bhutan, Bangladesh, Myanmar and China. Almost 70 per cent of the region is hilly. Population, except in the valleys and in Assam, is sparsely distributed. The region has been witness of historical confrontations and confusion. The territorial possession is disputed; the recognition of peoples' need is abysmal. More than 220 ethnic groups with equal number of dialects makes it extremely diverse region. Likewise, bio-diversity in the region, too, is very huge. It is matter of academic debate about the merit of clubbing the region as a socio-political entity, particularly in light of such diversity.

The entire region has roughly a population of 3.88 crores, of which 3 crore is concentrated in Assam. The rail network is poor and also concentrated in Assam. Compared to the national average of 73 km of road per 100 square km, the average road length in the region is low, at 53 km, with Arunachal Pradesh having the least length of roads—12.20 km per 100 sq km. Access to markets

FIG. 1

Progress of SHG-Bank Linkage Programmes

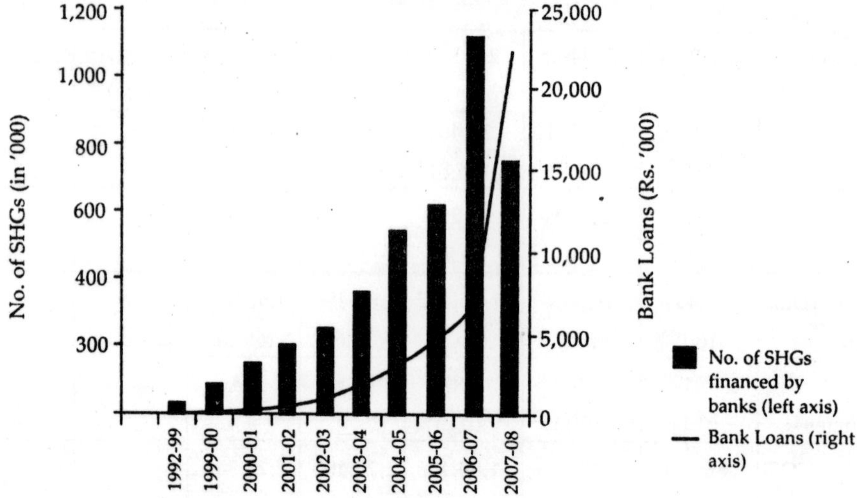

TABLE 3

Regional Spread of Credit Linked SHGs

Region	2000-01		2005-06	
	SHGs Credit linked to banks	Percent to total	SHGs Credit linked to banks	Percent to total
Northern	9,012	3.4	1,33,057	5.9
North Eastern	477	0.2	62,517	2.8
Eastern	22,252	8.4	3,94,351	17.6
Central	28,851	10.9	2,67,915	12.0
Western	15,543	5.9	1,66,254	7.4
Southern	1,87,690	71.2	12,14,431	54.3
Total	**2,63,825**	**100**	**22,38,525**	**100**

Source: *Report of Working Group on Gender Issues, Panchayat Raj Institutions, Public Private Partnership, Innovative Finance and Micro Finance in Agriculture for the Eleventh Five Year Plan (2007-2012), Volume One*

with the rest of India is difficult due to the poor infrastructure. Almost 75 per cent of the workforce in this region is engaged in the primary sector and agriculture is the mainstay of the economy. Most other economic activity is in small scale sector and heavily dependent on traditional skills of weaving and handicraft.

The Self Help Group and Bank Linkage Programme in India (SHG-BLP) is one of the key factors in the success of Microfinance Programme and have emerged as the largest Microfinance programme in the world. Under the programme a cumulative amount of Rs. 113.98 billion has been disbursed by

TABLE 4

Status of Microfinance in North Eastern Region

(Up to March 2005)

State	Cumulative no. of credit linked SHGs	Cumulative total amount of loan sanctioned	Average lending in Rs.
Assam	49,237	19,729.42	40,070
Arunachal Pradesh	229	58.01	25,330
Manipur	1,885	457.33	24,260
Meghalaya	1,315	475.62	36,170
Mizoram	251	188.61	75,140
Nagaland	442	259.97	58,820
Tripura	6,921	2,797.07	40,410
TOTAL	**60,280**	**23,966.03**	**39,757**

Source: *Office of the State Coordinator, Self Help Groups, Meghalaya, Shillong*

banks to as many as 22,38,565 SHGs till March, 2006. The southern states, especially Andhra Pradesh, shows the largest number of SHGs and also the amount of bank credit disbursed.

The North Eastern States, which had started the programme during the late nineties, show a relatively high growth rate. In the initial years the programme had a slow start and till the end of March 1999, the cumulative number of SHGs credit linked in the entire region was only 93, which was less than half a per cent of the cumulative number of SHG credit linked in the country under the programme. During March 1999 to March 2001, the cumulative number of SHGs in NER increased from 93 to 477, i.e. a little more than five times while at the India level it was increased by seven times.

Within the North Eastern Region, Assam and Meghalaya in 2001 accounted for majority share of the SHGs credit links (at about 58 and 34 per cent, respectively), and also that of the cumulative credit disbursed in the region (about 45 and 46 per cent, respectively) as against the very low share of States like Manipur (7 per cent), Sikkim (1 per cent) and Tripura (1 per cent) in the total cumulative number of SHG credit linked. The remaining States of Arunachal Pradesh, Nagaland and Mizoram did not have any SHGs credit linked under this programme by 2001. Until 2001 more than 90 per cent of the SHGs credit linked in the North Eastern Region was from the two States of Assam and Meghalaya.

It is seen that the performance of banks in providing credit to the SHGs has been good in the States of Assam and Tripura (Table 4), while it is poor in other States of the region. It is quite interesting that Mizoram has experienced a very poor movement of SHGs (only 251 number of credit linked SHGs), however, the highest amount per group was lent in this State. SHG movement in Assam has gained momentum during the last two years. So far, 49,237 SHGs has been credit linked to the extent of Rs. 197.29 crore as on March 31, 2005. The RRBs particularly Pragjyotish Gaonlia Bank, has been playing a lead role in the SHG movement. Presently, 47 Self Help Promoting Institutions (SHPIs) including 5 RRBs and 11 Farmers' Clubs were involved in the SHG-Bank linkaged programme in the State. During 2004-05, the joint liability Group (JLG) concept was introduced to all the 5 RRBs in the State and 98 JLGs had been financed to the tune of Rs. 53.22 lakh by three RRBs viz. Subansiri Gaonlia Bank, Pragjyotish Gaonlia Bank, and Langpi Dehangi Rural Bank.

In the district of West Tripura, each Gram Panchayat was to form one SHG in a month and 12 SHGs in a year under SGSY. The SHG movement received such equally enthusiastic response from other districts also and some Panchayats exceeded the target. It is expected that all the villages in the State will have around 20,000 new SHGs by the end of the year. As per reports, 4,000 SHGs have already passed first. In the gradation stage, 10,000 were eligible for such tests and 16,000 had passed second gradation. The Bharat Gyan Vigyan Samiti, Tripura micro-study, found that while group formation had a significant impact on social indicators and led to accumulation of handsome savings by SHGs, the impact on poverty alleviation was minimal, since SHGs concentrated more on thrift and credit activities in first few months and economic activities are taken up only later after Group stabilization. As reported, the subsidy was adjusted and no matching fund was sanctioned by some banks.

Within the NER States, banks have emerged as an important self-help promoting agencies. In Assam, in 2006, 79 per cent of the SHGs were promoted and financed by the banks themselves; while in Tripura and Sikkim more than half of the SHGs credit linked (51 and 75 per cent, respectively) have been promoted by banks. In the remaining states, such as Meghalaya (77 per cent), Manipur (68 per cent), Arunachal Pradesh (100 per cent) and Nagaland (93 per cent), majority of the SHGs credit linked have been formed by NGOs.

The poor performance in the progress of microfinance is mainly due to the sparse population in this region, lack of experienced NGOs for formation and nurturing of SHGs, and lack of homogeneity in Groups in the respective States. The local institutions like Marup in Manipur, Village Development Boards (VDBs) in Nagaland, Village Darbar in Meghalaya, Kebang in Arunachal Pradesh and Young Mizo Association in Mizoram could be activated to further the SHG movement in the respective States.

The Challenges of Microfinance in the North East

The model adopted in India for disbursing microfinance to the lower income groups through Self Help Groups (SHGs) will have to be suitably modified if the eight states of the north-east are to be included in financial services. A study carried out by the Indian Institute of Bank Management (IIBM), Guwahati, Assam, and commissioned by Sa-Dhan, shows that the SHG movement has not caught on in some north-eastern States for reasons that are peculiar to the region.

An association of Community Development Financial Institutions, Sa-Dhan was founded in 1999 and represents the emerging and rapidly growing sector of microfinance in the country. At present, Sa-Dhan has a collective outstanding loan of Rs 1,500 crore to seven million poor in the country. It is seriously concerned about the laggard growth of the SHG movement in the eight states of the north-east and hopes to lobby for policy changes to address the specific needs of each of these states.

The Government of India has set up a special zone for the north-eastern region (NER). The NER comprises Arunachal Pradesh, Assam, Nagaland, Manipur, Meghalaya, Mizoram, Tripura and Sikkim. Each of these eight states differs widely in terms of political and socio-economic environment. Almost 98 per cent of the land area in the NER runs along international borders with Bhutan, Bangladesh, Myanmar and China.

Almost 70 per cent of the region is hilly. Population, except in the valleys and in Assam, is sparsely distributed. The entire region has roughly a population of 3.88 crore, of which 3 crore is concentrated in Assam. The rail network is poor and also concentrated in Assam. Compared to the national average of 73 km of road per 100 square km, the average road length in the region is low, at 53 km, with Arunachal Pradesh having the least length of roads—12.20 km per 100 sq km.

The microfinance movement started late in the region and is confounded by many regional complexities that must be understood, appreciated and incorporated into policy if the plans to make affordable loans to low income groups in the region are to bear any fruit. The state of the SHG movement varies from State to State, and within States from one district to another. The SHG movement is yet to take off in any major way in Arunachal Pradesh. In Manipur, too, it is not significant despite, or perhaps because, many traditional systems of organizing savings and lending still hold sway.

The study outlines some of the traditional systems of savings and lending prevalent in the States in the region. For instance, Manipur has a wide network of marups started by the Metei community. Marup literally means friendship, and is a small group of friends and family who collect money from the group and either lends it on interest, or buy in bulk gadgets and materials required for any enterprise and distribute them to members of the group. The members then pay back the credit amount in instalments. By definition, therefore, marups are formed of people belonging to the same or similar income group and profession. It is very popular so that almost 90 % of the population of Manipur is involved in marups. There are small marups of only five members and there are moderately large groups of fifty members too. Since these operate mainly on trust, they are not very large. The contribution of members to marups and the interest rates charged also reflect the wide range of needs and the member's capacity to save and repay. Contributions range from Rs 10 to Rs 30,000 a month and the interest rates charged vary from 5% to 20% annually. In Manipur, such traditional systems still hold away.

In Arunachal, the lack of a banking network and the thin spread of population make the SHG model irrelevant. The few SHGs that exist are located in or around the capital, Itanagar, and the SHG model may not work here at all. We need to look at alternatives for this State, particularly low cost traditional institutions which utilize social capital and need not expand and scale up to be sustainable. Forming SHGs to fit the prescription of India's apex development bank, NABARD (National Bank for Agricultural and Rural Development), is an uphill task and may involve heavy operational costs that will render them unviable. For instance, according to NABARD, any SHG must have at least 20 members, which seems difficult to manage in the remoter and difficult to access areas of the region where it may be tough to find more than five people to join an SHG. Suitable modifications have sometimes led to dramatic changes. In Mizoram, the number of SHGs linked to banks was just 28 in March 2005. By March 2006 their number had jumped to 974, which means 946 new SHGs had opened accounts with banks. This dramatic turnaround was due to the local chief of NABARD who, taking into account the problems of the region, changed the focus of SHGs. In SHGs, the emphasis is on savings and credit is given later, after the banks have made their own assessment of risks involved. In Mizoram, the NABARD chief made it possible for SHGs to open accounts only when assured of a loan. That encouraged the formation of SHGs and their linkages with banks.

Meghalaya has been the most proactive in the formation of SHGs—notes the study. This was also the first State in which banks directly started SHGs. The State has 4,800 SHGs linked to banks. This has been possible because of the dedicated efforts of the State Government that not only allocated resources for development, but also set up a department on SHGs headed by a committed bureaucrat. What is required is a multi-pronged strategy to overcome the many challenges the region poses. Banks, policymakers and NGOs—the major actors in the field of microfinance—must come together to think through suitable modifications in policy. Banks may have to change their system of assessing risks. There is need for capacity building and expansion of infrastructure. In some cases, the SHG model may have to be replaced by other models. The Sa-Dhan survey has taken the first step towards understanding the many complexities of the region and the organization is now gearing up for follow-up action on many fronts including lobbying for policy changes.

References

1. Bandyopadhyay, Ashok (n.d.). Poverty alleviation: self help group-cooperatives within cooperative – 4th Model. Kolkata: West Bengal State Cooperative Bank (Mimeo).
2. Basu and Krishan Jindal (eds). New Delhi: Tata McGraw-Hill Publishing Company. pp. 208-218.
3. CMIE. 2000. *Profiles of districts.* Mumbai: Centre for Monitoring Indian Economy.
4. Das, S. K. and B. P. Nanda, B. P., 2008. Microfinance and Sustainable Rural Development, in S. K. Das *et al* (eds.), Microfinance and Rural Development in India, New Century Publication, New Delhi.
5. Government of India. 1998. *Debt and investment survey, household borrowings and repayments during 1.7.91 to 30.6.92.* Report No. 431. New Delhi: National Sample Survey.
6. Gulati, Ashok and Seema Bathla. 2000. *Institutional credit to Indian agriculture: defaults and policy options.* NABARD Chair Unit. Delhi: Institute of Economic Growth.
7. Harper, Malcolm, E. Esipisu, A. Mohanty and D. S. K. Rao. 1998. *The new middlewomen: profitable banking through on-lending groups.* New Delhi: Oxford and IBH and London: IT Publications.
8. Harper, Malcolm. 2000. Why are commercial banks not entering the microfinance market? In *Microfinance: emerging challenges.* Kishanjit Basu and Krishan Jindal (eds). New Delhi: Tata McGraw-Hill Publishing Company.
9. Hossain, M., 1988. Credit for Alleviation of Rural Poverty: The Grameen Bank in Bangladesh. International Food Policy Research Institute Research Report No. 65.
10. Hulme, D., and P. Mosley, 1996. *Finance Against Poverty.* London: Routledge.
11. Huppi, M., and G. Feder, 1990. "The Role of Groups and Credit Cooperatives in Rural Lending." *The World Bank Research Observer,* 5: pp. 187-204.
12. Jaffee, D. M., and T. Russell, 1976. "Imperfect Information, Uncertainty, and Credit Rationing." *Quarterly Journal of Economics* 90: pp. 651-66.
13. Jindal, Krishan. 2000. Successful efforts in microfinance: a case study of South Malabar Grameen Bank. In *Microfinance: emerging challenges.* Kishanjit.
14. Kanwar, Gautam *et al*,.2008. Microfinance in the Indian Scenario: A study on the Existing Models, *The Indian Journal of Commerce,* The Indian Commerce Association, New Delhi, Vol. 61, No. 2, April-June 2008, pp. 19-40.
15. Khander, S., 2001. "Does Microfinance Really Benefit the Poor?" Paper presented at the Asian Development Bank's Asia and Pacific Forum on Poverty, Manila, 5-9 February.
16. Kishanjit Basu and Krishan Jindal (eds). New Delhi: Tata McGraw-Hill Publishing Company. p. 233-252.
17. Lazar,Daniel and Palanichamy. 2008. Growth of Microfinance in India, in Daniel Lazar *et al* (eds.), Microfinance and Poverty Eradication—Indian and Global Experiences, New Century Publications, New Delhi.
18. lessons for banks in India. In *Microfinance: emerging challenges.* Kishanjit Basu and Krishan Jindal (eds). New Delhi: Tata McGraw-Hill Publishing Company Ltd. pp. 15-46.
19. Malhotra, R. and D. S. Chauhan 2000. Banking with the poor: innovations by Oriental Bank of Commerce. In *Microfinance: emerging challenges.*

20. Malveaux, J., 1997. "Another Way to Look at Banking." *San Francisco Chronicle.*
21. Micro-credit Summit Report, 1997. *Results Education Fund.* Washington, D.C.
23. MkNelly, B., and C. Watetip, 1993. "Impact Evaluation of Freedom from Hunger's Credit with Education Programme in Thailand." Freedom From Hunger, Davis, California. Mimeo.
24. Mosley, Paul. 2000. The microfinance experience of developing countries.
25. Muhammad Yunus. 2007: The Innate Entrepreneurs, *Business World,* 19 November, pp. 56
26. Nayak, Sudarshan. 2006. Empowerment of Poor through SHG and Microfinance, Cooperative Perspective, Vol. 41, April-March.
27. Shiralashetti, A. S. and S. S. Hugar. 2008. Microfinance—A Study of Self-Help Groups and Bank Linkage, *The Journal of Business Studies,* Department of Commerce, University of Kerala, Vol. 5, No. 9, pp. 31-44.
28. Singh, W. C. 2009. Microfinance and Economic Backwardness, in Komol Singha (ed.), Village Development in North-East India, Concept Publishing Company, New Delhi, pp. 230-235.
29. www.infochangeindia.org

8

Factors Affecting the Choice between Individual Liability and Joint Liabilities among the Micro-Credit Customers in Gedu Town of Bhutan

Jagadish Nath and Komol Singha

ABSTRACT: *With the increase in economic activities, the need for micro-credit system has been realized by the world, especially the poor countries. It is a viable tool to alleviate poverty and unemployment problem and the success of micro-credit system depends mainly upon its delivery system. Still, the complexity of its successful delivery arises when the scale is large. Moreover, traditionally, almost all implementing agencies favour the delivery of micro-credit through joint liability system—it may be Self Help Groups (SHGs) or Joint Liability Groups (JLGs). This paper tries to seek some basic factors which determine the choice between joint liabilities or individual liabilities among micro-credit customers. Among others, factors like age, gender, educational qualification, income levels, skill level, are some which have been considered in the study. The town of Gedu in Bhutan has been considered as the place of this study.*

Introduction

Joel Wassi Adechi, the Ambassador of Benin to United Nations, describes microfinance as, "... ... Microfinance represents a participatory approach to development where people can take control of their lives and because of self-sufficiency, one does not need to be an individual of significant means to have creative business ideas, save according to one's own priorities, and ultimately plan for the future."

Sustainable access to microfinance, so to say, which refers to loans, savings, insurance, transfer services and other financial products helps to alleviate poverty by generating income, creating jobs, allowing children to go to school, enabling families to obtain healthcare and empowering people to make their choices that best serve their needs.

The micro-credit (loans) has been, traditionally, the most prevailing type of microfinance till date, specially all across the SAARC region. Micro-credit can be delivered either under joint-liability or under individual-liability contract. But almost all implementing agencies, in most parts of the world, favour the delivery of micro-credit through joint liability system, mostly through Self Help Groups (SHGs) or Joint Liability Groups (JLGs). In this system, members are linked by joint liability in repaying the debt of any one of the group he/she belongs, who fails to repay. Which actually puts a inbuilt system within the group where non-borrower co-members of the group keep constantly monitoring the borrower group-member(s). Therefore, in the group lending under joint liability, the lenders need to put minimum effort in monitoring the repayment and is effectively risk-free.

But from the point of view of the beneficiaries, there are few problems associated with it. The above points regarding group liability are true only when the group as a whole has full control over all individual members. On the other hand, if, in contrary, the members are incontrollable, the programme may go haywire. Moreover, all potential customers may not be interested to be part of a group. Even otherwise, many potential customers would prefer individual liability over joint liability.

This paper is an effort to analyze the factors which might have some influence in determining the choice between joint liabilities or individual liability among micro-credit customers. Factors like Age, Gender, Educational qualifications Income levels, Skill level, Skill type are some of them which have been considered in the study. As this study is based at Gedu town of Bhutan, a bit of background about the said town would help to understand the socio-economic status of the area.

Gedu is a town under the Chukha dzongkhag in Bhutan and the village lies on either side of the National Highway from Phuentsholing to Thimphu. Before the establishment of Gedu Wood Manufacturing Industry in1980s in the present Gedu area, Gedu use to be a un-inhabitant area covered by thick jungles and people lived down in the Gedu village far away from the present town. With the establishment of the wood industry, many people were employed so they lived here to work and subsequently started residing in the present location. But with the construction of the buildings and work houses for the establishment of the Tala Hydroelectric Project in June 29th, 1997, as an association of mutuality between the governments of India and Bhutan, many people from different region—in Bhutans especially from the Chukha dzongkhag i.e. Tala and Daga village—migrated from their villages to Gedu in search of jobs. Few of them have also migrated here because there were no proper educational facilities and also other infrastructural facilities for their children's education.

The town that we have at the present time developed itself with the growing business transaction to meet the basic needs of the labourers hired in constructing the plant and also the people employed in the project. Low income earners were not provided housing facilities—the project management which resulted in slum settlements. Initially, before the completion of Tala project, the slum dwellers did not have well placed water and electricity facilities. It was only after the project has been completed that the slum dwellers were provided with electricity and water supply facilities by the project management. But with the changing time and the fast level of development in the country their living standard has improved a lot and their needs and wants also increased. This town has now become the home to a college, called Gaeddu College of Business Studies, the only Business college in the country which exemplifies its gaining prominence as a developing town.

Overview of Literature

Lenders' interest lies in the repayment by borrowers as repayment is the most important factor which determines a good borrower. Measure of repayment not only helps lender retain its good borrower base but also it attracts good borrowers which, in turn, helps in overall profitability and growth. Poor borrowers prefer a group liability loan over an individual liability loan—this has been established through a theoretical model by Madajewicz in 2008. In the model, it was established that group liability dominates individual liability up to a level of wealth. On the other hand, over that level of wealth, it is individual liability which is preferred by rural households. Interestingly, she also found that business funded with individual loans grow more than those funded with group loans.

Whereas, Lehner's (2008) in his theoretical model established that the microfinance institutions' decision of offering group loans or individual loans depends on the size of credit. Larger the loan size more is the likelihood of a group loan. And if the size of the loan is small, all microfinance institutions prefer to offer individual loans.

Not much of empirical research is available on the relative merits of the two methodologies of individual liability and group liability. Rather, much of the focus has been on higher repayment rates between the two (Ahiu, Townsend 2007).

If judged by only repayment rates, especially in case of micro-credit, the borrowers—whether with individual liability or group liabilities—are no different. In fact, the rates of repayment in both the types are usually very high, with more than 95% repayment rate.

A field experiment conducted in Philippines by Gine and Karlan (2006) found that individual loans can attract more clients for microfinance institutions but there is hardly any difference in the repayment rates of both types.

Our observation is that although almost all microfinance institutions across India deliver both individual as well as group loans, generally, it is only the group loan which is more common in practice though. It is our view that, if borrowers are given a choice, it will also add to the efficiency of the borrowers. With this study we are trying to find out if the same is also common in Bhutan and to identify factors associated with the choice of individual liability vis-à-vis group liability as far as micro-credit is concerned.

Objectives of the Study

1. To find out preferred choice of liability with respect to micro-credit.
2. To find out the factors (if any) influencing choice of Individual liability vis-à-vis Group liability with respect to Micro-credit.
3. To find out degree of correlation (if any) between different factors vis-à-vis choice of liability type with respect to Micro-credit.

Methodology Adopted

The affluent households usually enjoy greater accessibility to banks and post offices and also can meet the formalities of these formal institutions while seeking credit. Moreover, the size of the credit required is also large; thus micro-credit has traditionally been a matter of interest only for the 'not so affluent' categories. The reason behind selection of Gedu town of Bhutan is this and this is a small town where the concentration of households having annual income less than rupees five lakh per annum is highest and also there is provision of both group liability credit and individual liability credit is available.

The total population of Gedu town is around 15,000 and according to rough estimates 10 % (i.e.1,500) of the total population is covered under micro-credit programme. To obtain primary data on the patterns of the kinds of micro-credit liabilities vis-à-vis socio-economic and demographic factors and keeping in mind the 'not so affluent' categories, a sample size of 200 was picked up from the small traders within the income level up to Rs. 2.5 lakh per annum for the survey. The sample size of 200 was arrived by looking at the targeted total population set, i.e. population with income level up to Rs. 2.5 lakh per annum, which is around 15% of the total population totalling to roughly around 2,000. Therefore a total of 10% of the targeted population, i.e. 200, were taken as the sample size. A questionnaire was prepared for the survey and responses were collected through interview method. Out of the total 200 questionnaire, a total of 172 valid responses had been received.

The data collected thereby were tabulated and was analyzed with different statistical tools to find out the inferences and findings with respect to our objectives of the study.

Analysis and Findings

The following paragraphs show the analysis and findings of the proposed study. According to the survey, the micro-credit penetration, as of now, stands at 29%

for the population with income level up to Rs. 2.5 lakh per annum as against 44% of those who are interested in micro-credit. Since this is the category of population which has the potential of being most beneficial from micro-credit, it can be said that there is still a high gap (Table 1).

TABLE 1

Existing and Interested in Micro-credits

Total Respondents	172	%
Existing Micro-credit Customers	62	29
Interested for Micro-credit	82	40

The most preferred choice of liability is individual liability with almost 95% of the beneficiaries accounting for individual liability option amongst the existing micro-credit customers. Also among the total interested customers of micro-credit, almost 95% prefers individual liability. Although the preference of individual liability over group liability is predominantly higher for both male and female categories, in case of males it is 100% among both existing as well as potential customers whereas it is marginally lower at around 88% in case of females (Table 2).

TABLE 2

Individual Liability Preference among the Existing and Potential Micro-credit Customers

	Male	%	Female	%	Total (%)
Among Existing	28/28	100	30/32	94	58 (97)
Among all	32/32	100	44/50	88	76 (93)

With respect to age groups, it is found that 52% and 45 % of the total population in the age groups of 20 years to 40 years and 40 years 60 years, respectively, are interested to go for micro-credit as against the 33% and 25% of

TABLE 3

Age vs. Existing and Potential Micro-credit customers

Age (in years)	Interested in Micro-credit	Preferring Individual Liability	Preferring Joint Liability	Total	%
Up to 20 yrs	4	4 (100%)	0	12	33
20 yrs to 40 yrs	58	54 (93%)	4 (7%)	112	52
40 yrs to 60 yrs	18	16 (89%)	2 (11%)	40	45
Above 60 years	2	2 (100%)	0	8	25

the total population in the age groups of below 20 years and above 60 years category, respectively. The interesting observation here is that although in the age group categories of 20 years to 40 years and 40 years to 60 the interest level is higher, but likeability for individual liability is marginally lower with 93% and 89%, respectively, for the same categories among the potential micro-credit customers. However, in overall scenario, it can be inferred that age, as such, hardly has any correlation with the choice of the liability (Table 3).

TABLE 4

Income vs. Existing and Potential Micro-credit Holders

Income Level (in Rs. p.a.)	Interested in Micro-credit	Preferring Individual Liability	Preferring Joint Liability	Total	%
Up to 50,000	10	8 (80%)	2 (20%)	46	22
50,000-1L	30	30 (100%)	0	62	48
1L to 2L	34	30 (88%)	4 (12%)	52	65
2L +	8	8 (100%)	0	12	67

Income level does have a correlation as far as all micro-credit customers are concerned. It has been found that income levels from up to Rs. 50,000/- per annum till Rs.2,00,000/- per annum, between four different intervals, there is a gradual increase of the number of people preferring micro-credit. But in case of choice of liability type vis-à-vis income levels, no correlation is observed. (Table 4)

TABLE 5

Gender vs. Existing and Potential Credit Holders

Gender	Interested in Micro-credit	Preferring Individual Liability	Preferring Joint Liability	Total	%
Male	32	32 (100%)	0	66	39
Female	50	44 (88%)	6 (12%)	106	61

The survey clearly indicates that Micro-credit is favored more by women than their male counterparts. The percentage share between male and female micro-credit customers of total population is 39% and 61%, respectively, indicating clearly that female leads substantially. However, when it comes to the preferring liability types, 12% of the females among existing and potential micro-credit customers do prefer joint liability. In case of males, entire 100% of the existing and potential micro-credit customers prefer individual liability (Table 5).

TABLE 6

Qualification vs. Existing and Potential Micro-credit customers

Qualification	Interested in Micro-credit	Preferring Individual Liability	Preferring Joint Liability	Total	%
Below Matriculation	56	50 (89%)	6 (11%)	130	43
Matriculation to XII	22	22 (100%)	0	22	100
Graduation	4	4 (100%)	0	4	100
PG and above	0	0	0	2	0

With regards to educational qualification, the data indicates that in this particular locality, 100% of the respondents in both the categories with educational qualifications from Matriculation up to graduation are micro-credit customers (Existing and Potential). Whereas, in case of population below matriculation level, only 43% of the respondents are micro-credit customers. For the population group with educational qualifications of Post-graduation and above, there was no respondent preferring micro-credit. However, in the matter of choice of liability types, even in the category of 'Below Matriculation', preference in the individual liability is very high with 89% of the respondents preferring it. In other two categories, 100% of the respondents have opted for individual liability (Table 6).

TABLE 7

Reasons for preferring Individual Liability

Reasons		Easy to get	Others need not be involved	Liability burden	Independent decision	Total
Interested for Individual Loan	Male	10	10	0	12	32
	%	31	31	0	38	
	Female	4	10	0	30	44
	%	9	23	0	68	
	Total	14	20	0	42	76
Overall %		18.5	26.5	0	55	

The survey overwhelmingly indicates that individual liability is most preferred from amongst the two. The factors influencing respondents' choice of preferring individual liability over group type are: (Table 7)

1. Individual liability loans are easy to get (18.5% for overall, 31% for males and 9% for females).

2. There is no need to involve others (e.g. for group liability loans, formation of SHGs[1] or JLGs[2] are required) (26.5% for overall, 31% for males & 20% for females).
3. Individual liability credits give flexibility of independent decision making option (55% for overall, 30% for males & 68% for females).

Conclusions

From the data collected it is confirmed that, unlike in India, in Gedu town of Bhutan, individual liability micro-credit is more in practice and it is also the most favoured choice of the customers.

In this particular location where the study has been conducted, the influence of demographic factors like age, gender, educational qualification, income level in the choice of individual liable preference or group liability preference cannot be established and thus there is no question of having any correlation amongst them.

However, it can be inferred from the study that choice of individual liability over group liability is mainly for the following three reasons which are given in order of most important to least important one:

1. Flexibility of independent decision making option.
2. The involvement of others is minimum or nil as against group liability loans where formation of SHGs or JLGs are required—thus involvement of others becomes necessary.
3. It is easy to follow-up and get processed an individual loan.

Besides the above, study also confirms that micro-credit is preferred more by womenfolk than the males.

---

[1] **Self Help Groups:** SHG is group of rural poor who have volunteered to organize themselves into a group for eradication of poverty of the members. They agree to save regularly and convert their savings into a Common Fund known as the Group corpus. The members of the group agree to use this common fund and such other funds that they may receive as a group through a common management.

[2] **Joint Liability Groups:** This is formed by five to six members comprising of both men and women who have experience of handling funds previously. This is a credit group and savings is compulsory only after loaning. Since the group has no treasurer, each member is individually liable to each other.

REFERENCES

1. http://en.wikipedia.org/wiki/Muhammad_Yunus,31/10/2008.
2. http://en.wikipedia.org/wiki/Non-governmental_organization,31/10/2008
3. http://www.basixindia.com,31/10/2008.
4. http://www.iimahd.ernet.in/~mssriram/jmf.pdf,31/10/2008.
5. http://www.nabard.org/introduction.asp,31/10/2008.
6. http://www.sa-dhan.net,31/10/2008.
7. http://www.tn.gov.in/dtp/shg.htm,31/10/2008
8. http://www.un.org.in/iawg/icecd/section1.htm
9. Ahin, C. and Townsend, R (2007). 'Using Repayment Data to Test Across Models of Joint Liability Lending', Economic Journal, February, pp. F11-F51
10. Armendariz, de, Aghion .B. and J. Morduch (2005): 'The Economics of Micro Finance', MIT Press
11. Besley Timothy, S. Coat and G. Loury (1993), 'The Economics of Rotating Savings andCredit Association', American Economic Review, 83(4), pp. 792-810
12. Gine X. and Karlan D. (2006): 'Group versus Individual Liability – A Field Experiment in Philippines', World Bank Policy Working Paper, 4008, Washington.
13. Kundu, Amit (May 2009): 'Choice Between Microfinance System Operating on the Basis of Individual Liability Loan Contract or Through Joint Liability Loan Contract', MPRA Paper No. 14981, Department of Economics, Jadavpur University, Kolkata, India.
14. Madajewicz Malgosia (2008), "Joint Liability versus Individual Liability in Credit Contract", Discussion Paper, Columbia University, Department of Economics.
15. Maria Lehner (Nov. 2008): 'Group versus Individual Lending in Microfinance', Discussion paper 2008-24, Department of Economics, University of Munich.
16. Robinson, Marguerite S., 'Microfinance: the Paradigm Shift From Credit Delivery to Sustainable Financial Intermediation', in Mwangi S. Kimenyi, Robert C Wieland and J. D. Von Pischke (eds), 1998, Strategic Issues in Microfinance, Ashgate Publishing: Aldershot.
17. Sriram, M. S. (2007): IIM—Ahmedabad, Presentation in the NAC on Microfinance.
18. Sriram, M. S. (2001). Case study of SHARE group. In S. Datta and M. S. Sriram, Flow of Credit to Small and Marginal Farmers in India (report submitted to the Ministry of Agriculture, Government of India). Ahmedabad: Indian Institute of Management.
19. Sriram, M. S. and Rajesh S. Upadhyayula (2002): "The Transformation of the microfinance sector in India—Experiences, Options and Future" published in Journal of Microfinance, Vol. 6, no. 2.
20. Townsend, R. (1994), "Risk and Insurance in Village India", Econometrica 62: 3, pp. 539-91.

9

Microfinance as a Tool for Poverty Eradication: A Review of Literature

K. Hriyia Kayina

Abstract: *This study investigated through existing literature in an attempt to assess what has been studied about Microfinance Institutions and what needs to be addressed further. Following a discussion on literature, performance of microfinance in its goal of poverty reduction and how they have been measured is discussed. Based on information gathered from literature, a set of recommendations that could increase MFIs' efficacy is also offered. The reasons for the growth in importance of microfinance has been discussed and how far microfinance has actually helped in reducing poverty. Some issues such as high interest rates and group lending practices of Microfinance Institutions are discussed. Based on the existing literature, this paper finds that more and better data is required before any reliable conclusions on microfinance's success as a tool for poverty reduction is reached, success of microfinance as a tool should not be measured in terms of the performances of the various Microfinance Institutions but rather should be measured by adopting common standards that include social benefits.*

Introduction

With near three billion people living in abject poverty, the fight against global poverty has gained great importance and international attention. The issue of poverty in India has remained a prevalent concern. More than 37% of India's population of 1.2 billion still lives below the poverty line. More than 22% of the entire rural population and 15% of the urban population of India exists in this difficult physical and financial predicament.

For a long time the fight against poverty has been about building infrastructure to create employment opportunities with the objective to promote economic development and subsequently lift people out of poverty. These development efforts were done primarily by utilizing foreign aid in an attempt to increase the country's productivity. However, these efforts have produced limited results suggesting that macro development efforts alone are not sufficient for creating sustainable economic development or reducing poverty significantly. Considering these shortcomings of macro development, many countries have embraced microfinance as a new tool for economic development and poverty reduction. Popularized by Professor Mohammad Yunus and the Grameen Bank, microfinance has been credited with the economic development successes in some countries like Bangladesh, Brazil and Chile. The shortcomings of the earlier efforts of macro development and the claimed successes of microfinance and Microfinance Institutions have made microfinance a celebrated tool for economic development and poverty reduction. MFIs' importance in poverty reduction was further highlighted when the Nobel Committee's decided to award (2006) Mr. Yunus and the Grameen Bank the Nobel Peace Prize, on the ground that microfinance is helping people break out of poverty, which is an essential prerequisite to peace. With such great publicity more and more governments, international organizations, donors, and private companies has looked to microfinance as a basic tool for economic development and poverty reduction.

India has been no different. The last five years have seen a transformation in India: rapid economic growth, changes in the composition of that growth and a new vision of development, 'Inclusive Growth' aiming to integrate the county's poor in its growth trajectory, integrating the informal sector into the formal financial markets. The Self-Help Group-Bank linkage programme, India's large scale microfinance initiative, is an important tool in this strategy of Inclusive Growth. This model of microfinance in India has the dual challenge of 'financial inclusion' and poverty alleviation.

The recent growth in popularity of microfinance is, in part, due to its approach to poverty alleviation. The theory behind microfinance is that the poor, with access to credit, can push themselves out of poverty and also cause development giving a ground-up approach to development. With access to credit the poor will create or expand businesses that would bring sustainable income that eventually elevates them above poverty. The ground-up approach of microfinance is a contradiction to the traditional trickle-down approach. Microfinance promotes development through empowerment of the poor while the traditional theory of development is driven by the idea that benefits from the creation and expansion of key industries will eventually trickle down to the poor in the form of new and better paying job opportunities.

Although microfinance and traditional development differ in approach to poverty alleviation and economic development, both share the view that nonfunctional or missing credit markets is a major factor to persistence of poverty in developing nations. In the traditional theory, low incomes in less developed countries (LDCs) lead to low savings, which, in turn, result in low levels of investment. As a result, there is insufficient capital to build infrastructures that are necessary for growth and development. As such, the traditional approach to development aims to remedy the shortage in credit by providing foreign aid.

Microfinance theory also views credit constrains to be central in limiting the upward mobility of the rural poor. However, contrary to popular perception, the credit constraints on the poor are not caused by complete lack of access to credit. The poor in LDCs have multiple credit sources in village economies. In fact, borrowing from family members or professional lenders is common place. As such, the credit constrains are caused by limitations to available credit and not complete lack of access to it. The two main constraints in informal credit markets are high interest rates and dearth of funds. As noted by Abhijit Banerjee and Esther Duflo (2004), professional lenders charge very high interest rates, which dissuades many from borrowing unless absolutely necessary. Further, moneylenders often prefer lending to larger businesses instead of the poor seeking to smooth consumption, reducing available credit.

Problem Statement

While microfinance appears to offer a promising new strategy, academic and empirical research has not yet documented the efficacy of microfinance in poverty alleviation. At times the goals of MFIs are quite unclear although it is assumed that the main goal is of poverty reduction. Therefore, a careful assessment of microfinance and MFIs becomes necessary for understanding and clarifying the goals of MFIs to assess the efficacy of MFIs, also if MFIs are simply assumed to be successful, they might overlook crucial corrections that can adversely affect them and their borrowers.

History of Microfinance

The origin of modern day microfinance dates back to 1976 when Professor Mohammed Yunus experimented with microfinance by lending a small sum of money to a group of Bangladeshi women who wanted to expand an existing or start a new business. The initial success of that loan inspired Mr. Yunus to establish the Grameen Bank in Bangladesh with one simple goal: to provide credit to the poor. As Mr. Yunus observed, several factors contribute to the impoverished people's lack of access to credit. The first of these contributing factors is the poor people's lack of access to formal financial markets. This lack of access is partially caused by the poor people's lack of proximity to formal banks. Since formal banks often operate in larger cities, the rural poor are often too far from any formal banks. Even if proximity is not an issue, the poor could not get access to formal banks because they are considered to be uncreditworthy. Because the poor lack expertise or education, the banks assume that the poor cannot correctly utilize loans, and, as such, banks would be taking a higher risk lending to them. The perception that poor people are unable to correctly utilize loans is further perpetuated by their lack of documented loan experience. Furthermore, because the poor often lack any collateral to offer the banks as insurance against defaulting, the banks are forced to deny them credit.

Implementation concerns further hinder the poor people's access to formal markets, partially because collection and enforcement of bank contracts would be very costly and inefficient if the poor living in distant villages were to violate their agreements and default on loans. Lastly, there are cultural barriers that exclude certain sections of population,.generally women, from financial institutions. All these factors have contributed to impoverished peoples' lack of access to formal credit markets and have limited them to informal credit markets. The lack of credit access led to creation of Grameen Bank and establishment of microfinance. The theory behind microfinance is that the poor are creditworthy. In fact, given access to credit, the poor will utilize loans to increase their income flows and escape poverty. Mr. Yunus believes that with innovative uses of banking practices that lower risks of defaults, banks can lend to the poor. This banking philosophy has led to Grameen Bank's financial success, reporting an average overdue rate of a mere 1.6 percent. In fact, Grameen Bank's model has inspired numerous other MFIs to use similar banking practices. Presently, MFIs as whole report 95% repayment, which has forced many to rethink their position on the poor being uncreditworthy.

Another appealing factor of Microfinance is the low financial costs and the prospect of sustainability. Microfinance Institutes can operate with minimal infrastructure because, unlike formal banks, there is less need for bureaucracy and the amount of money lent to each borrower is fairly small. In addition to potential economic benefits, microfinance has potential social benefits as well. Most MFIs have made lending to women their top priority. In societies where women are often not even sure if they are even allowed to enter the banks, they are not only given access to credit but are also preferred to male borrowers. This access to credit and the ability to create businesses greatly empower women through financial power, which in turn gives them more social power and increases their involvement in household decision-making. The Grameen Bank has 97 percent of its clientele in women. These benefits of microfinance have made MFIs and micro-credit extremely popular.

Methodology Adopted

This study searches through existing literature in an attempt to assess what has been studied about MFIs and what needs to be addressed further. Following a discussion on literature, performance of microfinance in its goal of poverty reduction and how they have been measured will be discussed. Based on information gathered from literature, a set of recommendations that could increase MFIs' efficacy will be offered.

Literature Reviewed

MFIs' banking practices have been designed to promote two potentially conflicting goals. The main goal of MFIs is poverty reduction and, hence, MFIs' banking practices are designed to help alleviate poverty. But in recent studies, some of MFIs' lauded banking practices have been criticized as ineffective and at times counterproductive.

In microfinance the loan principle per borrower is fairly small which has some consequences—the amount of interest charged on the loans does not generate enough income for the MFIs to significantly expand and serve more clients and, at times, the interest generated from loans does not provide enough revenue for banks to cover operational charges, particularly because providing loans to the poor are more costly, partially due to the fact that MFIs must verify that the borrowers meet MFIs' criteria before issuing the loan. As a result, MFIs charge higher interest than the typical banking institute; although, MFIs' interest rates are still lower than the usury rates charged by professional village lenders who are the main alternative to MFIs in most villages. Nonetheless, as noted by Hudon (2006), many find MFIs' high interest rate ethically questionable. As MFIs try to become financially sustainable and independent, they are forced to increase interest rates on loans. MFIs justify higher interest rates by citing the importance of increasing revenues that would allow them to provide more services to more people. Furthermore, findings of Mel et al (2007) support the notion that borrowers' return to investment is large enough to cover MFIs' high interest rates.

Critics of high interest rates, however, have equated the profit seeking behavior of some MFIs and high interest rates in general to making a profit at the expense of the poor. The critics of MFIs argue that high interest rates are only justified with the assumption that the clients have sufficient return to capital to cover the interest rates. Datar et al (2008) contest that this assumption is problematic, particularly when empirical evidence shows sufficient returns on loans only when loans are used towards productive ends. Datar et al (2008) further cite that in cases where clients do not generate sufficient income from loans, they are forced to take extreme measures such as decreasing consumption or borrowing from professional lenders to repay the interest. This result is antithetical to the goal of MFIs. Still the greater question of impact of high interest rates on entrepreneurs' abilities and a potential trade off between business growth and repayment is yet to be empirically addressed.

Group lending is the most predominant method utilized by majority of MFIs. In the group lending paradigm, 3 to 10 individuals self-select and apply for micro-credit. After assessment, the loan is offered to the first two individuals in the group. Once the first two individuals repay the loan, usually after a few weeks, the next two in the group are offered the loan. This process continues until all members have been awarded and repaid loans. Once everyone in the group has repaid the loans, the group establishes itself as creditworthy and is awarded a higher credit limit. But, if during the process, any individual defaults on their repayment, the whole group losses access to the credit market. This method of lending has proved to be quite successful for a few reasons. First, the societal and group pressure helps guarantee timely payments and, secondly, by penalizing the entire group for shortcomings of a single member, the group often helps potential defaulting members in order to protect their own credit. The group also acts as a check on individuals to ensure the correct use of funds to avoid possible future repayment concerns. An alternative to group lending is village banking where larger groups with as many as 40 individuals are formed.

Group-lending is one of the innovative banking techniques practiced by most MFIs. This practice is often cited as the tool that enables MFIs to provide credit to the poor. The practice of group-lending mitigates clients' risk of defaulting by holding multiple people responsible for the issued loans. This shared risk allows MFIs to charge lower interest rates on loans. Furthermore, in group-lending, individuals self select into groups, which mitigates adverse selection problems. Meaning, responsible borrowers tend to choose other responsible borrowers to join their group, which, in turn, reduces banking costs of MFIs, who otherwise would have to bear the cost of verifying clients' creditworthiness. For these reasons, group-lending approach has been seen as the main reason for MFIs' success.

A recent study of social impacts of group lending by Annabel Vanroose (2007) casts doubt on this conclusion, however. She finds that while group-lending is effective in pressuring against defaults, it does so at the cost of borrowers' social capital. Vanroose explains that, in most developing countries, the poor heavily rely on social capital (their relationship with other members of their community) for survival. Vanroose (2007) finds that when individuals in the group cannot repay their loan, their social capital greatly deteriorates. As such, they find themselves in a worse situation than before borrowing from MFIs. Other studies have found group-lending to pose danger to those who fear the shame of defaulting. At times, to repay loans, borrowers are known to reduce consumption of food, sell furniture, and borrow from professional lenders. In some cases, borrowers commit suicide rather than face public humiliation. As such, some believe that at times the health of financial institutes is placed above the welfare of the poor and in these cases "microfinance exploits social relationships to obtain higher repayment rates and to reduce administrative costs."

In hopes of maintaining high repayment rates, numerous MFIs require frequent repayments. As noted by Sengupta and Aubuchon (2008), by demanding frequent small repayments before business ventures have reached maturity, MFIs are practically demanding that the borrowers have a second source of income, indicating that they are borrowing against their current consumption. Sengupta and Aubuchon (2008) claim that immediate repayments dissuade those without sufficient income and poorer individuals from borrowing. The requirement of frequent repayments, of course, serves as a disincentive to borrow for those who cannot afford quick repayments. As such, using frequent repayments allows MFIs to naturally select the better-off poor over the extremely poor.

Another banking technique employed by some MFIs is the compulsory saving programme. By forcing borrowers to save, MFIs reduce the risk of default. Sengupta and Aubuchon (2008) provide evidence that while this programme promotes long-term savings, it overlooks that many poor use savings to smooth consumption in difficult times. The lack of access to savings hinders borrowers who face unexpected difficulties. Also, the lack of access to savings raises the effective interest rate by limiting the amount of the savings available to borrowers. Most MFIs, however, no longer have compulsory saving requirements, partially because the programme limited borrowers by forcing them to save money rather than fully invest in productive ventures.

Predominantly lending to women is a well-known banking technique of MFIs. While the practice of lending to women is lauded for its social appeals, there are numerous banking benefits to lending to women. Aghion and Morduch (2005) explain three banking advantages of lending to women. The first is that, under neoclassical assumptions, "if women have less access to capital than men, return to capital for women should then be higher than for men." The second advantage of lending to women is based on their mobility. Women tend to be less mobile and more susceptive to social pressures. As such, MFIs have easier time tracking female borrowers and pressuring them to repay loans. Finally, as the consequence of the first two conditions, coupled with women's perception of credit as a chance for empowerment, women make safer business decisions, which is more beneficial for MFIs. While empirical evidence on the benefits of lending to women is limited, a study of repayment behaviour of men and women clients of The Grameen Bank by Khandker et al (1995) reveals that in 1991,15.3 percent of male borrowers were struggling for repayment compared to 1.3 percent of females struggling for repayments.

Many MFIs cite the success of their banking practices as evidence of reducing poverty. For instance, the MFIs who use low default rates as proof of poverty alleviation claim that repayment confirms that borrowers were able to create sustainable sources of income. Datar et al (2008) explain that using banking practices as proof of poverty alleviation relies on questionable assumption. Without actually investigating how loans were used and the sustainability of the created businesses, it is near impossible to make the aforementioned claims —particularly when individuals can resort to alternative sources to repay loans. Also, many MFIs measure success using consumer satisfaction, that is, if borrowers are satisfied with provided services, then the MFIs' services are creating positive impacts; using consumer satisfaction, however, has very limited explanation power regarding actual efficacy of MFIs. Some scholars have questioned the correlation between banking success and impacts on borrowers. Peter Crabb (2007) explains that MFIs' success can be explained by continual private and governmental support and its banking success are as a result of economies of scale, not because general improvement of borrowers. Furthermore, the correlation between observing success and causing success has not been shown. As such, "...the success of a microfinance institution is an indicator of improvement poverty conditions, not a factor in its improvement." Thus some argue that, general economic improvements and sound fiscal policies are the main driving forces that help the poor; MFIs simply act as vehicles that reallocate and redistribute private and public funds.

Income and Consumption changes as proof of efficacy, there are only few empirical studies that have studied the economic impacts of microcredit and MFIs. As previously mentioned, most empirical studies have focused on increases in income and consumption as proof of MFIs efficacy in reducing poverty. The claim of these studies is that an increase in income and consumption shows economic improvement, which suggests that the borrowers are rising above poverty. One such study, mentioned in section 2 of this chapter, is by Mel et al (2007), who find that small loans to existing businesses has significant returns to capital. In fact, the loans given to business owners increased real annual income by profits by 68 percent. This real annual return is significantly higher than nominal market rates of 16-24 percent for a two year loan. Although this study did not measure success of any particular MFI, it still shows that for that particular sample, there were significant gains from even small loans. Such high returns to capital at a minimum suggests that providing the poor with access to credit and financial services allows for consumption smoothing, which reduces risks and vulnerability as a result of life' financial shocks, a step in the right direction in the fight against poverty. As such, MFIs claim that at a minimum, even if data does not allow for wide-range efficacy measurements, their loans make clients more able to deal with financial crises.

But, some have noted that the above mentioned study specifically targeted existing businesses and kept those businesses under close supervision, to ensure that businesses utilize loans in a productive manner. But, vast majority of MFIs do not track the specific use of loans, nor do they only give loans to existing business owners. And as Arun et al (2006) observed, significant results are obtained only when loans are used for productive purposes, as was the case for the study by Mel et al (2007).

The main study of the efficacy of MFIs—one that is said to be the proof of MFIs' success—is a study carried out by Khandker (2005). The study's focus is The Grameen Bank, where panel data of income and consumption is used to measure the efficacy of given loans. Khandker notes that because the overarching objective of MFIs is poverty reduction and MFIs clients are people with little education and no land, any impact assessment of microfinance and poverty reduction should "assess whether programme participation increases household consumption over its level before programme participation." Khandker finds that consumption and income increase for both clients and non-clients. The study states that, between 1991/92 and 1998/99, the household annual per capita expenditure grew by 30.5 percent for all households, compared with the 34.5 percent for borrowers. Khandker also argues that the increase in all household consumption levels is in part due to spillover effects of borrowers' improved economic conditions. Khandker also finds that, based on increase in consumption in the sample villages, overall poverty declined by 17 percent between 1991/92 and 1998/99 and extreme poverty by 13 percent. These results led Khandker to conclude that "not only does the increase in consumption resulting from borrowing raise the probability that program participants will escape poverty, but the microfinance intervention also benefits nonparticipants through growth in local economy."

A recent study of literature on the efficacy of MFIs, performed on behalf of The Grameen Bank, lauds Khandker's findings and suggests that a raise in borrowers income is sufficient to show poverty alleviation. In accordance with numerous other studies, Khandker (2005) notes that the empirical studies based on available data are not incontrovertible and, in fact, more analysis and studies are needed to measure social impacts. A study of Khushhali Bank in Pakistan by Heather Montgomery (2005) finds that there is a positive correlation between borrowing from MFIs and income and consumption levels. While the study finds that borrowing from MFIs does not change food consumption, spending on children's education of borrowers increases significantly, annual per capita expenditure grew by 30.5 percent for all households, compared with the 34.5 percent for borrowers. Khandker also argues that the increase in all household consumption levels is, in part, due to spillover effects of borrowers' improved economic conditions. Khandker also finds that, based on increase in consumption in the sample villages, overall poverty declined by 17 percent between 1991/92 and 1998/99 and extreme poverty by 13 percent. These results led Khandker to conclude that "not only does the increase in consumption resulting from borrowing raise the probability that programme participants will escape poverty, but the microfinance intervention also benefits nonparticipants through growth in local economy." A recent study of literature on the efficacy of MFIs, performed on behalf of The Grameen Bank, lauds Khandker's findings and suggests that a raise in borrowers' income is sufficient to show poverty alleviation. In accordance with numerous other studies, Khandker (2005) notes that the empirical studies based on available data are not incontrovertible and, in fact, more analysis and studies are needed to measure social impacts.

A study of Khushhali Bank in Pakistan by Heather Montgomery (2005) finds that there is a positive correlation between borrowing from MFIs and income and consumption levels. While the study finds that borrowing from MFIs does not change food consumption, spending on children's education of borrowers increases significantly. Based on an 8 week questioner conducted in July 2005, the author found that there is a positive and significant correlation between education consumption of children. Critiques of Income and Consumption studies claimed that these studies merely establish an observable fact without deciphering the causal factors that led to it. The income-poverty studies carried out by MFIs that use proxies for measuring economic impact have come under great scrutiny. Hulme and Mosley (1996) explain that causes such as "...vulnerability to a sudden dramatic decrease in consumption levels, ill-health, and physical weakness, social inferiority, powerlessness, humiliation and isolation" are also essential and significant dimensions of poverty that must also be taken into account in any income-poverty analysis.

Furthermore, as stated by Hatch and Frederick (1998), national poverty lines are usually based on household income and food expenditure. They further note that these measures are complicated and quite possibly miss important qualitative forms of deprivation. Even proponents of income-poverty studies note the importance of looking deeper than changes in income before claiming improvements in the financial capital of borrowers. Furthermore, some critics charge that access to credit simply allows for consumption smoothing, not real economic development and poverty alleviation. But simply allowing for consumption smoothing would only allow for stability and not development. Any shock can quickly eliminate many of the benefits received from loans. As explained by Epstein et al (2005), claiming success for simply providing access to credit and consumption smoothing is not enough, particularly when MFIs have the opportunity to help their borrowers cross the poverty line.

Many other MFIs measure success using consumer satisfaction, that is, if borrowers are satisfied with provided services, then the MFIs' services are creating positive impacts. Alternatives to Income and Consumption Measurements as mentioned before, defining success is different for different MFIs. Financial-centered MFIs rely on income and consumption data, combined with banking success, to assess economic and social impacts. On the other hand, poverty-centered MFIs, operating under the assumption that income and consumption data do not accurately capture poverty levels, focus on behavioural changes, such as changes prioritization of health and education in households that were made possible through MFIs' services. These two different types of MFIs have two different methods in measuring success. Financial-centered MFIs assess banking and income success, which has already been discussed. The poverty-centered MFIs, however, assess poverty reduction without use of proxies or representative exogenous variables.

Conclusions and Suggestions

Prioritizing of financial sustainability has given more significance to banking performance. As noted by Murdoch (2005) there is still a lot of MFIs, even those working towards sustainability which are dependent on subsidies because many

MFIs have only recently implemented changes that can improve their financial standing making it difficult to make an accurate evaluation of MFIs' banking performance immediately. Nevertheless certain banking performances of MFIs have become well known, low default rates being one such performance measurement. According to Datar et al (2008) MFIs report a 95 percent repayment rate of loans, with some banks, such as Grameen Bank, reporting default rates as low as 1.6 percent. These figures present a significant banking accomplishment.

Despite the apparent banking success of MFIs, some critics remain skeptical. The main objection to MFIs' banking practices is lack of transparency. Most MFIs internally measure banking success and only selectively disclose results. As such, there is a general lack of transparency of MFIs' banking practices and banking calculations. This lack of transparency has led some critics to question reported success of some MFIs.

Furthermore, some have criticized MFIs for unconventional accounting practices. As noted by Morduch (1999) some MFIs calculate their overdue rate as the amount overdue by more than one year divided by current portfolio. This accounting practice under-reports the proportion of defaulted loans. Also, some MFIs, Grameen Banks in particular, operate under the assumption that the poor will eventually repay their loans. Therefore, as long as the clients are asking for extensions, the MFIs do not consider them to be defaulting, which further underestimate the number of clients defaulting on loans. Ultimately, the critics of MFIs argue that more transparency and time is needed before the success of MFIs as banking institutes can be assessed.

Examining literature on banking practices of some MFIs discussed above raises important questions regarding the socioeconomic impact of those practices. For instance, the economic impacts of high interest rates on loans are not fully examined. Some borrowers have difficulty repaying loans with high interest rates, which further exasperates their poor economic conditions. Simultaneously, MFIs rely on revenue generated from interest. Again, a trade-off between MFIs' interests and borrowers' interests becomes apparent. Further, at present no literature has substantially examined the impact of interest rates on growth of businesses. Therefore there is a need for further investigation on the socio-economic impacts of loans. The use of frequent repayments is another banking practice which needs to be further addressed. While frequent repayments are used to lower the risk of default, its socio-economic impacts have not yet been examined. Theoretically, having to repay loans almost immediately after the loan was issued would limit entrepreneurs and potentially limit creation or expansion of their businesses. Limiting borrowers and lowering their chance of success opposes the goals of MFIs. But, the actual impacts of this practice are unclear, dictating further investigation.

Similarly, as revealed by the literature review, the social impacts of other banking practices such as group-lending and lending to women are now under scrutiny. Some studies (Vanroose (2007), Murdoch (2005)) found that the aforementioned banking practices have negative social consequences, which at times leave clients more vulnerable than before obtaining the loans. While the aforementioned studies are not incontrovertible, the question still remains, what are social consequences of MFIs' banking practices? And if there are negative consequences to the banking practices, do the benefits received from them outweigh the costs?

Despite the impressive growth and expansion of MFIs, there is a dearth of studies that have assessed their socioeconomic impacts. There are two general problems with any study attempting to assess success of microfinance and MFIs. The first problem is what to measure. While the assumed goal of MFIs is poverty reduction, in reality the goals of MFIs vary, with some focusing on poverty reduction while others only seeking to provide financial services to the poor. As such, it is difficult to reach a consensus on what factors gauge MFIs' success.

Further, since MFIs serve dual purposes as banks and agents for social change, it is difficult to resolve which of the functions should be emphasized in efficacy measurements. As such, some MFIs claim that measuring banking success is sufficient to assess the efficacy of MFIs, while other MFIs claim that measuring real impacts (change in assets, education, health, etc.) on clients' lives, not banking performance, should gauge MFIs' efficacy. But, as noted by Epstein and Crane (2005), the general consensus amongst MFIs is that the ultimate goal is poverty reduction, even if they do not explicitly state it as a primary goal. As such, whatever methodology is utilized to access efficacy, it should ultimately address MFIs' impacts on poverty levels.

Moreover, most success stories of MFIs have been based using banking criteria such as high repayment rates, MFIs' expansion and profitability and the improvements in the general economy as proof of their efficacy in reducing poverty. Considering that the most important goal of microfinance is poverty reduction, MFIs must focus on their clients. Monitoring clients' performance and providing educational training for the staff and clients should be the priority than banking concerns.

Works cited and References

1. Arun, T. Imai, K. and Sinha, F. (2006)."Does microfinance reduce poverty in India? Propensity Score Matching, Based on a National Household Data (Development Economics and Public Policy-Working Paper)"
2. Crabb, Peter R (2007). "The success of microfinance: What really sustains this poverty relief effort" Northwest Nazarene University School of Business. Working Paper.

3. Datar, Srikant M., Marc J. Epstein, and Kristi Yuthas. "In Microfinance, Clients Must Come First." Stanford Social Innovation, Review 6, No. 1 (winter 2008).
4. De Mel, Suresh, David Mckenzie and C. Woodruff,(2007). "Who Does Micrfinance Fail to Reach? Experimental Evidence on Gender and Microenterprise Returns." BREAD Working Paper.
5. Epstein, M. J. and Crane, C. A. (2005). "Alleviating Global Poverty through Microfinance: Factors and measures of financial, economic and social performance".
6. Harraf, Omid. (2008). "Can Microfinance Eradicate Poverty? Analysis of the Efficacy of Microfinance Using Existing Literature". University of Nevada Reno.
7. Hatch, J. K and Frederick, L. (1998). "Poverty Assessment by Microfinance Institutions: A review of the Current Practices", Development Alternatives, Inc.
8. Hudon, M. (2006), Fair interest rates when lending to the poor: Are fair prices derived from basic principles of justice? Working Paper, WPCEB 06/15, Solvay Business School, Université Libre de Bruxelles.
9. Jalan, A. (2009). "Microfinance: does it affect rural poverty reduction? The case of two villages in southern India".
10. Khandker S. R. Microfinance and poverty: evidence using panel data from Bangladesh. World Bank Econ Rev. 2005; 19(2): pp. 263-286.
11. Morduch Jonathan and de Aghion, A. B. (2005). The economics of microfinance. Cambridge: MIT Press.
12. Morduch, Jonathan (1999). The Microfinance Promise, Journal of Economic Literature, Vol. 37, No. 4, pp. 1596-1614.
13. Sengupta, Rajdeep and Craig Aubuchon, (2008). The Microfinance Revolution: An Overview. Review 90(1): pp. 9-30.
14. Vanroose, A. (2007) "Microfinance: are its promises ethically justified" Working Paper Université Libre de Bruxelles, Solvay Business School, Centre Emile Bernheim (CEB) # 07-014.RS.
15. Weiss, John and Heather Montgomery (2005). "Great Expectations: Microfinance and Poverty Reduction in Asia and Latin America", Oxford Development Studies 33(3-4), pp. 391-416.
16. Yunus, M. "Grameen Bank II: Designed to Open New Possibilities." Grameen Bank, October 2002.
17. Yunus, M. "What Is Micro-credit?" Grameen Bank, September 2007.
18. Yunus, M. Banker to the Poor: Micro-Lending and the Battle Against World Poverty. New York: Public Affairs, 2003.

SECTION III

ROLE OF MICROFINANCE FOR RURAL EMPLOYMENT

10

Experience of SGSY in Backward Region: A Study in West Bengal

D. K. Dey

ABSTRACT: *The Swarnajayanti Gram Swarajgar Yajona (SGSY) as a self-employment programme has been implemented in rural areas with effect from April 1999 to eradicate poverty. The present paper is an attempt to critically examine the relevance of such programmes in respect of economically and socially backward areas including empirical evidences from the district of Purulia, West Bengal. It is observed that the success of any micro-credit programme can be evaluated in both quantitative and qualitative way. The study indicates that even in extremely deprived rural areas, women SHGs would have considerable impact upon the lives of the members. The common access of savings is perceived as a source of self-dignity apart from its financial implications.*

Introduction

Poverty reduction remains as one of the avowed goals in Indian planning exercise. Numerous committees had been formed followed up by adoption of prescribed strategies and now we are talking about an inclusive growth in Eleventh Plan Approach paper. The enactment of the right to get hundred days of employment through public works further confirms the persistence of absolute poverty in rural India. Moreover, the National Commission for Unorganised Enterprises in their report (2008) indicates the destitute condition of the Indian working poor. Since the Sixth Five Year Plan, Self-Employment programme has been executed to generate additional employment towards eradication of poverty. Currently Swarnajayanti Gram Swarajgar Yajona (SGSY) has been implemented universally in rural areas with effect from April 1999. The present paper is an attempt to critically examine the relevance of such programme in respect of economically and socially backward areas including empirical evidences from the district of Purulia, West Bengal.

India has accepted wage employment and self-employment as its core instrument to fight against poverty almost for the last three decades while other social security programmes like Public Distribution System (PDS), Old Age Pension or Mid-Day meal have been added for supplementary development process. Before SGSY, Integrated Rural Development Programme (IRDP) was implemented as the self-employment programmes in all blocks of the country for two decades. IRDP has been intensively evaluated by Researchers and Policy makers and numerous loopholes had been identified in these studies resulting in arrival of the new version of the programme as SGSY. The rest of the paper has been designed in the following manner. Section I presents a brief review of the existing literature on effectiveness of micro-credit programmes in poverty reduction found from empirical studies. Section II deals with India's effort in institutional lending in rural areas including a brief description of SGSY. Section III depicts empirical evidences from the district of Purulia followed by conclusion in last section IV.

I

Review of the Existing Literature

Meanwhile, the tide of micro-credit or microfinance from South Asia including Bangladesh and Latin America had reached our country also. National Bank for Agriculture and Rural Development (NABARD) had initiated a pilot project on microcredit in the early years of the nineties. These entire play pivotal roles in formulating this new programme named as SGSY in place of IRDP as per the recommendations of the committee formed by the Planning Commission to review the wage employment and Self-employment schemes in 1997.

SGSY differs from IRDP on four basic grounds. First, in place of individual targeting in IRDP the new one (SGSY) is a group based programme, thus it becomes "joint liability" in place of individual liability. This way of minimizing risk is a clear impact of microcredit wave. Second, rather than one time injection as designed for IRDP it is now based on "progressive lending" which is also one of the key principles of world wide microcredit programmes. Third, there remains scope for community organizations with the help of Panchayati Raj Institution (PRI) and Non-Governmental Organizations (NGOs), which was absent in its earlier version. Fourth, apart from credit, other inputs like training, marketing are embodied in the programme in its very design, while, in case of IRDP, other governmental agencies had to take care of these components. As per government claims these make SGSY of a holistic nature.

The growing spread and acceptance of microfinance is based on Win-Win proposition. The formation of CGAP (Consultative Group to Assist the Poorest) in 1995 as a resource centre for the entire microfinance industry is a reflection of this growing importance (World Bank, 2001). Vast literature on impact of micro-credit upon poverty has been developed in last couple of years. One of the early and most widely cited studies in this regard is Hulme and Mosley (1996). Programmes in a number of countries is considered including the Grameen Bank in Bangladesh and Bank Rakayat Indonesia (BRI). In general, a positive impact is found on borrower incomes of the poor. Gains are larger for non-poor borrowers and the increase in income of micro-credit borrowers is directly proportional to their starting level of income.

Another early empirical work was the surveys conducted in the 1990s by the Bangladesh Institute of Development Studies (BIDS) and the World Bank. This had provided data for several other studies such as Pitt and Khandker (1998). They found positive impact of micro-credit on total weekly expenditure per capita, women's non-land assets and women's labour supply. Strong impact was reflected on school going children as well as attitude of the village. Khandker (ibid) estimated that after repayment of loan of 100 taka, a female borrower is allowed to increase her consumption by 18 taka and in this way 5% of participant household are pulled above the poverty line annually. A detailed impact assessment study of BRAC in Bangladesh suggested that members who stayed in the programme for more than four years increased household expenditure by 28% and assets by 112 percent (Mustafa et al, 1996).

Another analysis of household level data demonstrated that access to financial services enabled BRAC clients to reduce their vulnerability through smoothing consumption, building assets and receiving services during natural disaster (Zaman, 2000). Following up his earlier work, Khandker (2005) finds a significant positive impact on consumption for female borrowers (10.5 taka increment per 100 taka repay). It is estimated that due to participation in micro-credit programme, moderate poverty decreased by 18.2 percentage points over the period of seven years in programme, villages. Using the same data set, Pit et al (2003) found that credit going to female has a large and significant impact in two out of three health measures for children—unlike that of the male borrowers.

MkNelley et al (1996) found positive benefits in village bank credit with education in Thailand while Coleman (1999) found no evidence of prorgamme impact. Chen and Snodgrass (2001) reported an average increase in income for bank's clients in a study on SEWA bank, India. They found little overall change in incidence of poverty but substantial movement above and below the poverty line. Coleman (2001), in another study on Village bank, Thailand, noted that credit programmes are not reaching the poor as much as they reach relatively wealthy people. Greater impact was observed on richer members compared to poorer one. Barnes (2001) assessed that participation in the Zambuko Trust led to positive impacts on consumption of high protein foods for extremely poor households.

II

Efforts in Institutional Lending

The term microfinance or micro-credit has got spectacular importance in development literature in the last one and half decades is mainly due to its many successes in combating poverty by reaching poorer families in a more effective way (Kaladhar, 1997). It has thus attracted support both from the redistributive left and the profitability-motivated right wing of the political spectrum (Hulme &Mosley, ibid). Intervention through credit is not new in Indian context, as it is reflected by the historic step of nationalization of commercial banks in 1969 followed by Integrated Rural Development Programme (IRDP) in 1980-81. Though the beginning of the institutional finance for agriculture in India dates long back to 1793 through taccavi loans, yet the first survey on rural indebtedness[1] by RBI shortly after independence reported that the share of banks in total rural household debt was only 1%. The vast spread network of rural banks [35,396 rural branches of commercial banks, 29 state cooperative banks, 367 district central cooperative banks, and over 90,000 primary agricultural societies (PACs) and 14,443 branches of Regional Rural Banks (RRBs)] was not sufficient to lend credit to rural masses due to their internal weakness and design defects and sectoral problems (Patil, 2005). Rural people needs credit for various purposes including productive purposes, credit as insurances against risk, and credit for meeting basic consumption needs like food, housing, health and education. The imperfectness of Indian rural credit markets and its adverse effects upon rural life have been well documented in existing literature. According to one estimate, moneylenders still cover more than 56 percent of rural people's credit needs (Khandelwal, 2007). The Rural Finance Access Survey (RFAS), 2003, reports that 41% of rural households have a deposit account while 21% of the same have access to credit from a formal source.

The SGSY is viewed in this larger context. How effective is the programme in reducing poverty in extremely poor pockets like our study area? How the poorest of the poor gets benefits from the programme?

The major criticism against micro-credit is its failure to address the poorest section of the society. Moreover, viability of the non-farm economic activities are crucial for the future of microcredit programme (Vatta, 2003). But access to credit by those slightly above the poverty line is not mis-targeting because credit to those sections generates much needed wage employment opportunities for the poorest (Mahajan, 2005). From empirical research it appears that while the programme had definite impact on building of social capital, it had marginal impact on income levels (World Bank, 2003). Apart from financial benefits SHG should be viewed as a participatory endeavour to secure three types of power—namely, social, political and psychological—to empower the group members (Vijaykumar, 2009). Thus it poses many unfinished tasks, especially for the backward region, also applicable for the rest of the country as per the performance indicators at national level.

According to the Annual Report (2007-08) of MORD, GOI, since the inception of the programme 27,41,082 SHGs have been promoted under this programme of which 82.5% are women SHGs. The performance of the programme at the national level is not as it is felt in the Mid Term appraisal of Tenth Five Year Plan that greater coordination between different government departments and banks are needed with more emphasis on Training and Marketing. It is mentioned in the CAG report of 2002-03 that only one SHG out of fifty have started economic activities.

A study on the SGSY covering the Bangalore district of Karnataka by V. Chetan and B. Krishnamurty (2002) concluded that 52.5% of the beneficiaries covered by the study took up employment on less number of days as a result of participation of the programme. Banerjee and Sen (2003), in their study conducted on the working of the SGSY scheme in West Bengal, found that the funding pattern under this programme is not only less transparent but simultaneously also involves several agencies without any chain of authority between them. Thekkekara (2008) pointed out that subsidy has made the programme less effective. Earlier, Purushottom (2006) stressed for training and other infrastructure support.

Concurrent Evolution of SGSY by Centre for Management Development (2003) indicated that the programme is carrying the legacy of IRDP. Performance of West Bengal in terms of available fund utilization is 54%—slightly below the national average (up to January 2008).

III

Empirical Study in Purulia District

Purulia is known as one of the backward districts of the country with highest proportion of tribal population in the state. The Government of West Bengal earlier had identified 994 villages of the district as 'backward'[2]. It is revealed from the official data of District Rural Development Cell (DRDC) that, at the end of 2007-08, 17 thousand Self Help Groups (SHGs) were formed in the district of which more than 90 percent are women groups. One may also notice that in the last five years the annual growth rate of new group formation is 20%. More than three-fourth of these groups passed Grade I[3] and availed first dose of Revolving Fund[4]. But only 0.5% of these groups could move to next stages where credit linkages are made for promoting economic activities (Table 1). It has also emerged that only 40 percent of the target in terms of group formation in backward villages had been achieved so far. This motivates for further probing to find the ground realities.

The study is based on field investigation done in two blocks of Purulia district of West Bengal. Purulia II and Jhalda II were selected purposefully as the first one is nearer to the district Headquarter and the latter is twenty kilometers from the district Centre. Two Gram Panchayats (GPs) from each block was selected randomly for field level enquiry. Five SHGs passed Grade I, from the backward villages of each GP were selected for the purpose of the study. Altogether forty SHGs were taken along with five members from each group including group leaders were selected for household level survey with structured questionnaire. Normally, microfinance impact assessment studies used two widely used methods: (a) comparing between "Treatment group"(formed by the programme participants), and "Control group" (formed by the non-participants) (b) comparison between "Old beneficiaries" and "New beneficiaries" (Jena, 2008). As the second one is beyond the scope of the study we have adopted the first one for our purpose. Non-Partcipants on one-third ratio of the Participants were selected randomly for household level survey from each block.

Group level information

It is revealed that groups were mainly promoted by the functionaries of Panchayats at the village level. It appears that there remains a target-achieving tendency on the part of the Panchayati Raj Institutions (PRIs) for their horizontal accountability[5] while vertical accountability[6] is almost absent in these backward areas. Sud (2003) mentioned that although the programme had been designed to be participatory one in papers, in reality it becomes another new programme of achieving target.

This sub section is presented in tabular form from Table 2 – Table 10. Most of the groups (67.5%) of our sample are 1-3 years old and their total savings varies accordingly. It is revealed that the programme provides the opportunity for these poor rural households of the backward villages to save safely. Robinson (2001) mentioned that this deposit service is valuable for the poor who don't have access to formal financial institutions. Members had jointly decided the amount of monthly contribution at the time of group formation. This amount has been simply divided by the number of meetings held during a month and that is used to be collected in meetings. Members of 72.5% of our groups save Rs. 20 per month with variation among the blocks. Most of the groups were formed with 10-15 members but the size of the groups remains unchanged. It means that self-selected members had joined in a group without drop-out, as well as new entry was also absent.

Public spaces have been used to conduct meetings though private places are also used in absence of public space. It is observed that in most cases members themselves maintain Accounts. In Purulia II the proportion of groups maintaining their own Accounts is high compared to Jaypur, lower literacy in the latter block may be a reason for this. It is important to note that all groups had opened their bank accounts in local banks and it has been operated on regular basis. Simultaneous involvement of Panchayat, DRDA and NGOs in this programme is responsible for this. As far as passing out of Grade I is concerned, groups of Purulia II are far ahead compared to Jaypur block in our sample. But it is not reflected in credit pattern as more members in Joypur have taken loan compared to Purulia II though more groups in Purulia II got revolving fund from DRDA.

One of the major advantages in micro-credit is its low defaulting rate. In our sample groups very few borrowers have delayed in repaying at the time of survey. It appears that groups of Purulia II performed better in some parameters presented above but, in terms of rotation of loan, Jaypur being far from the district town—performed better. In terms of pattern of loan utilization it emerges that in Jaypur high proportion (40%) of loans have been used for consumption purpose. One reason may be that the proportion of members enlisted in official BPL list is high in Jaypur compared to Purulia II.

Further decomposition of members of our selected groups shows that backward communities like ST and SC coverage is not high in both the blocks though considerable proportion of population in those areas belongs to these communities. As far as the selection of group leaders is concerned proportion of groups with at least one leader from the backward communities is not encouraging also. It is found that the percentage of married women belonging to the age group 18-35 is the major participants in our groups. Ramesh (2007) argued in favour of incorporation of SHGs in various public delivery systems.

It comes out from our study that groups of Purulia II are having the experience of involvements in Mid Day Meal and NREG, while groups of Jaypur has experience in Mid Day Meal. The other part of the story is that not a single member of our sample groups has gone through any kind of training of Accounts or capability generation. Therefore the members have to depend on traditional activities like goat rearing or poultry without any training, which will be described in next section where household level information will be presented.

Household level information

In this sub section household level information of SGSY beneficiaries as well as non-beneficiaries will be presented (Table 11 – Table 20). It has been attempted here to select non-beneficiaries from the same socio-economic background. It is interesting to see that though SGSY members and non-members come from poor background, all of them do not have Ration Card but almost all of them carry Identity Cards issued by the Central Election Commission. Very few portions of the members have individual bank account. Similar trend is followed for non-participants also. It appears that this non-bankable population of backward villages gets the access to bank through this programme.

Most of the members came from the nuclear family while female-headed families in the two blocks are less than 15%—implying that male members of the household may not pose obstacles for their female counterparts; to participate in the programme. It appears that most of the members live in *Kachcha* house; while a few use own toilet, almost all are dependent on open air. Less than 50% of the household avails electricity in Jaipur while the figure is quite lower in case of Purulia II. Even majority of the households have to depend on non-safe sources for drinking water. In the above two Tables, control group does not bear much differences from the treatment group.

It is observed that large proportion of households belongs to the landless category comparable with the BPL figures. Non-participants also mostly comprise landless, marginal and small farmers. It is observed that landlessness is high in Purulia II, but the pattern of distribution in terms of land holding is similar in both the blocks. It is likely that majority members have come from lower income groups, which is similar to the findings from the group level data, presented earlier. Members have little asset holding status, it emerges that 40% of the households are having bicycle and considerable sections of the household also have plow of their own. This is similar to the findings of Census 2001. There are not many differences among the members and non-participants in this regard also.

As far as the education status is concerned, it reveals that high illiteracy rate prevails among SHG members. But in both the blocks literacy rate is higher among the SHG members compared to non-members. Primary school enrolment ratio is high among the sample households. It is claimed by high proportion SGSY members (80%) and non-members (83%) that Mid Day Meal is one of the major reasons for this high enrolment. It is observed that in terms of employment the proportion of casual labour in agriculture is high in both the blocks. As landlessness is high in Purulia II and due to its geographical advantages in connection with district town, a considerable section of Purulia II are employed in 'other' category including non-farm and informal activities. Similarities between members and non members in terms of education and employment have been revealed.

There are many similarities among the members and non-members in terms of various socioeconomic indicators. The corollary question comes: Why the non-members didn't join the programme? Or, in absence of extensive credit rotation, what are the reasons for members to participate and maintain continuity in the programme?

There are various reasons for non-participation as expressed by the members of the control group. Lack of confidence about regular savings, uncertainty about using credit in productive ways, or various social factors are mainly responsible for this. Not being a member of SHG these households mainly depend on informal sources and relatives for their credit needs.

There are various reasons for savings as expressed by the members including festival and emergency. In both the blocks, high percentage of respondents indicate that saving in a group is useful in their distress while a considerable section of SHG members has the opinion that this regular saving has enhanced their confidence. So, in absence of credit related benefits, the groups survive because own savings is important for the members, as their dependence on moneylenders has significantly been reduced. It is reflected in members' awareness about rules, regulation and current state of affairs. Along with this, it is observed that members are currently enjoying greater mobility, accessibility to outside agencies including greater role in community affairs. It may be one reason for greater accessibility of members at the household level to other government programmes like NREG, Old Age Pension etc compared to non-participants.

The study was conducted in backward villages to document the impact of government sponsored micro-credit programme upon lives of the extreme poor. Khandekar (2005) found that the impacts of microfinance is greater on moderate poverty reduction rather than on extreme poverty. Apart from financial benefits, SHGs should be viewed as a participatory endeavour to secure three types of power—namely, social, political and psychological—to empower the group members (Vijaykumar, 2009). Empirical findings in earlier sub section also indicate that introduction of SGSY has created opportunities for women in backward villages to contribute towards family and society in meaningful ways. At the same time, it seems that without adequate forward and backward linkages only group formation may not have much influence upon poverty—especially in economically backward areas. It is evident that the sustainability of SGSY by its design depends largely on the efficiency of the implementing agencies, i.e., Panchayati Raj Institutions.

After ten years of inception it is now time to look back on the programme from critical angle. In last year, Government of West Bengal issued an order by which two leaders of SGSY groups are now incorporated as ex-officio members of the Gram Sansad. Two members of our sample groups were elected as members of respective GP in last election. It is also claimed by non-members that SGSY members are more exposed to the outside world due to their group related activities. Apart from financial performance, this indicates that SGSY has some relevance in terms of gender empowerment.

IV

Conclusion

The success of any micro-credit programme can be evaluated in both quantitative and qualitative way. Our study indicates that, even in extremely deprived rural areas, women SHGs would have considerable impacts upon the lives of the members. The common access of savings is perceived as a source of self-dignity apart from its financial implications. The integration with other social security programmes is a felt need in these backward villages. It needs supports from different agencies for succeeding self-employment programme in a sustained manner. Increasing participation of women in community related issues would only be assured by simultaneous efforts of different stakeholders.

TABLE 1

Block	No. of SHGs formed		Women group (%) 2007-08	% of SHG passed Grade and for which sanctioned (2007-08)	% of SHG for which 2nd instalment Revolving Fund sanctioned (2007-08)
	2006-07 (since inception)	2007-08 (up to March 2008)			
Bandwan	771	830 (7.6)	96.02	80.12	1.1
Hura	1,033	1,308 (26.62)	97.4	77.5	0.99
Manbazar I	960	1,097 (14.276)	96.99	86.8	0
Manbazar II	675	862 (27.7)	99.18	70.5	0
Puncha	655	801 (22.29)	100	82.6	0
Purulia I	682	830 (21.7)	97.3	65.66	0
Purulia II	922	1,224 (32.75)	92.97	73.7	0
Arsha	750	921 (22.8)	98.5	80.8	0
Bagmundi	1,064	1,151 (8.17)	91.3	82	0.35
Balarampur	659	871 (32.16)	85.6	71.5	0
Barabazar	646	759 (17.49)	91.3	65.21	0.13
Joypur	770	874 (13.5)	100	84.9	0
Jhalda I	561	765 (36.36)	95	60.4	0
Jhalda II	652	731 (12.11)	91.3	86.1	0
Kashipur	956	1,116 (16.73)	75.6	63.8	0
Neturia	375	444 (18.7)	55.4	73.9	0.22
Para	644	748 (16.14)	90.5	89.4	0.13
R.N Pur I	366	403 (10.10)	83.1	86.6	0
R.N Pur II	528	598 (13.3)	80.4	96.5	0
Santuri	456	476 (4.3)	99.3	88.2	9.5
Total	14,125	16,809 (19.00)	91.96	77.6	0.5

Source: DRDC, Purulia

Group Level Information

TABLE 2

Distribution of Groups based on Age of Formation

	Jaipur	Purulia II
Less than 1 year	5	2
1-3 years	12	15
3-5 years	2	3
>5 years	1	—
Total	20	20

TABLE 3

Distribution of Groups based on Number of Members

Number of members	Jaipur	Purulia II
5-10	3	7
10-15	13	11
15-20	4	2
Total	20	20

TABLE 4

Distribution of Groups based on Monthly Contribution

Monthly Contribution (Rs)	Jaipur	Purulia II
10	2	4
20	14	15
30	4	1
Total	20	20

TABLE 5

Distribution of Groups based on Total Savings

Total Savings (Rs)	Jaipur	Purulia II
<5,000	8	2
5,000-10,000	8	12
10,000-15,000	2	4
>15,000	2	2
Total	20	20

TABLE 6

Group Information

Group Information	Jaipur	Purulia II
No. of Groups using public space for group meeting	10 (50%)	12 (60%)
Accounts maintained by members themselves	11 (55%)	16 (80%)
No. of Groups opens Bank A/C	20 (100%)	20 (100%)
No. of Groups passed Grade I	7 (29%)	16 (80%)
No. of Groups gets Revolving Fund	5 (21%)	15 (75%)
Proportion of members taken loan	64 %	55%
Outstanding case	12 %	7 %
Groups with leaders from backward communities	5 (25 %)	4 (20%)
No. of Groups involved in Mid-Day Meal	5 (21%)	15 (75%)
No. of Groups involved in NREGS	—	5 (21%)

TABLE 7

Reasons for taking loans (in %)

	Jaypur	Purulia II
Emergency	15	30
Children's Education	15	–
Festival	10	15
Productive Purpose	20,	30
Marriage	–	–
Illness	–	5
Consumption	40	20

TABLE 8

Classification of SGSY Beneficiaries of Sample Groups (in %)

Name of the Block	ST	SC	Others
Jaipur	20	18	62
PuruliaII	12	16	72

TABLE 9

Age Composition and Marital Status of SGSY Beneficiaries of Sample Groups (in %)

Name of the Block	Age composition			Marital Status
	18-35	36-50	>50	Married
Jaipur	33.33	48	18.66	92
Purulia II	37.33	42.6	20	86

TABLE 10

BPL Status of SGSY Beneficiaries of Sample Groups (in %)

Name of the Block	Proportion of members (%) belong to the official poverty			
	ST	SC	Others	Total
Jaipur	100	80	74	82
Purulia II	100	72	68	75

Household level information

TABLE 11

Proportion (%) of members and non-members holding Ration Card, Voter ID and own Bank A/c

	SGSU Members			Non-Participants		
Name of the Block	**Ration Card**	**Voter ID**	**Bank AC**	**Ration Card**	**Voter ID**	**Bank AC**
Jaipur	76	97	5	70	92	—
Purulia II	79	98	1	75	95	4

TABLE 12

Family Status of the Members

	Nuclear Family		Female Headed	
Name of the Block	**SGSY Members**	**Non-Participants**	**SGSY Members**	**Non-Participants**
Jaipur	78	83	14	8.3
Purulia II	82	79	10	12

TABLE 13

Structure of House and Facilities

	SGSU Members		Non-Participants	
Household Amenities	**Jaipur**	**Purulia II**	**Jaipur**	**Purulia II**
Kachcha house (%)	84	80	83.3	79
Pacca roof (%)	4	5	25	12.5
Own Toilet (%)	4	2	—	8.3
Electricity (%)	27	34	50	25
Drinking water from safe source (%)	37	42	33.33	41

TABLE 14

Distribution of Families (%) based on Land Holdings

	SGSU Members		Non-Participants	
Landholdings	**Jaipur**	**Purulia II**	**Jaipur**	**Purulia II**
Landless	54	65	58.3	62.5
0-1Bigha	22	10	20.8	20.8
1-3 Bigha	12	8	8.3	8.3
3-5 Bigha	8	5	8.3	8.3
Above 5 Bigha	4	2	4.2	—

TABLE 15

Durable Assets of the Family (in %)

	SGSU Members		Non Participants	
Household Asset	**Jaipur**	**Purulia II**	**Jaipur**	**Purulia II**
Radio	8	10	12.5	8.3
Cycle	41	38	40.00	42.00
Television	15	6	12.5	10.00
Motor Cycle	4	4	4.00	—
Plow	60	29	66.00	37.5
Telephone	3	2	4.00	4.00

TABLE 16

Education and Employment Status

	SGSU Members		Non-Participants	
	Jaipur	**Purulia II**	**Jaipur**	**Purulia II**
Illiteracy Rate (%)	62	55	66.6	62.5
Enrolment ratio of the age group 5-10	85	92	83.3	91.6
Employment (%)				
Casual labour in agriculture	52	32	41.6	29.2
Artisan	7	2	16.6	8.3
Trade	12	26	29.2	25
Others	29	42	12.5	33.33

TABLE 17

Reasons for Non-participation (%)

	Jaipur	Purulia II
Lack of confidence regarding regular savings	42	41
Lack of capability to utilize credit properly	33	21
Other reasons	25	38

TABLE 18

Reasons for Savings (% of the total respondents)

Reasons	Jaipur	Purulia II
Consumption needs	70	58
Insurance against major shocks	60	65
Festival	60	35
Emergency	73	80
Social Status	50	55
Still depends on Money Lenders	11	—

TABLE 19

Proportion of Members (%) aware about Different Group Activities

Activities	Jaipur	Purulia II
Rules and regulations	95	82
Cash in box	75	78
Bank Savings	85	74
Group Savings	84	71
Defaulter	80	70
Number of loan	81	75

TABLE 20

Participation (%) in other Government Programmes

Programme	Jaipur		Purulia II	
	SGSY member	Non-member	SGSY member	Non-member
NREG	32	21	42	29
Old age Pension	21	16	28	25
Janani Surakhya Yajana	55	25	67	33

Notes

1 All India Debt and Investment Surveys (AIDIS)

2 Backwardness has been identified on the basis of two crude indicators: (i) ratio of Marginal workers and Non-Workers more than 60 percent. (ii) Female literacy rate less than 30%. This has been done on the basis of Census 2001.

3 After six month of formation, groups are being evaluated by banks and DRDC on the basis of some indicators and qualified groups are marked with Grade I.

4 Any group passed Grade I is able get a Fund of Rs. 5,000/ as their capital for rational use of the members for income generating activities.

5 It refers to the coordination between different departments.

6 It is used to mean hierarchical arrangements within any department.

References

1. Barnes, Carolyn (2001); Microfinance Program Clients and Impact: An Assessment of Zambuka Trust, Zimbabwe, USAID-AIMS Paper, Washington, D.C.
2. Chen, M. A. and Snodgress, D. (2001); Managing resources, activities, and risk in urban
3. India—the impact of SEWA Bank, Washington D.C: AIMS, September 2001
4. Chethan Vanitha and B. Krishnamurthy (2002): 'Swarnajayanti Gram Swarozgar Yojana for Empowerment and Rural Women in Karnataka ' in Prasad Kiran (Eds): 'Communications and Empowerment of Women, Strategies and Policy Insights for India' Delhi, the Women's Press.
5. Coleman B. E. (1999); The impact of group lending in Northeast Thailand, Journal of Development Economics, Vol. 60, pp. 105-141.
6. Coleman B. E. (2001); Measuring impact of Microfinance Programme, *Finance for the Poor*, Asian Development Bank, Vol. 2, pp. 5-7
7. Hulme, D. and Mosley, P. (1996); *Finance against Poverty* , Routledge, London.
8. Jena, Sayantan (2008): Programme Design and Impact Assesment: 'Success' of Microfinance in Perspective, *Economic and Political Weekly,* August 9, 2008.
9. Kaladhar, K. (1997): Microfinance in India: Design, Structure and Governance, *Economic and Political Weekly* Vol. 329(42).
10. Khandelwal, A. K. (2007): Microfinance Development Strategy for India, *Economic and Politica Weekly. 42(13).*
11. Khandkar, S. R. (1998): Fighting Poverty with Microcredit, OUP.
12. Khandkar, S. R. (2005): Microfinance and Rural Poverty: Evidence using panel Data from Bangladesh, World Bank Economic Review, Vol. 19, pp. 263-286
13. Mahajan,V. (2005) From Micro-credit to Livelihood Finance, *Economic and Political Weekly*, Oct 8
14. MkNelley and Dunford (1998); Impact of Credit with Education on Mothers and Their Young Children's Nutrition (Ghana).
15. Mustafa, S. I Ara, et al (1996); Beacon of Hope: an Impact Assessment of BRAC's Rural Development Programme, Dhaka, Bangladesg, BRAC.
16. Pit et al (2003): Does Micro-Credit Empower Women? Evidence from Bangladesh, World Bank Policy Research Working Paper No. 2998.
17. Purushottom, P. (2006): A Process Study on SGSY, NIRD.
18. Robinson, M. (2001): The Microfinance Revolution: Sustainable Banking for the Poor, The World Bank, Washington DC.
19. Sud, N. (2003): Experiences of SGSYin Gujarat: From Process-Oriented Theory to Deterministic Practice *Reflecting changes in policy theorization* September 27.
20. Thekkekara. T. F. (2008): 'Impact of SGSY on SHG: Bank Linkage' in 'Microfinance', Edited by K. G. Karmakar, Sage Publications, Delhi, pp. 188-214.
21. Vijaykumar. R. (2009): Reinstating the Self-Help Group Perspective in Microfinance, *Economic and Political Weekly,* April 11, 2009, Vol. XLIV(15).

22. Vatta, K(2003); Microfinance and Poverty Alleviation, *Economic and Political Weekly,* Feb. 1, pp. 432-433.

23. World Bank (2001); Engendering Development through Gender Equality in Rights, Resources and Voice, New York: (OUP).

24. World Bank (2003); Microfinance in India: Issues, Challenges and Policy Options, Washington DC: World Bank.

25. Zaman, H. (2000); Assessing the Poverty and Vulnarability Impact of Micro-credit in Bangladesh: A Case Study of BRAC, Washington D.C., World Bank.

11

A Study of Microfinancing in Centre for Rural Development, Guwahati, Assam

Nilotpal Saha and Deba Prasad Sharma

Abstract: *Often the term microfinance is limited to the narrow definition of micro-credit to micro-enterprise. It is considered as providing financial services like saving, credit, insurance, money transfer to the so far un-served strata of population—those who earn low income, own a few assets and are constrained in voicing out their interest. However, it may include a wider range of services and it represents something more than micro credit. The Centre for Rural Development, Guwahati, popularly known as "Rickshaw Bank" to the local people, is serving the so called non-bankable population by providing a different type of credit. The paper discusses how the centre for Rural Development innovatively is acting as a social intermediator and the method which is used by them.*

Preamble

The *World Bank* estimates that 456 million Indians (42% of the total Indian population) now live under the global poverty line of $1.25 per day (PPP). This means that a third of the global extreme poor now reside in India[1]. Poverty is the shortage of common things such as food, clothing, shelter and safe drinking water, all of which determine the quality of life. It may also include the lack of access to opportunities such as education and employment which aid the escape from poverty and/or allow one to enjoy the respect of fellow citizens. It is typically analyzed as an economic issue with level of income as a common measure of determining individual well being. The concept of poverty has evolved as also involve other deprivations such lack of food, housing clothing, education, health care and civic participation.

Microfinance is financial intermediation through the distribution of small loans, acceptance of small savings and provision of other financial products and services to poor. The basic hypothesis behind microfinance is that underprivileged people who desire to escape from poverty can do so if they are able to access a micro-loan and thereby establish a micro-business or enter self-employment or otherwise engage in very small scale informal commercial activity. This new activity, in turn, can raise individual and household income, and thereby increasing the purchasing power of them. Increased purchasing power translate into higher consumption often involving the purchase of locally produced goods and services, including additional spending on health, education and many other products and services which may also mean additional local jobs through standard employment multiplier effects. The idea, rediscovered by Nobel Laureate Mohammed Yunus, has already traversed three decades of development. It has touched lives of millions, uplifting many poor families and has improved their living standard.

Microfinance has been primarily driven by philanthropic objectives, funded by subsidized credit/soft loans grants and donor money, and run by NGOs and charities. Microfinance's contribution in poverty alleviation is reflected in United Nation declaring 2005 as the International Year of Microfinance. Private sector banks then start taking more interest on microfinance and it has undergone a transition from an informal sector to a regulated formal sector

Many scholars describe microfinance as 'miracle cure' for eradication of poverty. It is beyond doubt that microfinance has been able to reduce poverty for decades—so the methods must be very effective—but still poverty persist, One of the reason may be that the benefits are limited to size and scope.

Some of the probable barriers to success of microfinance may be:

- **Not understanding the real need.** Most of the poor consume the money for their domestic requirement and may not use it to start any micro-enterprise—so the benefit of sudden liquidity extinguish as the money is spend. Solution may not be in supplying money but provide means to earn.
- **Lack of responsibility and accountability.** Working in a group is always tough. A group which is formed solely to avail the loan may not work as a team and take the full advantage of micro-credit they have availed.
- **Inability to give overall progress to socio-economic conditions.** Financial products like loan, grant, and subsidy etc. give benefit to only two parties —namely borrower and lender. But for sustainability of micro-enterprise or commercial farming, infrastructure and other factors need to be in favour. For a MFI the possibility of modifying the infrastructure and social conditions is very low
- **Failure to give a social dignity.** Often the poor belong to the so-called lower class of population. Their overall development is not possible unless the social status is uplifted along with the economic condition.

Introduction and Genesis of CRD

The Centre for Rural Development (CRD) is an organization of repute with its expertise in social mobilization, community skill-upgradation, microfinance, rural marketing, and other livelihood supports in Agriculture, Animal Husbandry, Fishery and its allied entrepreneurship activities.

The genesis of CRD can be traced back to more than a decade ago, while there was upheaval of many professional Non-governmental Organizations (NGOs) in the rest of India. In the North eastern region, there was the **Rashtriya Gramin Vikas Nidhi (RGVN),** a national level supporting and funding organization with its headquarter at Guwahati along with a few renowned voluntary organizations which were mainly working with the Gandhian ideology. Then a young veterinarian with his urge in social entrepreneurship was serving as Veterinary Assistant Surgeon **Dr. Pradip Kumar Sarmah** in the Dept. of Animal Husbandry & Veterinary, Govt. of Assam (who later became one of the **Ashoka Fellows** in India). The very urge of Dr. Sarmah made him to resign his service with the Govt. of Assam and join RGVN in 1991. Being one of the Senior Executives in different parts of the region, Dr. Sarmah came to realize the scope of broad based Agriculture development—especially Animal Husbandry—and the miserable plight of the farmers and entrepreneurs due to lack of adequate backward and forward linkages for sustenance. The inquisitiveness of Dr. Sarmah led him to plan for a supporting organization that can sufficiently substantiate the need of the farmers, entrepreneurs and Rural Producers' Organizations (RPOs) in broad based Agriculture in the region. He shared his plan along with a few likeminded professionals and entrepreneurs. His plan was accepted and that has finally led to the formation of **Centre for Rural Development (CRD)** in 1994-95. Subsequently, Dr. Sarmah left RGVN with a new-fangled spirit and has been leading CRD thereof.

This is the humble beginning of the organization and since then CRD has been escalating in its diverse fields of livelihood sector. Failure is the pillar of success and success is the encouragement for upbeat. During this decade of journey since 1994-95, CRD has witnessed a good deal of ups and downs. It has been reviewing, learning, propagating and progressing withstanding all the odds on its way. CRD also works as a **Nodal Agency** under Assam Rural Infrastructure and Agricultural Services Project (ARIASP)—a **World Bank** funded programme—Government of Assam. CRD has proven its efficiency in many multi-dimensional activities in various fields—but for this paper we shall keep the discussion confined to the Rickshaw Bank only.

Working of CRD as Rickshaw Bank (RB)

Rickshaw is a modified tricycle, which is used extensively as a mode of transport for carrying passengers and luggage. There are currently estimated to be 8 million rickshaw-pullers in India. About 95 percent of rickshaw-pullers don't have their own rickshaws. They have to pay Rs. 25-30 per day to the owner of the rickshaw. Annually they are paying 6-7 thousand rupees and have been doing the job for last many years, even may be for lifetime; still they don't have their own rickshaws. So all these rickshaw pullers are victims of high daily rental fees making it nearly impossible to earn enough income to ever own a rickshaw in their lifetime. In addition, similar to other rental services, they have to bear the cost of any accidental damage to the vehicle on which there is no insurance option. Unable to bear the cost of a large damage, the puller is subject to harassment and this leaves the pullers with no choice but to flee the locality. The underlying cause behind this vulnerability is that Rickshaw Pullers are constrained by lack of access to basic formal banking services such as loans, savings, insurances, lack of disposable income to access basic utilities or provide adequately for families.

The principles of the social business venture, the Rickshaw Bank, are three-fold: to remove constraints of the targeted community, to increase earning capacity, to ensure sustainability and scalability of program. The Rickshaw Bank addresses each of these opportunities. It releases the pullers from the constraints of access to basic financial services, provides identity proof to protect them from the social stigma and harassment. The second advantage is the enhanced financial gain. When the pullers pay off the loans for their rickshaws, the future income goes into their own pockets, to their families, and eventually back into the local economy. Through additional collaborations with local institutions, the Rickshaw Bank has been able to tie up for free healthcare, affordable clothing, licensing and procuring cooking gas licenses—all critical expenditures for the household. Third, the business aims to provide both 'in-reach' and 'outreach'. In-reach or depth of the service means providing access to affordable products, services, and information to the existing clients by means of negotiating at a large scale. For outreach, the model is commercially sustainable for the service to be adopted or expanded to other needy areas.

So CRD took initiative to provide them a micro-credit in the form of a rickshaw. The pullers pay the same amount daily, which they use to pay to the owners as instalment and the encouraging aspect of this is that they become the owner of their rickshaws just in 15 months. After that they go back with a smile, with an asset which provides them daily bread. CRD also incorporates some other services like uniforms, driving license, insurance, health support services and a dignity with their bread earning asset.

Collaboration and support taken from other institutions

Indian Institute of Technology (IIT), Guwahati: The organization got hand holding support from **Indian Institute of Technology (IIT),** Guwahati, from the very beginning. With their technical assistance CRD could modify the existing rickshaw to more spacious, comfortable and lighter vehicle and give it a new

Fig. 1: Deep Bahan, The Rikshaw of CRD

identity as 'Deep Bahan' (Fig. 1). However there are some modifications, minor changes occurred year after year. Regarding technical aspect the organization got some practical experiences of the choice of people of in different regions of the country. Based on their regional preference CRD has to keep in mind all these aspects.

Municipal Corporation: CRD felt the importance to have a good network with Municipal Corporations in different parts of the country for handhold support to the project to acknowledge the rickshaw drivers by the following services:

- Facilitation in preparing the required number of License to the pullers in bulk.
- Recognize the service of the pullers by avoiding any kind of harassment.

Police: The Coordinator of the organization also met the senior officials of Department of Police to overcome some of the issues relating:

- Verification of identity of rickshaw pullers whenever CRD requires on request.
- Minimize unnecessary harassment of the pullers of Rickshaw Bank by the police constable.
- Traffic rules like no parking zone, no entry zone etc. and to provide the latest information relating traffic rules.

Procedure in short

The first step is of formation of group of 5 homogenous members. Then verifying the proof of identity and residence and collecting photograph. Then the officials of CRD complete other formalities like fill up of Family Details Form, Puller License Application Form. One *Shapathnama* (oath) is also filled up, where the rickshaw puller ensures the certificate of good character and is responsible for abiding by the rules and regulations of Rickshaw Bank project. The rickshaws are manufactured locally, either in an in-house manufacturing unit or by local suppliers. After that five brand new rickshaws are handed over to the group.

CRD also ensures:

- Democratic election of leader by the rickshaw pullers themselves.
- The members of one group deposit their daily instalment to the Leader which is collected by the Field Coordinator of CRD daily.
- CRD also encourages the group members the rotation of leader after every 3 months.
- Collective responsibility of the group while seeking leave or non-payment of daily instalment.
- Set up of Garage against 25 rickshaw pullers for daily rickshaw servicing and act as daily collection centre.
- Focus group discussion and to tie up some economic activities of the wives of rickshaw pullers for enhancement of their livelihood.
- Organize need base training to the rickshaw pullers from time to time.

This asset is accessible by a five-member common liability group that acts as the social collateral towards the 'loan'. The concept of garage is introduced as the meeting point for the 25 pullers or 5 groups and it also serves as a collection centre for the daily repayment. The garage owner is creation of another point of entrepreneurship initiated by loan from the Rickshaw Bank. The product available to the target community is the Rickshaw; the insurance facility for the puller, the license for puller and the vehicle, medi-claim, the uniform and the identity card. Additional benefits tied in on fee basis are cooking gas connectivity, emergency loan or need based purchase items.

Features of Rickshaw Bank

1. Rickshaws are technologically superior leading to increased customer demand: Designed by the Indian Institute of Technology (IIT) and assembled by CRD's production centre, the rickshaw is more aerodynamic, lighter than the traditional vehicle and has safer seating arrangements. This makes it easier on the puller and more comfortable for the passenger, thus creating heightened consumer demand for Rickshaw Bank vehicles.

2. Rickshaws are provided to pullers in groups of five. The pullers, who are members of the Rickshaw Bank, form garages in different parts of the city to manage their savings, repair the rickshaws, update business records, and collect rent.
3. Repayment is collected on a daily basis. Since the puller has a daily earning pattern, the repayment is collected on a daily basis. This revenue for the Bank is applied towards the cost of the rickshaw, insurance premium, license, uniform, and operating costs.
4. Finance is raised on a Loan cum Advertisement based model. Formal financial institutions provide the loan on commercial rates; grant money is targeted to leverage greater financial access to bank loans and for internal capacity building; advertisement space behind rickshaws is sold to local businesses or interested corporate houses and is an additional source of revenue. The advertisement revenue also helps to reduce risk in case of delayed repayments from pullers.
5. Additional loans given to the Rickshaw Pullers community to address other community needs. Pullers own their Rickshaws in a maximum of 15-18 months—with most owning this asset within 10-12 months. The link with the Rickshaw Bank continues for a loan towards second product or service and especially for negotiating better advertisement rates with businesses, and for accessing insurance services.

Who are getting benefit from Rickshaw Bank of CRD and how?

1. **Rickshaw pullers**
   - Enables Rickshaw pullers to become owner of the rickshaws.
   - Provide the Rickshaw pullers a superior quality rickshaw.
   - Increases Rickshaw Driver's Income Levels and Standard of Living.
   - Provides a Financial Resource for Rickshaw pullers.
   - Provides Better Health Services to the Rickshaw pullers and their families.
   - Clothing.
   - Proper cooking fuel.
2. **Community and environment**
   - Convenient mode of public transport.
   - Decreases Fossil Fuel Emissions from Auto Travel.
   - Creates a Positive Work Environment.
   - Jobs for youths.
3. **Corporate**
   - Avenue for Corporate Social Responsibility.

- 'Mobile' advertisement facility at 96% cheaper rate for corporate.
- Flexible term options on advertising (1 month to 3 yrs).

4. **Donors**
   - Donors get 100% tax exemption.
   - Donors can participate in the programme monitoring process.
5. **Banks and financial institutes**
   - Participate with purely commercial terms.
   - Getting the commercial return as per the prevailing terms.
   - 100% repayment.
   - Better investment opportunity.
6. **Government and local authorities**
   - Improves law and order.
   - Less corruption.
   - Better documentation through availability of licenses.
   - Safer roads.
   - Additional revenues.

Feathers in the cap of CRD — awards and recognition

The innovative and effective activities of CRD have received many national and international awards and recognition. Some of them are:

- The Rickshaw Bank has got its recognition in the **Limca Book of Records** as First Rickshaw Bank under the business section in 2006.
- *The* **Citizen Base Investment Award** *2003* for its concept at National Stock Exchange Building, Mumbai, in November 2003.
- IIM, Bangalore, selected Rickshaw Bank project under their Microfinance Incubation Programme, during November – December 2005.
- **Global Change Makers Award,** National Press Club, Washington on April 5, 2006.
- The **Microfinance Process Excellency Award, 2006,** at New Delhi on April 7, 2006 given by the Planet Finance and the ABN Amro Bank.
- Srijan 2007 **Microfinance Business Plan Competition** 3rd Prize at Hyderabad on April 25, 2007.
- Asian Innovation Awards 2007 on 13 November, 2007 at Singapore for Rickshaw Bank.

Postscript

Often the term microfinance is limited to the narrow definition of micro-credit to micro-enterprise. Common perception is that micro-credit means formation of SHG, then getting a bank loan and repaying in weekly manner. It includes providing financial services like saving, credit, insurance, money transfer to the so far un-served strata of population—those who earn low income, own a few assets and constrained in voicing out their interest who are—according to traditional banking definitions— 'non-bankable'.

From the above discussion about CRD we can get that the principles of microfinance can be used in a modified manner by providing other amenities for a micro-enterprise and not exclusively money. Through Rickshaw Bank, CRD could overcome some of the lacunae of microfinance. It provide loan but not in terms of money, but the means of earning the 'rickshaw', it benefits society, corporate and government. It is successful in providing the rickshaw pullers a social recognition as well as health to the family members of the rickshaw pullers.

Bibliography

1. http://en.wikipedia.org/wiki/Poverty_in_India
2. 'Microfinance Prospective and Operation', published by Indian Institute of Banking and Finance.
3. Rajagopalan S., Purswani Radha 'Commercial Microfinance' text and cases.—ICFAI University Press, Hydrabad.
4. Dey N. B., Adhikari K. 'Microfinance Emerging Need and Problems' Banijya, Vol. 1, No. 1 July 2008. pp. 19-24.
5. Haque S. M. I. 'Microfinance An Answer to Poverty' Professional Banker July 2009. pp. 11-15
6. Sharma K. C. 'Microfinance in India—Status and Challenges' Professional Banker, July 2009. pp. 16 – 19.
7. Prahalad C. K. 'The Fortune at The End of Bottom of The Pyramid – Eradicating Poverty' Wharton School Publishing, p. 72, pp. 292-94
8. Human Development Report, 2003. p. 5, 8.
9. Annual Report 2008, CRD.
10. http://www.crdev.org/rb.asp
11. http://picasaweb.google.com/crd4ev/AFNA

12

NGOs in Microfinance: A Case Study on Anchalik Gram Unnayan Parishad of Jania Block, Assam

Bhabananda Deb Nath

Abstract: *The Non Government Organizations (NGOs) in the field of Microfinance processing, utilization and its monitoring has a major role by different ways. The NGOs movements towards social upliftment, especially for the poor people are well-working and the Govt. of India and some other countries takes these organizations as their helping hands. Because, many government departments assume that, a step with NGOs will bring more success due to their local informational awareness in which the government departments may lack. This innovative and alternative to government organization concept with their bold aims and objectives has made tremendous success in many fields. Millions and millions NGOs have been establish all over the world with their individual and innovative aims in particular and social transformation in general. The study has been confined on the role of NGOs in microfinance.*

Introduction

Microfinance is a bold attempt of Gramin Vikas Banks of India to alleviate the Poverty from the Society by financing a small amount of fund for their sustainable development. Microfinance is the provision of credit (loans of small amounts), deposits of small amounts, insurance facilities and other financial helps (like caution money etc.) for the poor or economically disadvantageous people living in rural, semi-urban and urban areas for their all-round development.

According to Joel Wani, the prominent economist of the United Nation, "Micro-finance represents a participatory approach to development where people can take control of their lives and because of self-efficiency one does not need to be an individual of significant means to take creative business ideas, save according to one's owns priorities and ultimately plan for the future."

Further, according to the Reserve Bank of India,, Microfinance means the provision of thrift, credit and other financial securities and products of very small amount of the poor in rural, semi-urban or urban areas for enabling them to raise their income levels and improve their living standards.

From the above interpretation it is found that Microfinance is a system of financing a small amount of fund to the economically disadvantage masses of India for their all-round development. Though there is a primary provision to finance for the economic development of downtrodden masses of both rural and urban areas, in some cases it is found that economically sound masses are also considered at the time of providing financial assistance under the Microfinance policy of Gramin Vikash Banks.

NGO

The NGO-sector has often been described as extremely diverse, heterogeneous and populated by organizations with hugely varied goals, structure and motivations. It is, therefore, not an easy task to find a common definition of the term "non-governmental organization". It cannot be based on a legal definition given the wide variations in laws relating to NGO activities, according to which an NGO may have, for instance, the legal status of a charity, non-profit association or a foundation.

The term "NGO" can nevertheless be used as shorthand to refer to a range of organizations that normally share the following characteristics:

- NGOs are not created to generate personal profit. Although they may have paid employees;
- and engage in revenue-generating activities, they do not distribute profits or surpluses to members or management;
- NGOs are voluntary. This means that they are formed voluntarily and that there is usually an element of voluntary participation in the organization;
- NGOs are distinguished from informal or ad hoc groups by having some degree of formal
- or institutional existence. Usually, NGOs have formal statutes or other governing document
- Setting out their mission, objectives and scope. They are accountable to their members and donors;
- NGOs are independent, in particular of government and other public authorities, and of political parties or commercial organizations.

NGOs are not self-serving in aims and related values. Their aim is to act in the public arena at large, on concerns and issues related to the well-being of people, specific groups of people or society as a whole. They are not pursuing commercial or professional interests of their members.

Though these common characteristics can help describe the notion of the term "NGO", it must be borne in mind that their size as well as their scope of activities can vary considerably. Some NGOs consist of a rather limited number of persons; others may have thousands of members and hundreds of professional staff. In functional terms, NGOs can focus on operational and/or advocacy activities. Operational NGOs contribute to the delivery of services (such as in the field of welfare), whereas the primary aim of advocacy NGOs is to influence the policies of public authorities and public opinion in general.

NGO Registration Methods

1. Trust, 2. Society, and 3. Non profit Company. In India, non profit/public charitable organizations can be registered as trusts, societies, or a private limited Non Profit company, under Section 25 of The Companies Act, 1956. Non-profit Organizations in India (a) exist independently of the state ;(b) are self-governed by a board of trustees or 'managing Committee'/governing council, comprising individuals who generally serve in a fiduciary capacity; (c) produce benefits for others, generally outside the membership of the organizations; and (d), are 'non-profit-making', in as much as they are prohibited from distributing a monetary residual to their own members. Thus, the Formation and Registration of a Non-Profit organization (NGO) in India are done under:

(1) Trust
(2) Society
(3) Section 25 Companies Act 1956.

The role of NGOs can be outlined as:

How an NGO works

(1) It arranges frequent meetings with the local and targeted people to provide current information i.e. fulfil the informational needs.
(2) It generates awareness and empowerments among the poorest of the poor.
(3) It also reduces superstition, which is very dangerous among rural poor.
(4) It provides training to the poor and also avail them with new and innovative business ideas.
(5) It provides planning about making them financially viable and strong.
(6) It generates awareness about making use of waste materials to best ways and also to take benefits of their local resources.
(7) Act on Microfinance to make the poor financially viable.
(8) Act as social mobilizers or as social volunteers.
(9) Provide information about the various government. schemes and policies and how to get benefit of then.

(10) Minimum documentations as regards any action (like easy financing etc.).
(11) It works as monitor, liaison officer to channelize them in the field.
(12) Arranging exhibitions and melas to boost them.
(13) Selfless service, so, corruption level is very low, etc.

So, generally NGOs assume the above responsibility to have overall development and social transformation.

But, exactly how an NGO works in Microfinance with all other Banks , FFIs, and other government agencies etc. and the special role of NGOs in that respect are given below. The different role of NGOs with the above mentioned institutions bring different models in microfinance dealings.

A brief explanation about some of the models generally followed is given:

Direct Linkage Model

In this model NGO is not the financial intermediary. The NGO's role is only in group evaluation and stabilization, whereas the financial linkage is directly with the group.

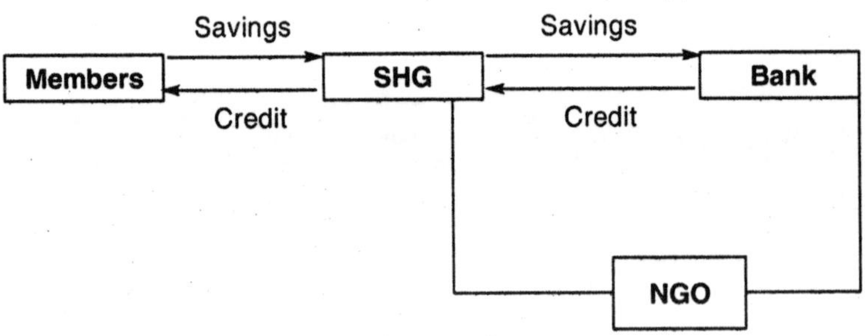

Indirect Linkage Models

In this model basically the fund flows through the NGO, i.e., the NGO is the financial intermediary. In case of this Linkage model various types exist as:

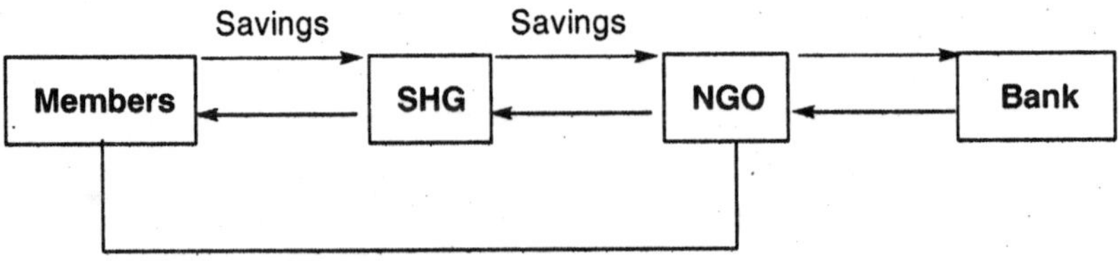

Modified Indirect Model

This model exists in cases where the groups are artisan/handicraft groups and NGO support for marketing is also available like SEWA, LUCKNOW:

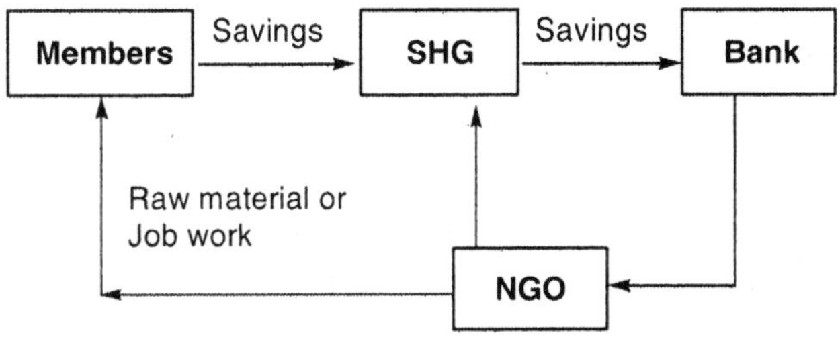

In the above models, apart from two-way flow of funds, there is also flow of services, extension, consultancy, training etc. from the Banks, NGOs and other voluntary agencies and it has been found that NGOs follow all the models as regards financial dealings, especially in Assam.

Anchalik Gram Unnayan Parishad (AGUP)

While specifying the role of NGOs in our home district, *Barpeta*, the Anchalik Gram Unnayan Parishad (AGUP), a leading NGO, established in 1986, registered under Societies Registration Act XXI-1860, No. 1819/88-89, is considerable. It has also registration under FCRA, 1976, No. 020770002, with the vision to form a society where, people can live in peace, co-existence, love, justice and in common brotherhood and with some mission

- To establish a moral human society in ground of truth and justice and harmony.
- Act on Microfinance, especially on SHGs and Personal loan model.
- Technology implementation and awareness generation.
- Bring standard and healthy life style among the people of her surrounding.

To achieve the above the NGO is under the following initiatives according to their priority or importance:

- Social development;
- Financial stability by engaging the rural people in some regular activities;
- Develop the saving habits among the poor people, i.e., capital formation for their future needs;
- Removal of child labour, by giving otherwise means to sustain;
- Removal of illiteracy;
- Improving poor health conditions;
- To bring cent percent sanitation facility to the poor;
- Knowledge about the use of pesticide to agriculture and making beware about its misuse (use of science and technology);

- Bring the behaviour change communication among the people of its surrounding;
- Open the definition.

The primary objectives of this NGO was to serve the people, where the government facilities are yet to reach and thereby remove exploitation and also to provide assistance to the underprivileged groups and the financial stability and soundness only can bring 80 % solution of their problems. Taking note of all the above, the NGO received Microfinance loans under Swarna Jayanti Gram Swarojgar Yojana (SJGSRY), before 1993 and also form Rashtriya Gramin Vikas Nidhi (RGVN) about Rs 20 lakh. The fund received first being utilized through SHG mode. Initially, it was formed 113 of SHGs of that 85 SHGs provided with loans, amount ranging form Rs 10,000 to Rs30,000 to each group.

It also received financial assistance from Rashtriya Mahila Kosh (RMK), Ministry of Women and Child Welfare, Rs 17 lakh in 1999 and also For Individual Lending, House based and non-House based under National Water Development Programme for Rain-fall Areas (NWDPRA) under the Agricultural project of Rs 6 lakh.

The NGO has been able to gain lots of financial assistance and grants, since its inception; following are some of the leading financiers:

1. CAPART.
2. NABARD.
3. DRDA, Barpeta.
4. Nehru Yuba Kendra (NYK), Barpeta.
5. SIDBI.
6. Rashtriya Gramin Vikas Nidhi (RGVN).
7. Rashtriya Mahila Kosh (RMK).
8. Assam Science Society.
9. Assam Science, Technology and Environment Council.
10. Entrepreneurship Development Institute of India, Ahmedabad.
11. Central Social Welfare Board.
12. Ministry of Environment and Forest, Govt. of India.
13. Indo German Social Science Society, (IGSSS).
14. Ministry of Agriculture, Government of India.
15. Ministry of Youth Affairs and Sports.
16. Khadi and Village Industries Commission.

It is to be mentioned here that, with the changes of time, some agencies become more active and some of them has stopped their helps. At present the following are the funding agencies which provide financial grants to this NGO.

- KVIC.
  - (a) People's Education Programme.
  - (b) Entrepreneurship Development Programme.
- Bamboo Cluster (under SFURTI).
- Bamboo Mini Cluster Programme.
- Prime Minister's Employment Generation Programme (PEGP).
- SIDBI.
- Child Development and Nutrition Programme (under UNICEF).

The performance of NGOs found very successful and in some cases the NGO movements are such that they are doing better then any other formal organization can do with such a little resources. It is needless to have any evidence about their services and honesty, as in some govt. dept. they have already appointed some NGOs for monitoring and supervision. For an example, the National Rural Health Mission (NRHM) a health sector project of government of India, that is supported by the World Bank, Unicef, State Govt. etc. to bring revolution in health service sector, specially in rural areas to reduce the MMR, IMR & TFR, has engaged an NGO called "DISCOVERY CLUB" of Kokrajhar district to access the evening OPD services provided by the hospitals. While the role of NGOs in Microfinance arena is concerned, it is really working well from long back as negotiator, rural financer or so called semi formal bank to cover the people. On the other hand, dealing with Microfinance is a matter of risk as no collateral is charged and the loan is disbursed to the poor people having less credit-worthiness. The Banks and other financial Institutions have to face lots of trouble due to recovery problems. The basic problems are to select the right beneficiaries to sanction the loans, who have the creditworthiness.

Again, poor people are very poor—having no access to Banks due to their illiteracy and lack of awareness. Now, these Institutions have to face with problems as they have been ordered to finance the rural poor to sustain their vulnerable conditions. Again, non-recovery of debts is also a question for answer to the authority concerned, otherwise its leads to bank bankruptcy. In this critical phenomena, the NGO concept and its role plays an important role, as it assume the responsibility of finance taking note of their creditworthiness. Again, the beneficial issues lying with NGOs is that, they know about their local habitant, so, also know their transactional behavior and creditworthiness, accordingly they choose the beneficiaries, while sanctioning the loans, either personal or by group finance, i.e., through SHG model.

The formal financial institutions (FFIs) now assume that only the NGOs can do this job well and also make it happen; as a result the FFIs do not hesitate to provide crores of rupees Microfinance through NGOs leadership. The leading financial intermediaries, like RGKN, KVIC, NABARD, RMK, Gramin Banks, MFI's Cooperative Banks etc, are ready to provides financial support through NGOs.

Achievements

AGUP, the NGO, is in service from a long time in Jania block with manifold activities. Its existence in that area becomes an only hope for the poor because of trustworthy, selfless service and for her social leadership towards the surrounding people thereby. The NGO is able to gain confidence, support by its loyal service. The change and development has been observed in financial viability and life style among the poor by accepting the microfinance policies under the management of AGUP.

The changes has also been as regards Education, Health and hygiene, awareness about population, poverty alleviation, Entrepreneurial force and employment generation etc. The NGO has been able to engage more then 3,000 people under its various schemes with handsome income. During 2008 a "Common Facility Centre", was establish at Raipur side by the popular B .H. College—here 2,000 artisans can work together and presently 500 artisans are working in the same. The NGO has also taken some initiatives to bring the village Bamboo Artisans under their project, giving them necessary training and machinery to increase their quality, productivity and income. The NGO is presently engaged in bamboo products under SFURTI and it become a profitable business for the NGO. The bamboo product made by the NGO are being sold in different parts of the country by way of Exhibition/Melas or by direct sale form their showroom. This year the NGO proposed to receive some export order from United States, China, under the marketing leadership of Target Corporation Pvt. Ltd., Kolkata. In an average, Rs 40 to 50 lakh turnover comes in a year from the bamboo products, as the Secretary of AGUP said and also believes to have more in coming days.

The honest and the sincere service of AGUP have been noticed by many departments and personnel from time to time and its good historic record is a matter of praise by all. The year 2008-09 was really remarkable for the NGO, when it was selected for **National Award 2008**, for all round development, and the prize being handed over to by our Hon'ble Prime Minister Dr. Manmohan Singh, New Delhi in an august gathering.

Regarding this NGO everything was going well, but the noticeable thing is that, the NGO received financial assistance as Microfinance more than Rs 20 lakh in 1993 and it was utilized for the purpose granted for, by farming more than hundred SHGs covering greater amount of rural people of that area. The programme of microfinance and SHGs were gone well up to 2003 in terms of loan utilization and its repayments to the concern authority. But, after 2003, the NGO did not apply for any Micro-credit assistance to RGVN, SJGSY, and RMK etc. It is not so that the credit needs of the poor of that surrounding area are completed nor all of them are unproductive or misuse the funds received. Their reports says that, the earlier funds have been recovered successfully (about 95%) from the fields and also returned the same to the concerned authority. On a discussion with the officials of the NGO, they depict the facts of Microfinance in the practical field. The micro-credit is a financial assistance meant for poorest of the poor, which is given without any collateral and creditworthiness which is never able to recover cent percent return from the parties. But the authority concerned wants cent percent return from the dealing NGOs. Lots of SHGs unable to repay their loan in spite of regular efforts and monitoring. The condition of those people is such that by no means the loan can be recovered. This fact is not the concern of the authority, though intimated, and they are strictly adhering to their norms. As a result the gap amounts are to be managed by the dealing NGOs, their rewards being wiped-up due to this practice make them weak and create lots of problems for their existence. So, we have decided to stop doing so and to channelize the people in some other innovative and low risk profile activities.

This is the practical scenario and serious issue with the Microfinance. If a leading NGO like AGUP has to think otherwise, then what will happen to other newly formed and upcoming NGOs in field of Microfinance? The Microfinance becomes a global issue and again, it is the only ray of hope for the poor. But the problems face by the dealing heroes (i.e. NGOs/ intermediaries) should be considered first and to remove it soon, if the dreams with microfinance are supposed to be materialize.

Science and Technology Model/Packages, brings under the management of NGOs and followed by the AGUP

There are several NGOs with strong grassroots base active in rural India to represent the interests of the poor. They are playing an active role across the rural economy in areas as diverse as animal husbandry, horticulture and food processing etc. to strengthen the linkage amongst the science and technology institutions, agricultural universities and village people, especially, small and marginal farmers having small land holdings. Their role in these sectors becomes crucial as they are ideally placed to **innovate, design** and disseminate field tested proven technologies with appropriate modulations. Such organizations with inhouse S & T capabilities and technical back-up support from nearby S & T institutions can play crucial role in helping village community to translate the new technology packages to the grassroots level activities under demand driven system. In this process, a number of S and T based field groups in different parts of the country are actively working to empower the rural community with new skill and knowledge through participatory approach.

The development approach of several of these organizations based on the above systems approach have resulted in sustainable model of activities, where application of S & T has resulted in improved living conditions as well as new opportunities for gainful employment to the rural poor, including women. In this direction, several technology based development projects have been implemented under the Science and Society programme, Department of Science and Technology (DST), Delhi, through a network of science based NGOs and S & T institutions which have resulted in some potential replicable technology models/packages for rural application and poverty reduction. For instance, in a collaborative program between the Council for Advancement of People's Action and Rural Technology (CAPART), New Delhi, and DST, New Delhi. CAPART has taken up large scale replication of some of the technology models as packages of appropriate technologies evolved and proven by the latter through their partners i.e., field group, NGOs along with collaborating S & T institutions through system approach.

The development approach of some of these has resulted in sustainable models of activities. Some of them are given below to access the S & T field groups/NGOs' involvements in the field with small and marginal farmers, women weaker sections, Scheduled Castes and Scheduled Tribes.

1. Rural Women Technology Parks: Model with Integrated and Multi-Sectoral Approach.
2. Reaching the Un-reached: Model with Network Approach.
   (a) Case of Processing and Preservation of Horticultural Produce: Technology at village level.
   (b) Rural Artisans and Decentralized Technologies for value Addition.
3. Local Capacity Building: The Case of Mushroom and Vermi Technology Transfer in Hill Area: Household Level Model.

The experience has brought to light the fact that there is vast potential, intelligence, strength and ability in our rural people that can be tapped and used for sustainable development.

As regards use of scientific technology this NGO has taken certain steps and has implemented scientific technology to have quality products and incomes, the following are some of the methods that are used by the AGUP:

(i) Water pollution Control & Training on Safe Drinking water to the rural People.
(ii) Solar Electricity Generation for local use.
(iii) Training to have Scientific Irrigation with use of little pesticides.

(iv) Production of Cane and Bamboo items using machinery of modern types.

(v) Food processing training with scientific process to produce the local fruit juices of papaya, watermelons, pineapples etc. for outside markets.

Conclusion

The exemplary success of the NGO is due its honesty, hardwork and perseverance towards its mission and due to support of the people, as they believe. But, while the Microfinance aspect of this NGO is taken into consideration, the present efforts of AGUP makes us a bit disappointed. The UN General Assembly had designated the year 2005, as the International Year of Micro-credit to draw global attention on it, taking its importance, growth potentiality-especially in rural areas. It is really a matter of immediate attention to cope-up with the practical phenomena or problem that, the dealing hero's (NGOs and other intermediaries) are facing in the practical field. If the existence of these Intermediaries comes to survival, them the Microfinance dreaming will never come to expectancy.

The foregoing discussion on the NGO's role in Microfinance in special reference to AGUP has been able to gain the following points to have special attention:

1. The NGOs should be more selective in identifying the schemes and the beneficiaries.
2. The NGOs need to be more generous in augmenting their role in micro-finance.
3. The NGOs can play an effective role in creating an environment to foresee the far-reaching impact of microfinance for rural transformation.
4. NGOs can undo the problem of microfinance in terms of identification and continuation of relation with the financing institutions.
5. NGOs can introduce and popularize area approach in microfinance opening the scope for more and more SME products.

Exploring the Women Empowerment and Leaderships through Microfinance: Evidences from Grassroot

Deepak Bhagat

Abstract: *With a small start by Muhammad Yunus, Microfinance has spread worldwide. It is the financial lending with the participation of group of people (SHG) which is called as microfinance in contemporary parlance. But SHG has a larger role in addition to financial intermediation. It acts as a forum which unites and organizes the people to learn from the peers and help the peers. The SHG is also an opportunity for unity and empowerment of women, providing them the space and voice to negotiate and participate as equals both within the family and in the society in general. This paper focuses on topic that has drawn attention of the researchers over the years and is seen as an integral part of microfinance. Based on the field experience, I explored what empowerment and leadership means in context of poor women and SHGs. To supplement the view, few cases were also discussed.*

Introduction

When Muhammad Yunus, an economics professor at a Bangladesh university, started making small loans to local villagers in the 1970s, it was indistinct where the thought would go. Today, Muhammad Yunus is recognized as a visionary in a movement that has spread worldwide, claiming over 65 million customers at the end of 2002. His Grameen Bank model has now been replicated on five continents (Armendariz, Morduch, 2007). It has been now realized that the poor can save, can borrow, can decide on loans to fellow poors; and will certainly repay loans.

According to the Task Force on 'Supportive Policy and Regulatory Framework for Microfinance' (NABARD, 1999), microfinance is "provision of thrift, credit and other financial services and products of very small amounts to the poor in rural, semi-urban or urban areas for enabling them to raise their income levels and improve living standards." Microfinance is largely synonymous to rural finance as practiced in India. Except that, of late, semi-formal institutions such as non-governmental organizations (NGOs) and non-banking financial companies (NBFCs) have entered the rural credit business, bringing in a new (rather renewed) approach of lending to groups of people popularly known as Self- Help Groups (SHGs). It is this type of lending involving SHGs which is referred to as microfinance in the modern parlance (Satyasai, 2003). The Self-help Group is a particular form of microfinance institution consisting of a small group of people from a similar class and region, who come together to form savings and credit organization. They pool financial resources to make small interest bearing loans to their members (MYRADA, 2002).

This paper focuses on a topic that has drawn the attention of the researchers over the years and is seen as an integral part of microfinance. Based on the field experience, I explored what empowerment and leadership means in context of poor women and SHGs. To supplement the view, few cases were also discussed. I believe that these insights will stimulate further debate and model development on this critical but important topic. I have not tried to get bogged down in definitions about empowerment and leadership. What I have tried is to focus on those initiatives, may be apparently small but very important in the lives of the rural poor women.

Methodology

The study draws on the rich experience of Professional Assistance for Development Action (PRADAN), a well reputed and professional non-governmental organization (NGO) working in some of the most resource poor and difficult regions of India. I also got an opportunity to work with PRADAN. This paper is based on some of the striking incidences that shows how SHG led microfinance can bring real empowerment to the people that touched me on my visits to SHGs during my association with PRADAN.

SHG-Bank Linkage Approach of Microfinance Delivery

Among the diverse microfinance delivery approaches, SHG-bank linkage can be easily considered as the most leading model in contrast to the financing through MFIs which can be taken up as an promising model in microfinance. A SHG is a homogeneous group of about 15 to 20 members (mostly women from weaker sections) where every member saves a small amount regularly. NABARD initiated the "SHG-Bank Linkage Programme" in 1992 as a pilot project and mainstreamed it in 1996. The objective of the programme is to enable formal banking services to provide financial services to the rural poor through the process of savings and credit linkage of Self Help Groups. This scheme has made incredible progress in the recent years. As on March 2006, banks have cumulatively linked 22.38 lakh groups and disbursed loans of Rs. 11,397.55 crore. The trend in disbursement of bank loans to SHGs since inception is presented in Table 1.

TABLE 1

Progress in Credit Linked SHGs

Year	New SHGs finance by banks			Bank Loan (Rs. in crore)		
	During the year		Cumulative	During the year		Cumulative
	No.	Growth %	No.	Amt.	Growth %	Amt.
1992-99	32,995		32,995	57.07		57.07
1999-2000	81, 780	148	114,775	135.91	138	192.98
2000-01	1,49,050	82	263,825	287.89	112	480.87
2001-02	1,97,653	33	461,478	545.47	89	1,026.34
2002-03	2,55,882	29	717,360	1,022.34	87	2,048.68
2003-04	3,61,731	41	1,079,091	1,855.53	81	3,904.21
2004-05	5,39,365	49	1,618,456	2,994.25	62	6,898.46
2005-06	6,20,109	15	2,238,565	4,499.09	50	11,397.55

Note: In addition to this, 1,71,669 existing SHGs inn 2003-04, 2, 58, 092 in 2004-05 and 3,44, 502 existing SHGs in 2005-06, were given repeat finance by banks.

Source: Report of Working Group on Gender Issues, Panchayat Raj Institutions, Public Private Partnership, Innovative Finance and Micro Finance in Agriculture for the Eleventh Five Year Plan (2007 – 2012), Volume One.

TABLE 2

Regional spread of Credit Linked SHGs

Region	2000-01		2005-06	
	SHGs Credit linked to banks		SHGs Credit linked to banks	
Nothern	9,012	3.4	1,33,057	5.9
North Eastern	477	0.2	62,517	2.8
Eastern	22,252	8.4	3,94,351	17.6
Central	28,851	10.9	2,67,915	12.0
Western	15,543	5.9	1,66,254	7.4
Southern	1,876,90	71.2	12,14,431	54.3
Total	2,63,825	100.0	22,38,525	100

Source: Report of Working Group on Gender Issues, Panchayat Raj Institutions, Public-Private Partnership, Innovative Finance and Microfinance in Agriculture for the Eleventh Five Year Plan (2007 – 2012), Volume One.

The southern region currently constitutes about 54 percent of the credit linked SHGs in the country. The share of southern region has come down from 71 percent in March 2001 to 54 percent in March 2006 (Table 2). The share of Northeastern region has increased to 2.8 percent in 2005-06 from a mere 0.2 percent in 2000-01.

Microfinance, SHG and Women Empowerment

Though microfinance through the use of SHG has gained substantial accomplishment, the SHG has a larger role in addition to financial intermediation. It is an institution based on the concept of "peer learning" as against learning that is externally controlled.

TABLE 3

Logical Matrix

SHG Role	Role Manifestation	Prerequisite Conditions	Determining Factors
MUTUAL HELP	• Pooling resources • Internal (Personal) financial mediation • Livelihoods support	• Security of funds • Flexibility of services • Easy access to services • Fair play and equity	• Mutual rust • Equality among members • Transparent systems • Open and rational process
FINANCIAL MEDIATION	• Linkage with banks and financial institutions for supplementary	• Social collateral • Productive loaning • Mutual disciplining • Strict norms	• Access to information about each other • Peer pressure • Financial discipline • Concern for the very weak • Autonomy
EMPOWERMENT	• Making demands on the external world-panchayat, government, society and family	• Forum for solidariry • Influencing social climate and standing	• Awareness generation • Collaboration • F/Peer learning • Risk taking • Enhancing confidence

This is an influential procedure that enables growth and progress in a society. Members learn from each other in a group and SHGs learn from other SHGs, which then lead to collective evolution. The SHG is also a forum for solidarity and empowerment of women, providing them the space and voice to negotiate and participate as equals—both within the family and society in general. Therefore an SHG plays three roles simultaneously (Table 3). It provides mutual help and internal financial mediation. It facilitates external financial mediation, and it empowers women to make demands on the external world (Narendranath, 2001: 2, 4, as sited by Ajit Kanitkar in beyond Micro-credit: Putting development back in microfinance in an edited book by Homas Fisher and M. S. Sriram).

Few studies are available on SHG and microfinance and women empowerment.

I have tried to review the following:

Micro-credit as a tool of poverty alleviation and empowerment, particularly of women, has gained credence in development dialogue the world over (Deshmukh-Ranadive and Murthy, 2005). Pitt and Khandeker (1995) found in their study that credit was empowering, since the outcome 'increased income earning time spent in credit-based activities' was assumed to automatically increase women's influence in household decision making. Women's Empowerment Project in Nepal, for example, showed 68% of women experienced an increase in their decision making role in the areas of family planning, children's marriage, buying and selling property, and sending their daughters to school (Jeffrey and Parrott, 2001). World Education found that the combination of education and credit put women in a stronger position to ensure more equal access for female children to food, schooling and medical care (Sherpa, 2001). Hashemi and Schuler (1996) found a reduced incidence of violence among women who were members of credit organizations than among the general population. WWF (2000) found 41% of its members who had experienced domestic violence were able to stop it due to personal empowerment, and 29% were able to stop it through group action. Most of the SHGs that are formed under the current micro-credit initiatives are those of women. Since women are supposed to be good credit risks, and women-run enterprises benefit their families, micro-credit is seen as a tool to empower women. There is no doubt about the fact that, given the current system of micro-credit, women have access to credit. However, empowerment is not dependent on mere access but on control of both the credit and the use to which that credit is put. The concept of empowerment is defined as the process by which women take control and ownership of their choices. The core elements of empowerment have been defined as agency (ability to define one's goals and act upon them), awareness of gendered power structures, self-esteem, and self-confidence (Kabeer, 2001).

Osman (2000) in his article remarked that microfinance schemes alone can not alleviate poverty. The battle for total eradication of poverty requires combining microfinance schemes with parallel, complementary programmes addressing the social and cultural dimensions of want, privation, impoverishment and dispossession. Kapur (2001) opined that women's empowerment is much more likely to be achieved if women have total control over their organizations, which they can sustain both financially and managerially without direct dependence on others. Malhotra (2004) in her book has examined how women entrepreneurs affect the global economy, why women start business, how women's business associations promote entrepreneurs, and to what extent women contribute to international trade. It explores potential of microfinance programmes for empowering and employing women and also discusses the opportunities and challenges of using microfinance to tackle the feminization of poverty. According to her, the microfinance programmes are aimed to increase women's income levels and control over income leading to greater levels of economic independence. They enable women's access to networks and markets, access to information and possibilities for development of other social and political role. They also enhance perceptions of women's contribution to household income and family welfare, increasing women's participation in household decisions about expenditure and other issues leading to greater expenditure on women's welfare. Cheston and Kuhn (2004) in their study concluded that microfinance programmes have been very successful in reaching women. This gives microfinance institutions an extraordinary reach to act intentionally to empower poor women and to minimize the potentially negative impacts of some women experiences. Sahu and Tripathy (2005) in their edited book views that 70 percent of world's poor are women. Access for the poor to banking services is important not only for poverty alleviation but also for optimizing their contribution to the growth of regional as well as the national economy. Self Help Groups (SHGs) have emerged as the most vital instrument in the process of participatory development and women empowerment. The rural women are the marginalized groups in the society because of socio-economic constraints. They remain backward and take lower position in the social hierarchical ladder. They can lift themselves from the morass of poverty and stagnation through microfinance and formation of Self-Help Groups.

Evidence from the Field

Evidence from the field supports literature analysis. In this section, I have tried to present some of the evidences that I have seen during my visits to SHGs:

1. ***TWC Horticulture Scheme:*** Sanso, Sarjama and Kurag are three villages in the block Ghaghra of Gumla district in Jharkhand where the government decided to implement the plantation of Mango and agro forestry under the Tribal Welfare Commissioner (TWC) fund. PRADAN was the implementing agency. The scheme was to be implemented in two phases. In both the phases the fund was to be released in two installments i.e after submission of bill of the 1st instalment. Initially everything was fine. Nine of the SHGs selected for the programme and the money came directly to their account as per their entitlements. Apart from the regular SHG meetings as savings and credit group, the women started sitting weekly after the normal meeting to keep track on the progress of the scheme and utilization of money as it was a SHG which was made responsible for completing the project. It was the SHGs of women only.

   But the money in the scheme was comparatively less. Only Rs.29,778.00– which was supposed to cover the cost of pit digging, pit filling, fertilizer, pesticide, sapling, transportation, and a well was also to be constructed in the plot because in this part of Jharkhand there is a problem of water scarcity. So the women decided that as far as possible they will provide the labour from their family. And the work started. But the problem in these villages was the huge drinking habit of males. So after few days they stopped coming to work and engaged in drinking. At the same time a serious problem was around the corner. Being an agriculture crop the mango has to be planted within a specific time. As it requires water after plantation, July end at the time of onset of monsoon was selected for planting. But the attitude of the male was making the implementing agency worried. An emergency meeting was called to discuss the serious issue. Only solution was to bring the men to the field since women alone cannot finish the pit digging job in time which was really hard, especially in the sunny days of June. Recognizing the seriousness of the issue Sukro Devi, a 50 year old illiterate lady stood up and said, "I will bring my husband to the work." Everyone went with her to see how she is convincing her old husband. Her husband was lying in the corner of a house with his other drunken friends. She pulled her husband and slapped him on his cheek, held him with one hand, took the spade in other and reached to the pit digging site almost pulling him. Other men automatically went to their home, took their spade and reached their respective field. As a result, mangoes were planted in time. Everyone in the nearby villages recognized the power of women. From now onwards men were partners of women in every initiative they took.

After the plantation, then comes the second-most important work. Digging a well—that is not a family based job. People who are trained can only do it and they have to be hired. For that money is required. But problem was that even after the submission of bills for the first instalment the district administration was not releasing the second instalment. The best time for digging well is after harvest of paddy and before the onset of monsoon. The time was running out. So, the SHG members took the decision that they will organize a function and invite DC and request to visit the field and see the condition of the dying plants due to water scarcity. The DC came to the function, gave a nice speech. When the members requested DC to visit their field, the answer was in negative because of very busy schedule. But the women forced DC to go to their field and see the ground reality. This incidence made the DC to recognize the seriousness of the issue and to assure them for timely release of money. And it happened.

The success of this scheme is only because of the SHG which was formed 4 years ago as a medium to help the women through microfinance. It was that initiative only which made the women organize into groups and become empowered to fight for their rights.

2. ***Women Managing their own Bank:*** Every 25th of month 14 women traveling a distance which goes even up to a maximum of 16 km from all the direction of Ghaghra block reaches to the office of Mahilla Vikas to give payments to their postmen and computer munshi, to take decisions on buying new computer equipment or its accessories, discuss the various coming issues while smooth running of their Mahilla Vikas Mandal which is above the cluster level of around 150 SHGs. There are 7 clusters in the Ghaghra block. All the SHGs of a particular cluster send two members along with Rs.2 per member (depending upon member in group) to the cluster meeting held once in every month. It is a forum to learn from the experiences of other SHGs. There they deposit the money also. From this cluster, again, 2 members will go the Office of Mahilla Vikas Mandal monthly. There they deposit the money which will be paid as mentioned above. Remaining money is deposited in the bank. They have selected three bank signatories who will do all the bank transactions on their behalf.

To keep complete and proper record of all the transactions in a group, after every meeting in the group, the SHG sends one copy of RMTS (Regular Meting Transaction Sheet I) to the Mahilla Vikas office where the computer munshi enters the data and takes a print out of the RMTS II having information on the loans, interest to be collected from the members. The postman will deliver the sheet to the group.

These women are running their own MFI which is sustainable. Their capacity to handle such an institution is now appreciated by everyone.

Conclusion

All the sections of the paper and the cases suggest that SHGs are beyond a financial device for extending financial services to the poor. Though they perform this role, SHGs are self-governing organizations having strong impacts on their members that go further than access to financial services. SHGs can support better or new livelihoods for their members; empower them, provide opportunity to show and develop leadership qualities and form a major revolution of grassroots level democratic institutions.

Note

I am grateful to the PRADAN professionals in the Gumla and Lohardaga team in the state of Jharkhand.

References

1. Armendariz, B. and Morduch, J. 2007. The economics of microfinance. Prentice- Hall of India Private Limited. New Delhi.
2. Cheston, Susy and Lisa Kuhn (2002), "Empowering Women Through Microfinance", Unpublished Background Paper for the Micro-credit Summit 15, New York, 10-13 November (www.microcreditsummit.org).

3. Deshmukh-Ranadive, J. and Murthy, R, K. 2005. Micro-credit, Poverty and Empowerment: Linking the Triad. Sage Publications, New Delhi.
4. Fisher, T. and Sriram, M. S. (2006). Beyond Micro-credit: Putting Development Back into Microfinance and presentation in the NAC on Microfinance in India on 10th May 2007 by M. S. Sriram.
5. Hashemi, Syed, Sidney Schuler, and Ann Riley (1996) "Rural Credit Programs and Women's Empowerment in Bangladesh." *World Development* 24:4 (1996): 635-653.
6. Helen Sherpa. World Education response to email survey. October 20, 2001.
7. Jeffrey Ashe and Lisa Parrott. *Impact Evaluation of PACT's Women's Empowerment Program in Nepal:A Savings and Literacy Led Alternative to Financial Institution Building.* (Cambridge, MA: Brandeis University, 2001) .
8. Kabeer, N. (2001), "Resources Agency Achievements: Reflections on the Measurement of Women's Empowerment – Theory and Practice", SIDA Studies, No. 3.
9. Kapoor, Pramilla (2001), *Empowering the Indian Women*, Publications Division, Ministry of Information and Broadcasting, Government of India.
10. Malhotra, Meenakshi (2004), *Empowerment of Women*, Isha Books, Delhi.
11. NABARD. 1999. Task force on supportive policy and regulatory framework for microfinance. Mumbai: National Bank for Agriculture and Rural Development (http://www.microfinancegateway.com/section#Q1).
12. Narendranath, D. 2001. Group Dynamics. News Reach. New Delhi.
13. Osman, Khalil, 2000 "Microfinance Institutions: Effective Weapon in the War against Rural Poverty", www.muslimedia.com
14. Pitt, M. and Khandeker, S., 1995, Household and Intra-household Impacts of the Grameen Bank and Similar Targeted Credit Programmes in Bangladesh' Paper presented at the workshop on *Credit Programmes for the Poor: Household and Intra-Household Impacts and Programme Sustainability*, 19-21 May, Dhaka: World bank and Bangladesh Institute of Development Studies.
15. Report of Working Group on Gender Issues, Panchayat Raj Institutions, Public Private Partnership, Innovative Finance and Micro Finance in Agriculture For the Eleventh Five Year Plan (2007-2012), Volume One retrieved on October 11, 2007 from the website http://planningcommission.nic.in/aboutus/committee/wrgrp11/wg_subland.doc
16. Sahu and Tripathy (2005), *Self-Help Groups and Women Empowerment*, Anmol Publications Pvt. Ltd., New Delhi.
17. Satyasai, K. J. S. 2003. Microfinance in India: Progress and Perspectives. Institutional change in Indian Agriculture, NCAP, New Delhi.
18. Swarnjayanti Gram Swarozgar Yojana Guidelines, Government of India, Ministry of Rural Development,New Delhi.
19. Working Women's Forum. *Social Platform Through Social Innovations: A Coalition with Women in the Informal Sector*. Chennai, India: Working Women's Forum, 2000, pp. 22.

14

Microfinance and Women Empowerment: An Exploration

Dipanwita Deb

ABSTRACT: *The term microfinance is an alternative source of credit for the rural poor which includes financial services to them in small amount which enables them to sustain in different dimensions. The term women empowerment means the transformation of women in social, political and economic terms which gives them a status in the society and enables them to take decisions at household and society levels. The microfinance with women empowerment came into limelight when the concept of Grameen Bank started by Mohammad Yunus gained grounds in Bangladesh. Subsequently many NGOs and other financial institutions started the programme of micro-credit. An attempt has been made in this paper to review the different studies on impact of microfinance on women empowerment. It is observed through different studies that microfinance is of immense benefit to women as it helped many poor women in their upliftment which has enabled them to take up livelihood generating activities and be independent, and has ultimately resulted in the development of their entire household. It can be said that microfinance and women empowerment has a close link and microfinance has the potential to help the rural poor.*

Introduction

Microfinance is a concept which has developed in the 1970s. The simple nature of this concept has made it universally accepted. It has been taken up by many developing countries as a new measure to uplift the socially backward. Sometimes called "banking for the poor," microfinance is an amazingly simple approach that has been proven to empower very poor people around the world to pull themselves out of poverty. Relying on their traditional skills and entrepreneurial instincts, very poor people, mostly women, use small loans, other financial services, and support from local organizations called microfinance institutions (MFIs) to start, establish, sustain, or expand very small, self-supporting businesses. A key to microfinance is the recycling of loan dollars. As each loan is repaid—usually within six months to a year—the money is recycled as another loan, thus multiplying the value of each dollar in defeating global poverty, and changing lives and communities.(Grameen Foundation: 2001). The basic principle behind the concept of microfinance is explained by the then UN Secretary-General, Kofi Annan, as "Sustainable access to microfinance helps alleviate poverty by generating income, creating jobs, allowing children to go to school, enabling families to obtain healthcare and empowering people to make choices that best serve their needs" (Batra, 2007).

Microfinance has played a crucial role in transforming the lives of poor women, particularly in the Indian sub-continent. All earlier poverty alleviation programmes were more male-oriented and were not specifically targeted at women who have to bear the greater scars of poverty. The success of microfinance is largely due to the fact that these tiny loans have not only helped in combating poverty but have also brought about a big change in the social status of women. It has enabled them to provide better health, nutrition and education to their children. In fact, poverty had deeply affected the overall development of the family, the worst sufferers being the women who are at the core of the family nucleus and perform the triple role of caring for the home, hearth and the farm.

Commonly, empowerment is described as a process whereby women become able to organize themselves to increase their own self-reliance, to assert their independent right to make choices and to control resources which will assist in challenging and eliminating their own subordination. Empowerment has been conceptualized differently by different writers. However, for all of them, the goal of the empowerment process is to address issues relating to women's subordination, inequality and inequity. Furthermore, women's empowerment is seen as entailing a shift from positions of powerlessness towards strategic social, economic and political participation. This implies taking on power—both at the individual and social levels. All the conceptualizations of empowerment emphasize four main dimensions: individual or personal, economic, collective/ social group and political. Most see the empowerment process as addressing a combination of these dimensions and affecting different domains: Household, community, national, and international. These views of empowerment are grounded within different concepts of power, the root concept within which empowerment is located, leading to different mechanisms for social change and transformation. They can broadly be organized along a continuum, with personal and political empowerment forming the two ends.

A review of the literature on women's empowerment suggests that there is still little primary research at the grassroots level to contribute to our understanding on what empowerment means in daily life. There are many definitions of empowerment. The World Bank defines empowerment as "the expansion of assets and capabilities of poor people to participate in, negotiate with, influence, control, and hold accountable institutions that affect their lives."

Empowerment implies a more participatory, bottom up approach to development objectives than has been taken in the past, a result of the increasing consensus that "giving poor people more freedom to make economic decisions enhances development effectiveness at the local level in terms of design, implementation and outcomes".

Empowerment approaches focus on enhancing poor people's freedom of choice and actions. Empowerment of poor people is an end in itself and is also critical for development effectiveness. It is not a stand-alone strategy but a way of doing development, grounded in the conviction that poor people themselves are the most invaluable partners in the task of poverty reduction. Empowerment approaches include behavior that build people's self-confidence and their belief in them, and respect their dignity.

Objectives of The Paper

Over the years Microfinance has contributed to women empowerment and has brought many positive changes. In the present era, where almost 70% of the population lives in rural India, the concept of Microfinance has acted as a financial gateway to help the rural poor, it is the only way through which access to finance is easy for the poor. This paper is aimed to establish a close link between Microfinance and Women Empowerment and to explain the potential of microfinance in alleviating the rural poor. In the present article, an attempt has been made to explain how microfinance has helped in empowering of women and how it has helped the downtrodden.

Establishing a link between Microfinance and Women Empowerment

From the early 1970s, women's movements in a number of countries identified credit as a major constraint on women's ability to earn an income and became increasingly interested in the degree to which poverty-focused credit programmes and credit cooperatives were actually being used by women. SEWA in India, for example, set up credit programmes as part of a multi-pronged strategy for an organization of informal sector women workers. Since the 1970s, many women's organizations worldwide have included credit and savings, both as a way of increasing women's incomes and to bring women together to address wider gender issues. The 1980s saw the emergence of poverty-targeted micro-finance institutions like Grameen Bank and ACCION and others. Many of these programmes see themselves as empowerment-oriented. In the 1990s, a combination of evidence of high female repayment rates and the rising influence of gender lobbies within donor agencies and NGOs led to increasing emphasis on targeting women in microfinance programmes (Linda Mayoux).

The contribution of microfinance in women empowerment is categorized as:

Financial self-sustainability paradigm: Currently dominant within most donor agencies and in the models of microfinance promoted in publications by USAID, World Bank, UNDP, CGAP and the Micro-credit Summit Campaign. Here the main consideration in programme design is provision of financially self-sustainable microfinance services to large number of poor people, particularly micro- and small-entrepreneurs. The focus is on setting of interest rate "right" to cover costs, to separate microfinance from other interventions to enable separate accounting, to expand programmes so as to capture economies of scale, to use groups to decrease costs of delivery. Gender lobbies have been able to argue for targeting women on the grounds of high female repayment rates and contribution of women's economic activity to economic growth. In this paradigm, it is assumed that increasing women's access to microfinance services will in itself lead to individual economic empowerment, well-being and social and political empowerment.

Poverty alleviation paradigm: Underlies poverty-targeted programmes. Here the main considerations are poverty reduction among the poorest, increased well-being, and community development. The focus is on small savings and loan provision for consumption and production, group formation, etc. This paradigm justifies some level of subsidy for programmes working with particular client groups or in particular contexts. Some programmes have developed effective methodologies for poverty targeting and/or operating in remote areas. Gender lobbies in this context have argued for targeting women, because of higher levels of female poverty and because of women's responsibility for household well-being. Poverty alleviation and women's empowerment are seen as two sides of the same coin. The assumption is that increasing women's access to microfinance (together with other interventions to improve household well-being) will in itself induce women to bring about wider changes in gender inequality.

Feminist empowerment paradigm: Underlies the gender policies of many NGOs and the perspectives of some of the consultants and researchers looking at gender impact of microfinance programmes (Johnson, 1997). This paradigm did not originate as a Northern imposition. It is rooted in the development of some of the earliest microfinance programmes in the South—particularly SEWA and WWF in India. Here the underlying concerns are gender equality and women's human rights. Microfinance is promoted as an entry point in the context of a wider strategy for women's economic and socio-political empowerment. The focus here is on gender awareness and feminist organization. Some programmes have developed very effective means for integrating gender awareness into programmes and for organizing women and men to challenge and change gender discrimination. Some also have legal rights support for women and engage in gender advocacy (Linda Mayoux). Further, the close link of microfinance and women empowerment is established and is explained as:

Economic empowerment: Women's access to savings and credit gives them a greater economic role in decision-making through their decision about savings and credit. When women control decisions regarding credit and savings, they will optimize their own and the household's welfare. The investment in women's economic activities will improve employment opportunities for women and thus have a 'trickle down and out' effect. The financial sustainability emphasizes women's own income-generating activities. In the poverty alleviation paradigm, the emphasis is more on increasing incomes at the household level and the use of loans for consumption. In the feminist empowerment paradigm, individual economic empowerment is seen as dependent on social and political empowerment.

Increased well-being: Access to savings and credit facilities and women's decision about what is being done with savings and credit strengthens women's say in economic decisions of the household. This enables women to increase expenditure on the well-being of themselves and their children. This is the main concern in the poverty alleviation paradigm. Women's control over decision-making is also seen as benefiting men through preventing leakage of household income to unproductive and harmful. Other welfare interventions are advocated in addition to microfinance, typically nutrition, and health and literacy campaigns to further decrease vulnerability and improve women's skills. In the financial self-sustainability and feminist empowerment paradigms, improved well-being is an assumed outcome from increasing women's economic activities and incomes.

Social and Political empowerment: A combination of women's increased economic activity and control over income resulting from access to microfinance with improved women's skills, mobility, access to knowledge and support networks. Status within the community is also enhanced. These changes are reinforced by group formation, leading to wider movements for social and political change. The financial self-sustainability paradigm and the poverty alleviation paradigm assume that social and political empowerment will occur without specific interventions to change gender relations at the household, community or macro-levels. By contrast, the feminist empowerment paradigm advocates explicit strategies for supporting women's ability to protect their individual and collective gender interests at the household, community and macro-levels (Linda Mayoux).

An example of SEWA Bank is cited in this article to make the subject more clear:

A small number of self-employed poor women formed their own organization in 1972 when the Self-Employed Women's Association (SEWA) was registered as a trade union in Gujarat. Its main objective was to strengthen its members' bargaining power to improve their income, employment and access to social security.

Self-employed women are caught in the vicious circle of poverty, indebtedness, no government assistance and low incomes. A possible solution to free these women from this vicious cycle involves linking them with registered banks. But attempts to link self-employed women with national banks through SEWA as an intermediary met with many difficulties. The gap between sophisticated bank staff and women in shabby clothes accompanied by noisy children was not bridged, because the banks were not able to relate to these women as their clientele.

In 1973 the members of SEWA came forward with an answer; a bank of their own where they would be accepted in their own right and not made to feel inferior. Four thousand women contributed a share capital of Rs 10 each to establish a women's' cooperative bank. In May 1974, SEWA Bank was registered. Since then, it has provided banking services to poor, illiterate, self-employed women and has become a viable financial venture.

The main objective of SEWA Bank is to help poor women reserve the process of recapitalization at the micro level and to begin the process of capitalization. This is accomplished by providing financial services like savings, credit and insurance which help women:

- To escape from the clutches of moneylenders;
- To rescue their mortgaged/pledged assets, such as land, ornaments and cattle;
- To create their own assets, such as house, savings, and equipment;
- To expand their business through productive credit;
- To cope with losses due to sickness, accidents, death, floods and riots;
- To increase their bargaining power;
- To improve their living conditions; and
- To improve themselves, ultimately.

References

1. Ahmad, Rais. Role of Microfinance in Empowering Women, Grameen Foundation: 2001.
2. *Linda Mayoux,* Microfinance and the empowerment of women—A review of the key issue J:\ilo_data\public\english\employment\ finance\download\wp23.wpd
3. Qazi, Moin. Microfinance and Women's Empowerment.
4. Vyas, Jayshree, "Banking with Poor Self-Employed Women".

SECTION IV

INSTITUTIONAL INNOVATIONS AND IMPACT ASSESSMENT

15

Conceptualizing Alternative Method of Studying Microfinance Organization

Maya Kant Awasthi

Abstract: *Conventional approach for studying impact of microfinance initiatives have been that of identifying factors which contribute to high loan repayments or assessing socio-economic impacts of microfinance programmes on borrowers. Such impact studies largely overlook the effects of group dynamics on microfinance processes even though it is critical to study the process through which group members interact with each other and collaborate. As such, this process has tremendous impact on outcome of any microfinance scheme. Effectiveness of this collaborative process also has serious sustainability implications for Microfinance Organizations (MFOs). Collaborative process may also yield behavioural changes in beneficiaries of these schemes. These behavioural changes often work as defensive mechanisms aimed at overcoming risks, vulnerability, powerlessness and isolation (Ana Marr 2002). The paper, therefore, conceptualizes an alternative framework which can be used to study group dynamics and blueprint new channels of impact effects on the individuals participating in microfinance schemes.*

Conceptual Framework

Conceptual framework developed in this paper is based on the logic that microfinance programmes and schemes are based on collaborative process. Therefore, any attempt to study effectiveness of microfinance organization has to be assessed by looking at the processes involved. A typical MFO initiative can be studied by exploring dynamics of the following sub processes:

1. **Dynamics of Assortative Matching Process:** Earlier work by Stiglitz and Weiss (1981), Varian (1990), Becker (1991), and Ghatak (1999), suggests that socially and economically vulnerable groups do not have complete information and have high chance of exclusion from financial products. Under such situations self-selection process leads to a positive assortative matching, where groups self-select members of the same risk type—this

leads to formation of homogeneous groups. Therefore, for assessing effectiveness of microfinance initiative or organization we need to study level of cohesiveness by assessing the degree of assortative behaviour among members of microfinance organization.

2. **Dynamics of Peer Auto-monitoring Process:** Stiglitz (1990), Banerjee et al (1994), Besley and Coate (1995), Conning (1996), Madajewicz (1998) and Armendariz (1999) studied the incentives and monitoring structures of microfinance schemes. Findings of the their studies suggest that peer monitoring instruments such as social sanctions and benefits are effective in resolving problems of moral hazard and costly enforcement and may reduce the loan default rate. Therefore, estimation of level and effectiveness of peer monitoring may reveal quality of microfinance organization.

   However, assortative matching and peer monitoring work on environment is that members of microfinance organization have complete information about one another and can obtain information with no additional cost. Alternative model developed in this paper does not have any such requirements. In such situation we study intra-group dynamics and the performance of monitoring, auditing, and enforcement of contracts. We may also study group collaboration process and its influence on positive assortative matching process along with influence of MFO staff on group behaviour.

3. **Microfinance Process Dynamics:** There is a two-way influence between group dynamics and socio-economic impacts of microfinance organizations on beneficiaries and their ecology. Intermediate impacts affect group dynamics via group and members' behaviour, their poverty-reduction strategies, and the ultimate impacts on individuals, households, enterprises and community-based networks that give groups origin, in a specific social and historical context (Chrish Huxham, Siv Vangen, 2005).

The effectiveness of MFO, therefore, is best assessed by examining group dynamics. For assessing group we may study how groups are organised, evolve and transform over time. As evolving social interactions within groups affect members' behaviour as their attitudes towards risks, cooperation and private rent-seeking become heavily influenced we may try to capture it. Ultimate impacts on poverty are the tangible and intangible effects of microfinance-induced strategies that groups, members, households, enterprises, and communities put in motion to reduce poverty (Chrish Huxham, Siv Vangen, 2005). This should be part of impact assessment exercise.

Analysis of main ingredients of Group Dynamics

Group dynamics can be studied exploring the following three key ingredients of group dynamics:

1. Drivers of group dynamics.
2. Dynamic process of distribution of roles and responsibilities distribution.
3. Nature of outcomes of group dynamics.

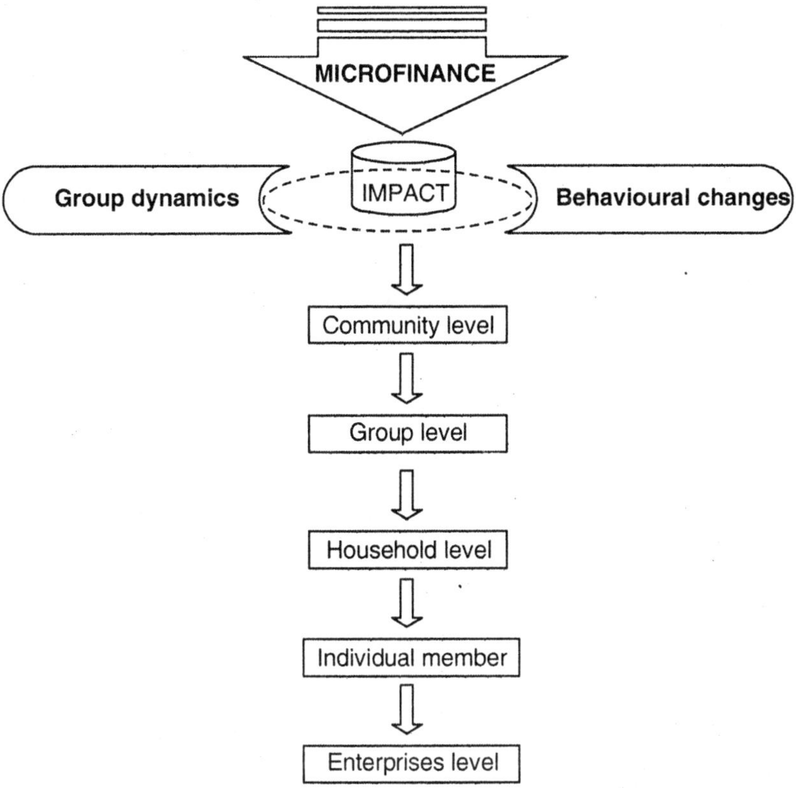

Fig. 1: Impact Path of Microfinance Initiative

Drivers of Group Dynamics

Strong backward and forward linkages across these ingredients generate possible outcomes of group dynamics, which mark the path of impact effects on poverty reduction etc. objectives of MFO. The financial sustainability and organisational sustainability are two drivers of group dynamics. In microfinance, organization groups try to achieve financial sustainability of their groups by securing prompt repayments of loans from the external, internal and complementary accounts. These groups also progressively increase loan sizes and induce higher savings growth rates and capitalizing their internal accounts for this purpose.

Dynamics of Process of Roles and Responsibilities Distribution

A typical MFO develops its own system of self-management by evolving internal rules and regulations that members agree to comply. These regulations introduce

TABLE 1

Costs and benefits of Group Dynamics

FINANCIAL SUSTAINABILITY	
Parameter	**Indicator**
COLLECTIVE ACTION	• Group loan repayment • Individual member's access to • Progressively increasing external loan account • Internal loan account • Complementary loan account • Social sanctions for non-repayment
PRIVATE COSTS	• Costs of monitoring and auditing • Cost of exercising enforcement norms and rules. Opportunity costs of compulsory savings. Alternative sources of credit and savings • Returns accrued from investments of group's • Savings
COLLECTIVE BENEFITS	• Use of savings to repay loans of defaulters. Group's loss of access to loans when some members do not repay
ORGANISATIONAL SUSTAINABILITY	
COLLECTIVE ACTIONCOSTS	• Self-management of the group as an organisation • Skill development • Empowerment • Mutual support in times of need. Participation in positions of power. Social sanctions for non-cooperation • Fee charges of non-attendance to meetings. Penalties for non-collaboration in activities. Opportunity costs of time spent in meetings. Alternative sources of skill/empower development. Independence as a social network • Linkages with other social networks • Erosion of social ties • Fracturing of group as social network.

Source: Chrish Huxham, Siv Vangen (2005)

the idea of joint-liability and joint profit sharing to members. This process involves intensive interactions amongst microfinance members. Similarly, for smooth functioning of MFO, responsibilities of monitoring, auditing and enforcement are distributed between members. Analysis of this process of responsibility distribution for its effectiveness and transparency is essential to the analysis of group dynamics.

Outcomes of Group Dynamics

Group dynamics in MFO initiative has number of private and collective costs and benefits to group members (Table 1). These explicit and implicit benefits and costs serve as incentives or disincentive for MFO members to perform the assigned duties and responsibilities. Over time, members negotiate and accommodate within the group to maximize private and collective net benefits. Assessment of effectiveness of this process in generating equitable benefits and cost sharing mechanism can be used to peep into functioning of MFO.

Possible Outcomes of Group Dynamics

In order to maximize net benefits, members of MFO initiate certain actions which generate areas of potential friction within the group. These frictions work as hindrance for achieving financial and organisational sustainability of MFO. Presence of friction of high magnitude also affects the organisational sustainability and may result in the fragmentation of groups. There may be number of factors which might be responsible for creating friction in the group. These factors may be in the area of inadequacies of institutional contracts, selection criteria, MFO officers' training, lack of communication and inadequate mechanisms for the management and prevention of crises. Therefore, analysis of group dynamics from the perspective of positive and negative outcomes of group interaction process and mechanism is one of the important impact assessment areas.

Units of Analysis

Impact of MFO can be felt at various levels. Analysis may, therefore, focus on any such level. The analysis may be undertaken at following levels or units of impact:

1. Group level
2. Individual member level
3. Household level
4. Enterprises level
5. Community level

Group Level Analysis

MFO work essentially as a group or very often as a self-help group. Impact of MFO initiative, therefore, can be best captured at the group level. Level and intensity of interactions at group level is determined by the types of contracts, responsibilities and the personal characteristics of the group members. The effects of MFO activities on group behaviour will be reflected in enforcement and collective actions at the group level. Group level analysis may focus specially on seeking answers to questions such as how changes in behaviour affect the functioning of groups and how members able to strengthen group's collective processes ? Members of groups are affected by the evolving dynamics of groups as their behaviour is influenced by the actions of fellow members and the MFO officers supervising them (Chrish Huxham, Siv Vangen, 2005).

Individual Member Level

MFO initiatives are essentially initiatives of the people, by the people, and for the people. Such initiative, therefore, is bound to impact its members. This multi-dimensional impact can be captured by assessing impact of MFO on its members. At individual level MFO activities also affect flow and quality of information—positively or negatively. Depending on the extent to which group dynamics affect individual behaviour, members develop their own group and interpersonal strategies and exercise greater influence in decision making process related to benefit sharing, utilization of loans on high-risk investments such as on-lending MFO loans to non-members, working hours of MFO, and the management of debts.

TABLE 2

Units and Causes of Impact

Units of impact	Behavioural changes	Strategies
Group	Risk attitudes on monitoring and enforcement. Perceptions of power structure within the group. Intensity of interaction between members Cooperative tendencies. Exclusionary tendencies? • Staff/group extent and quality of interaction	Strengthening of group's collective benefits. Conflict mgmt/ resolution. Delegation of monitoring. Substitution of joint-liability mechanisms. Organization of communal adhoc activities. Self-management? • Enhancement of sanctions
Individual	Risk attitudes on use of loans and savings. Rent-seeking behaviour. Free-riding on monitoring. Attitudes towards revealing private information. Responses to degree of fairness of social sanctions. Attitudes towards finance, business, and work ethics? • Ability to voice concerns	High-risk investments. Lengthening of personal working hours. Temporary job migration On-lending. Debt management. Reliance on informal finance for loan repayment. Positioning oneself within the group power structure? • Exercise influence
Household	Temporal time preferences. Divergence/convergence of individual preferences on use of loans/savings. Quality of interaction between members. Attitudes towards women's position within household? • Cross-generational investments	Insurance building (animals, grain stock, etc). Housing improvement. Stability of children's school enrolment. Preservation of health. Migration of offspring. Negotiation amongst member Conflict resolution? • Asset building for offspring

Contd.

Contd.

Units of impact	Behavioural changes	Strategies
Enterprise	Risk attitudes on investment. Influence of group peers' Choice of business. Separation of consumption and production. Attitudes towards business, and work ethics. Profit-maximization as goal. Attitudes towards women and child labour? • Cross-generational investments	Initiation of enterprise. Stabilisation of enterprise. Self-mgmnt of financial reports. Technology adaptation. Growth of enterprise. Labour of household members at enterprise. High-risk investments. Hiring external labour. Change/addition of business? • Offspring control over old and new enterprises
Community	Demonstration effects on people's perceptions of institutional finance. Members' competitors reaction to profit margins. Perceptions of degree of fairness in programme selection of members? • Local markets' response to members' use of finance	Growth of informal finance. Entry of financial NGOs. Creation of similar micro-enterprises. Re-structuring of community-based organisations. Re-setting of market prices for goods and labour. Creation of jobs? • Innovation on business types

Source: *Chrish Huxham, Siv Vangen (2005)*

At the Household Level

Members of MFO are part of their respective basic social unit, i.e., family or households. Therefore, any behavioural change also affects the way these members interact with the other family members. At the household level most of the income and resources are pooled and responsibilities are shared. Individual demands are then aggregated to optimize satisfaction and welfare at household level. Behavioural change affect process of negotiation between family members related to resolving of conflict, prioritization of households needs and asset purchase. Therefore, impact of MFO activities need to be continuously reassessed in the context of household dynamics.

At the Enterprise Level

MFO induced changes in behaviour of members of MFO influence the way they makes decisions and influence their choices of businesses and their attitudes towards work ethics and the involvement of women and children in the running of their own enterprises. Microfinance programmes also affect perception of fairness in the selection process and local markets. As a natural consequence to this members may decide to formulate new strategies to take advantage of emerging opportunities and creation of small enterprises.

Impact Domains and Variables

For analyzing impact of MFO activities we have to identify relevant impact domains and variables. Domains of impacts are the spheres of activity and processes. Whereas variables of impacts are specific indicators of changes within the impact domains at each level of analysis. Table 3 (A) and (B) suggest few generic impact domains and variables which can be used.

To assess impacts of MFO activities on the group's organisational sustainability several quantitative and qualitative variables such as growth and stability of membership, criteria for exclusion and inclusion of members, the governance structures, level of sharing, management of internal accounts, social sanctions and rates of attendance at meetings can be used.

TABLE 3A

Impact Domains and Variables

IMPACT DOMAINS	IMPACT VARIABLES/INDICATORS UNIT OF IMPACT: GROUP
Collective Action	• Growth and stability of external and internal loan sizes • Arrears rates of external and internal loans • Savings growth • Loan repayment rates • Frequency of loan collection • Fine rates and interest rates for internal account
Organisational Sustainability	• Growth and stability of membership • Meeting attendance rates • Voting system • Degree of exchange of members skills • Frequency and types of participation in community activities • Criteria for exclusion and inclusion of members • Criteria for loan size eligibility • Degree of self-management • Types of joint-liability • Benefits and costs of social sanctions • Quality of information
Staff/members stability	• NGO officers profiles • Performance-related incentives • Staff turnover • Length of supervision of a given group • Degree of delegation of duties to group members • Frequency and quality of members/group auditing

Contd.

Contd.

IMPACT DOMAINS	IMPACT VARIABLES/INDICATORS UNIT OF IMPACT: GROUP
	• Channels of communication between members and management
Asset accumulation	• Stability and growth of personal income and expenditure • Nutritional intake • Non-CB loans
Skill accumulation	• Perceived value of NGO training courses • No. of topics covered in group meeting • Book keeping
Empowerment	• Information about members' business and livelihoods • Ability to perform responsibilities • Degree of participation in group meetings • Involvement in organisations control • Financial independence from husbands/ others
Self-esteem	• Ability to voice own concerns within groups and households • Degree of participation in decision-making Perceived treatment by others
Asset accumulation	• Stability and growth of income, expenditure, net worth • Restoration and acquisition assets
Consumption-smoothing	• Stability and growth of consumption • Savings diversification • Motives for saving (insurance, precautionary, etc) • Expenditure in emergencies
Long-term investment	• Actual and perceived returns of investments • Fixed assets (tangible and intangible returns; maturity periods) • Percentage of investment on young and grown-up children
Power structure and intra h/h relations	• Degree of participation in decision-making members with respect to finance, expenditure • Short and long-term investments • Degree of unequal control over household resources • Intensity of interaction between members • Incidence and severity of violent conflict resolution

Source: Chrish Huxham, Siv Vangen (2005)

TABLE 3B

Impact domains and variables

IMPACT DOMAINS UNIT OF IMPACT: ENTERPRISE	IMPACT VARIABLES
Existing enterprise	• Stability and growth of income, net profits, net cash flows • Acquisition of assets • Sales on credit • Formal and informal debts. Types of waged and non-waged jobs, new enterprises
Diversification of economic activities	• Risks, returns, maturity periods • Co-variance of risks between enterprises
Business management	• Financial management • Women and child labour hours • Skill development • Productivity • Creation of jobs/enterprises
Employment Technology	• Labour-reducing technologies • Cost-reducing, efficiency-enhancing technologies
Organisational Governance	• Degree of influence in decision making process • Criteria for exclusion and inclusion of members
Horizontal and vertical linkages of social networks	• Extent of participation • Frequency of meetings • Intensity of interactions • Extent of coordination
Empowerment	• Degree of participation in local organisations • Displacement of community members • Increased control over common properties
Financial market	• Growth of informal and formal sources of finance • Types of emerging financial products
Labour market	• Number of members that leave CBs to join other financial schemes • Growth of temporary and permanent jobs • Levels, number of working hours • Growth of economic activities (by type) • Degree of displacement of existing businesses
Real market	• Changes in market prices • Degree of competition • Number of new market niches being opened

At the household level we may use four impact domains, i.e., asset creation, nutritional intake, investment on productive activities and empowerment within intra-household relationships. Whereas, at the enterprise level, impact domains such as diversification of business, business management, employment and adoption of modern technologies may be used.

At the community level, impact domains include the horizontal and vertical linkages that develop between MFOs, financial institution, local organizations and local markets. Analysis of these variables helps in evaluating whether or not the prosperity of MFO members is coming at the cost of non-MFO community members.

Summary and Conclusion

Paper proposes an alternative comprehensive analytical framework for assessing impact of activities of any microfinance organization. Under this methodology, impact is assessed by tracing impact of microfinance initiatives on group dynamics and impact as consequence of changes on members of MFO group, households, individuals and enterprises. This analytical methodology allows us capturing impacts from process perspective which is not possible through traditional methodologies. Such dynamic impact assessment can reveal new impact paths and effects which may provide critical input in policy planning related to Microfinance organization.

References

1. Armendariz, B. (1999) "On the design of a credit agreement with peer monitoring". In Journal of Development Economics 60 (1), pp. 79-104
2. Banerjee A., T. Besley and T. Guinnane (1994) "Thy neighbor's keeper: the design of a credit cooperative with theory and a test". In Quarterly Journal of Economics 109 (2), pp. 491-515
3. Becker, G. (1991) A Treatise on the Family. Harvard University Press: Cambridge
4. Besley, Timothy and S. Coate (1995) "Group lending, repayment incentives and social collateral". In Journal of Development Economics 46 (1), pp. 1-18
5. Chrish Huxham, Siv Vangen (2005) "Managing to Collaborative Advantage: The theory and practice of Collaborative Advantage. Routledge Publishing, New York
6. Conning, J. (1996) "Group lending, moral hazard and the creation of social collateral" IRIS Working Paper #165. University of Maryland at College Park
7. Ghatak, Maitreesh (1999) "Group lending, local information and peer selection". In Journal of Development Economics Vol. 60, No. 1, pp. 27-50
8. Hatch, John and Mimi Hatch (1989) FINCA Village Banking Manual.
9. Madajewicz, M. (1998) Capital for the poor: the effect of wealth on the optimal loan contract. Working Paper, Stockholm School of Economics

10. Stiglitz, Joseph and A Weiss (1981) "Credit rationing in markets with imperfect information". In American Economic Review 71 (3), pp. 393-410
11. Stiglitz, Joseph (1990) "Peer Monitoring and Credit Markets". In The World Bank Economic Review, Vol. 4, No. 3, pp. 351-366
12. Varian, H (1990) "Monitoring agents with other agents". In Journal of Institutional and Theoretical Economics, p. 146.
13. Ana Marr (2002) Studying Group Dynamic: Alternative Analytical framework for the study of Microfinance Impact on Poverty Reduction. Journal of International Development. Vol. 14, pp. 511–534 (2002)

16

Microfinance Institutions (MFIs): A Study on its Dynamics in a District of Assam

Arup Roy, Chandana Goswami and Sujit Sikidar

ABSTRACT: *Microfinance has raised the standard of living of the poor and brought significant increased productivity among the rural poor. The MFIs have reached out to over 33 million clients whereas the potential is around 100 million. Looking at the number of poor yet to be served by microfinance, the growth potential is huge. The process of growth of MFIs must capture the hope and aspirations of the poor. Microfinance sector can manage its business but addressing poverty is a major challenge. With the changes of microfinance phenomenon, regulation, performance management and inbuilt accountability has become critical because MFIs operate in diverge forms in different places with entirely different operational mechanisms. It should be reflected in terms of transparency, governance, operational norms, disclosure norms and social audits. In this paper we try to understand the micro-credit delivery system of the Microfinancial Institutions (MFIs) in a District of Assam which will help to understand the operational mechanism and tries to find out the micro-credit assessment and micro-credit monitoring system that is practiced in Assam.*

Introduction

Microfinance—since the works of McKinnon (1973) and Shaw (1973)—gained importance, especially as a tool for socio-economic development. Microfinance has become, in recent years, a fulcrum for development initiatives for the poor, particularly in the Third World countries. It has been practiced in varying forms in different countries and has come to be regarded as an important tool for poverty alleviation. The process of growth of Microfinancial Institutions (MFIs) must capture the hope and aspirations of the poor. Microfinance sector can manage its business but addressing poverty is a major challenge. The microfinance revolution, particularly the success stories of institutions like Grameen Bank in Bangladesh, Banco Sol in Bolivia, and Bank Rakyat in Indonesia, attracted several economists to study microfinance in the latter half of the 1990s. Some studies argue that microfinance has very beneficial economic and social impacts (Holcombe, 1995; Hossain, 1988; Otero and Rhyne, 1994; Remenyi, 1991; Schuler, Hashemi and Riley, 1997).

Among Asian countries, the root of microfinance originates in ancient India as indigenous finance in the form of moneylenders, Chit Funds and Rotating Savings and Credit Associations (ROSCA). Money-lending became an organized and subsequently regulated profession in India around 1,700-2,200 years ago. In 1975, the government introduced a new network of government-owned Regional Rural Banks (RRBs), regulated and supervised banking institutions with a low capital base of around $250,000, each covering with its branches a designated service area of 1-3 districts. In 1982, NABARD started its operation for providing credit for the promotion of agriculture, small scale industries, cottage and village industries, handicrafts, and other rural crafts and other allied economic activities in rural areas with a view to promoting IRDP and securing prosperity of rural areas. NABARD has changed the philosophy of rural finance from credit-driven to savings-oriented. A need for more innovative financial instrument was felt which could incorporate some amount of flexibility for the poor. In 1991, NABARD entered into a policy dialogue with RBI to make preparations for a pilot project linking informal groups (SHGs) to banks. In comparison to the Grameen Bank model, NABARD found that "the SHG linkage model appears more sustainable and appropriate in the Indian conditions where (India has) in place a vast network of rural bank branches... (and) SHGs which are functioning on their own and waiting to be linked to the banking system" (Nanda, 1995).

The past two years have seen a series of critical developments in the Indian MFI sector. These are both positive and negative. On the positive side, MFIs have started to leverage their new fund management expertise to achieve scale and to spread their operations well beyond their traditional operational areas. Thus, rating data from a large sample of the leading MFIs shows that these have recorded high growth rates of the order of 80% per annum in terms of numbers of borrowers and around 40% per annum in terms of portfolio reaching from 300,000 to one million clients each. Also positive is that a significant part of that expansion has been either to less developed areas of the country— Orissa, Jharkhand, Rajasthan, Madhya Pradesh, Tripura, Assam—or to areas such as Maharashtra that also have substantial numbers of low income families in some regions even if their overall development indicators are not as low as those for the other states (Sector Report on Microfinance in India, 2007).

On the negative side, MFIs have been under attack from politicians and bureaucrats in some of their traditional operational areas in Andhra Pradesh and Karnataka (with questions even being asked in Orissa). Their loan recovery practices have been questioned and their interest rates described as exorbitant. The related publicity has vitiated the credit culture in the traditional microfinance states forcing a lowering of interest rates and increasing the necessary level of loan loss reserves and provisioning. Operationally, the increase in costs has been compounded by the spread of the operations of individual MFIs simultaneously (and inorganically) to a number of non-traditional states. This has put pressure on operating efficiency and resulted in slowing the trend to lowering unit costs.

Microfinance is one of the many intervention strategies for socio-economic development, poverty alleviation, income generation, employment promotion and entrepreneurial development among the poor. MFIs not only provide risk capital and financial services to the rural poor but also act as a launching pad for social development livelihood intervention. The poor require a range of financial services, such as opportunities to safeguard earned income and credit to enable them to maintain minimum levels of consumption throughout the year. The rural economy is entirely different from urban economics and the majority of poor people live and work by numerous small transactions. The magnitude of the financial transactions is quite small but the frequency is high. These small transactions are essential components of rural livelihood. MFIs are such type of organizations which offer financial solutions to the very small needs of the poor.

Microfinance, over the years, has raised the standard of living of the poor and brought significant increased productivity among the rural poor. The MFIs have reached out to over 33 million clients whereas the potential is around 100 million. Looking at the number of poor yet to be served by microfinance, the growth potential is huge. The major strength of an MFI is its ability to unite growth and help poor people to move out of their poverty. Poor people are defined in monetary terms by the World Bank according to two poverty thresholds: 1$ or 2$ a day *per capita* (CGAP, 2003). According to the 1997 World Micro-credit Summit, the poorest are those who belong to the lower half of the group of people who live beneath the 1$ a day *per capita* poverty threshold. The best manner to help the poor accessing financial services causes debates between *welfarists* and *institutionalists*. Although they share the objective of poverty alleviation, the former emphasizes impact on the borrower as the core mission of MFIs whereas the latter aims at integrating microfinance in the financial markets (Cornée, 2007). This "microfinance schism" (Morduch, 1998) stands as a trade-off between targeting the poor and ensuring the profitability of MFIs. There are many options that have the potential to reduce poverty and increase economic growth and profit making capacities. Microfinance is one of the options which can reduce poverty and increase economic growth in a sustainable manner in a people-centered approach.

Need for the Study

Microfinance industry is an emerging industry and growing at a fast rate, spreading its benefits mostly to the poor people. With the changes of microfinance phenomenon, regulation, performance management and inbuilt accountability has become critical because MFIs operate in diverge forms in different places with entirely different operational mechanism. It should be reflected in terms of transparency, governance, operational norms, disclosure norms and social Audits. In India, NABARD has been involved since 1990s for the development of microfinance industry. India as a whole is performing well in this industry. The average outreach rate in India is 5%. But for the state of Assam, it is less than 2%. Thus we see there is lot of potential for the growth of microfinance industry in Assam. In case of Assam, it is only in 1997-98 that microfinance movement had really begun and has been rapidly picking up since then. Over the years, the growth in the number of members of the SHG linked banks and the amount of credit disbursement of MFIs has been quite impressive. Nobel Laureate Professor Muhammed Yunus has agreed to extend his help to Government of Assam for introducing a microcredit scheme for upliftment of the standard of living of the people of the rural areas of the State. In this context, the present study tries to understand the micro-credit delivery system of the Micro Financial Institutions (MFIs) in Sonitpur District of the State of Assam. The study also helps to understand the operational mechanism and tries to find out the micro-credit assessment and micro-credit monitoring system that is practiced in Assam.

Research Methodology

The entire study is conducted in Sonitpur district of Assam. The district that has been selected to launch the study is Sonitpur District. Sonitpur District is considered because, according to a study by the RBI in 2008, this district has the largest population outside the ambit of the formal banking system in Assam. Recently, Government of Assam has drafted a micro-credit project to be implemented in Sonitpur District in a period of three years in two phases with an amount of Rs 835 lakh. So it is important to understand the mechanism and performance of MFIs in this place as very few studies have been conducted in this area. The objective of the present study is to find out the latest microfinance practices in Sonitpur District in Assam. The study tries to evaluate the micro-credit delivery systems of the various MFIs in reaching the dual objectives of outreach and profitability in the state of Assam. The present study is conducted during the period January 2009 and June 2009, using qualitative research tools – principally the case study methodology. This was supplemented by quantitatives research tools through collection of both primary and secondary data. Various social research tools like interviews and focus group discussion were used for the study. Rapid assessment was done to understand the depth of the underlying issues. The method involves direct observation, informal conversation, key-informant interviews and participant observation concerned with employment scenario, entrepreneurship scenario, potential areas which would involve large labour forces, entrepreneurship related behaviours, knowledge, attitudes and practices (KAP), crucial entry points for intervention and local responses to entrepreneurship development. Conceptual issues included the structure of incentives, the complex relationship between cognition and behaviour, and how people respond to the components and factors of labour and entrepreneurship issues. Cases were analyzed through financial ratios and simple statistical tools. The sampling was done by Judgment Sampling Technique. Since only few NGOs/MFIs are working in Sonitpur District, and not all are involved in micro-credit, only three MFIs are selected viz., Sonali SHG Unnayan Samiti, Mahila Sakti Kendra (MASK) and GRAMIN (Microfinance) in Sonitpur District which have been involved in micro-credit operations from 2005 onwards.

Organization Philosophy, Equity Shareholders and Structure of MFIs

In this study, we have surveyed three organizations: (i) Sonali SHG Unnayan Samiti, (ii) Mahila Sakti Kendra (MASK), and (iii) GRAMIN (Microfinance).

Each of these has its own organisational philosophy and operational structure:

Sonali SHG Unnayan Samiti (MFI) is a federation of Self-Help Groups (SHGs) and was established on 1st April 2000. Subsequently it was registered as an NGO on 8th February 2005 under Societies Registration Act, 1960. The SHGs that formed the federation in April 2005 were originally promoted by 122 SHGs with 1,830 SHG members. The aim of Sonali MFI is organizing dedicational service in the field of vocational, productive, financial programmes and activities through self-support system and means along with the target of inculcating congenital socio-economic, ecological atmosphere in the society. At present, 122 SHGs are the shareholders of Sonali MFI. Minimum and maximum number of members in a SHG according to Swarnajayanti Gram Swarozgar Yojna (SGSY) is 10 and 20, respectively. Hence, total number of equity shareholders is 1,830. The General Body Members are 244 from 122 SHGs. The members are the Presidents and Secretaries from each of the 122 SHGs. Executive Committee members is 31. There is a Financial Advisory board which distributes duties and responsibilities of members/staffs/office bearers and has the sole authority to prepare any other financial programmes.

MASK, a federation of Self-Help Groups (SHGs), was established on 1st April 2002 and was registered on 8th February 2006 under Societies Registration Act, 1960. The SHGs that formed the federation in April 2002 were originally promoted by Gana Chetana Samaj (GCS), Balipara. The vision of MASK is to empower the poor and marginalized, especially women, to bring about social change in their status, and transformation in society. At present there are 86 SHGs comprising approximately 1,500 members in MASK. All the members contribute Rs.20 each per month to their respective SHG and the total amount so collected forms a source of finance for the SHG to their individual members.

All these SHG members are the equity shareholders of MASK. The seed money of MASK was Rs.10,00,000. This money was collected from numerous donors from Mumbai and some amount from the local donors. The present President and the Secretary Mr. Eliza Boro and Mr. Sushila Orang, respectively, went to Mumbai for a seminar and requested for some seed money to help the poor people through microfinance in some seminars and conferences. They received a positive response and formed a corpus of ten lakhs. This money is used to help the various SHG members through microfinance if the applicant's respective SHG is having insufficient fund. The Governing Body has the authority to take principal key decisions and it consists of 7 members. Moreover, there is a General Body comprising of 26 members. The Area Co-ordinators Committee of MASK is the loan sanctioning authority. Two Governing Body members of MASK, along with the Area Coordinators representing clusters of SHGs, form the Area Co-ordinators Committee. The President or the Vice-President or the Secretary of MASK will be in the Committee along with any other Governing Body members of MASK.

GRAMIN was founded in 1995 with the aim of organizing the rural people into SHG, motivating them to develop their socio-economic conditions by engaging in income generating schemes, organizing skill development training for them, linking them with banks for their microfinance requirements and arranging links for marketing their products. However, over the years, it was found that the pace of development was rather sluggish and in most cases it was because of non-availability of bank loans for investment and, in some cases, because of lack of proper training for the chosen activity. It was for these reasons that GRAMIN decided to open its microfinance operations in 2005 and, by the end of the year, GRAMIN Microfin had a outstanding of INR 4.6 million. GRAMIN is for rural income generation, for socio-economic development of the rural people, for betterment of the society; and thus GRAMIN Microfin has decided to be the most sought after microfinance Institute in the region. The aim of GRAMIN is to be growth oriented and client friendly microfinance product and service provider to the poor and prospective entrepreneurs in a transparent and equitable manner with respect to its client.

The Vision of GRAMIN (Microfin) is to emerge as the most sought after and trusted MFI in Assam by 2020. There are 12 members in the Governing Body of GRAMIN. The Governing Body comprises of Chairman-cum-CEO and General Manager at the top hierarchy. Below them are the Operational Manager, HR Manager and Finance and Accounts Manager. Next level is Zonal Managers followed by Branch Managers. The Branch Managers work with the Credit Officers (also called Field Officers). GRAMIN has borrowed the seed money from APEX Bank, ICICI Bank, and SIDBI.

Thus we see that each of these three MFIs has uniqueness in their philosophy, fund raising style, and organisational structure.

Microfinance Products and Services

Sonali MFI has three range of products—Fixed Deposit, Recurring Deposit, and Micro-credit. The recurring deposits amount starts from Rs.5 to Rs.200 daily. The Loan Officer collects the recurring deposits instalments visiting the place of the beneficiaries either daily or weekly. The Micro-credit scheme is again divided into two forms—Demand Loan (DL) and Advanced Term Loan (ATL). The quantum of Demand Loan is generally 80 % of the total deposit in the form of either Recurring Deposit or Fixed Deposit and is disbursed within an hour. This Demand Loan largely helps the beneficiaries for their urgent medical and educational requirements. The other form of loan given by Sonali Microfinance is the Advanced Term Loan (ATL).

The Advanced Term Loan (ATL) amount ranges from minimum Rs.5,000 to maximum Rs.20,000. In some special cases, if the loan demand by the beneficiary is more than Rs.20,000, say Rs.40,000, then the loan is sanctioned in the name of two members of the same family. Duration of the loan is very much flexible in nature. The loan officers ask the beneficiaries about how much they can afford to repay from the loan amount per month and, accordingly, the duration of the loan is fixed. Minimum period of the loan is 3 months. Any beneficiary can repay the loan even after a single day, but an interest of at least 3 months has to be paid.

MASK offers only micro-credit to the members of its member SHGs. The quantum of loan given to the tune of 1:4 of the group's total capital. For the first time loan is given up to a limit of Rs.10,000, for the second time, the loan is in the ratio of 1:3 and the third time it is in the ratio of 1:4 of the groups capital. The maximum limit is 1:4 of the group's capital. Loans are given for a maximum period of three years. The Area Coordinators Committee has the authority to sanction loans up to Rs.1,00,000. Any application for a loan above Rs.1,00,000 will be decided by the Governing Body of the MASK.

GRAMIN, on the other hand, offers micro-credit to the members of SHGs, Joint Liability Groups (JLG), Individuals and Businessmen. For the members of SHGs and JLGs the amount of loan starts from Rs.3,000 with a maximum amount of Rs.5,000 to each member. But for financially sound individuals and businessmen, GRAMIN grants loan maximum up to Rs.25,000. There is a fixed repayment period of 50 weeks for the beneficiaries of the loans. In case of any earlier loan settlement, the beneficiary has to pay full interest of 50 weeks.

Microfinance and Interest Rates

Sonali MFI charges a flat rate of 2% interest per month on the principal amount Therefore, the annual rate of interest is 24% and the interest is charged on reducing balances. For example, if the loan amount is Rs.10,000 and if the beneficiary agrees to repay the principal amount of Rs.500 per month, then his loan repayment schedule is given in Table 1:

TABLE 1

Repayment Pattern

No. of Months	Principal	Interest	EMI	Balance Amount
1	500	200	700	9500
2	500	190	690	9000
3	500	180	680	8500
4	500	170	670	8000
5	500	160	660	7500
6	500	150	650	7000
7	500	140	640	6500
8	500	130	630	6000
9	500	120	620	5500
10	500	110	610	5000
11	500	100	600	4500
12	500	90	590	4000
13	500	80	580	3500
14	500	70	570	3000
15	500	60	560	2500
16	500	50	550	2000
17	500	40	540	1500
18	500	30	530	1000
19	500	20	520	500
20	500	10	510	0

Thus, Total Loan Taken = Rs.10,000

Total Interest Paid = Rs.2,100

Therefore, Effective Rate of interest paid by the beneficiaries

= (Total Interest Paid/Total Amount of Loan) * 100

= (Rs.2,100/Rs.10,000) * 100 = 21 %

Thus we find that the effective rate of interest is 21% which is 1.75% per month.

Loan Duration = Total Loan Taken / Affordable Amount

= Rs.10,000 / Rs.500 = 20 instalment

MASK charges an interest rate of 0.5% per month which is around 6% per annum on reducing balances. Following the same procedure above, the effective rate of interest is found to be 5.25% per annum. Interest has to be paid on quarterly basis. MASK can give loan at such a low interest rate because the loan is given out of the seed money Rs.10,00,000 which is collected from the donors and this amount need not to be repaid.

GRAMIN (Microfinance) offers different rates of interest for different categories of beneficiaries. An interest rate of 18% per annum is charged from the SHG members whereas 24% per annum interest rate is charged from individuals and businessmen on reducing balances. The interest charged to the JLG loan is flat 15% per annum on reducing balance. The mode of payment of interest and principal is weekly for the JLG members and monthly for the SHGs, Individuals and Businessmen.

Prerequisites for Microfinance

Sonali MFI provides loan only to the persons who are members of the society and the membership period should be at least 6 months old irrespective of any amount of their deposit.

MASK offers loans in the form of Micro-credit Assistance only to the SHGs and not directly to individuals. Loans are given only after a year of formation of a group. The groups must have an experience of at least six months in internal lending (i.e., from its own resources). Once any SHG qualifies the above criteria, then the group will be rated based on some parameters. If the group secures 75% and above, then only it is eligible for the loan.

For GRAMIN (Microfinance) the eligibility criteria vary for different categories of beneficiaries. For loan given to JLG and SHG members, the beneficiary has to be a member of the respective groups. There are no fixed criteria for the loan to be given to individuals and businessmen. Credit Officers along with the Branch Managers decides the individual creditworthiness of the borrower and forwards the loan application to the higher authorities.

Micro-credit Delivery System

When a person seeks a loan from Sonali Microfinance, he is referred to the nearest Area Collector (also called the Agent). At present, Sonali Microfinance has more than 315 Area Collectors. Then the person contacts the Area Collector and writes an application with his assistance. The Area Collector is a local agent and generally knows the loan applicant and his creditworthiness. Then depending upon the applicant's creditworthiness, Area Collector forwards the application to Head office which is located at Khelmati. There is an Advisory Council comprising of 7 members and the Council has the authority to sanction the loan. Initially the Council again forwards the application form to the Loan Officer and asks them to verify the actual loan requirement. The Loan Officers then visits the family of the applicant. He surveys the authenticity and genuineness of the loan amount and type of business proposed to be conducted. Once the Loan Officers are satisfied with the genuineness of the loan requirement and success of the proposed business, then the application is forwarded to the Advisory Council who in turn sanctions the loan. Then, if the loan is sanctioned, the applicant is asked to come to the Head office with relevant documents to collect the loan amount. Documents are in the form of residence certificate given by Gaon Panchayat Mukhiya, electricity bill, photograph, ration card representing the loan applicant's identity and address proof. The applicant is also asked to bring a Stamp Paper on which an agreement is made between the loanee and the Sonali Microfinance and the required loan amount is delivered to the beneficiary.

When any SHG member requires loan from MASK, the loan application form has to submit to the Area Coordinator of the respective Cluster. MASK forms SHG in various villages in Clusters. The number of members in a SHG ranges from 10 to 20. If there are more members, then MASK forms different SHGs in a village and combines them into a single Cluster. The Area Coordinator will handover the application to a field staff of MASK. The field staff will, in turn, submit a report on a prescribed format on the functioning of the group after interacting with the members and also inspect its books of accounts and various relevant records. The field staff will then return the application form with his comments on the report and forward it to the respective Area Co-ordinator. The Area Coordinator will then present the application along with his comments at the Area Coordinators' Committee Meeting which is held once a month. The members present in the Area Coordinators' Committee Meeting will seek for explanation and clarification about the authenticity of the loan. After a through discussion, a resolution is taken. In case the group has not been assessed, an assessment of the group is done based on the NABARD format. However, a loan could be sanctioned conditionally before the assessment report of the group. Loans are given by cheque. Only in emergencies like hospitalization etc. loans are given in cash based on a request made by the President and the Secretary of the SHG and the formalities are completed later. The Area coordinator of the respective group informs the SHG of the Area Coordinator's decision. In case the loan is sanctioned, the President and the Secretary of the Group would collect the cheque from the the Head office of MASK within a week on any working day from 9 am to 11 am. Before receiving the loan all the members of the group will have to sign a Promissory Note in a prescribed format. The President and Secretary has to affix their stamp and sign on the reverse of the cheque, payment voucher and repayment schedule of MASK. This completes the micro-credit delivery process to its beneficiaries.

GRAMIN (Microfinance) adopts different mechanism of micro-credit delivery to its beneficiaries. When any category of loan application—whether it is from SHG or JLG or Individual or Businessmen—is received in the Branch Office, the application is forwarded to the Credit Officer who works under direct supervision of the Branch Manager. The Credit Officer visits the place of the loan applicant and interacts with his neighbors and family members and tries to find the authenticity of his loan requirements. Once the Credit Officer is convinced about the genuineness of the loan, then the Branch Manager along with him again visits the place of the applicant. The Branch Manager then investigates about the past credit history of the applicant from his neighbours.

He also evaluates the business model proposed by the applicant with respect to the current market scenario and finds out whether the business would be profitable or not. Once the Branch Manager is satisfied with the authenticity of the loan requirement and profitability of the proposed business, he forwards the application to the Operational Manager. Operational Manager puts his comments and forwards the application to the General Manager. Finally, the Chairman-cum-CEO approves the loan. The Branch Manager is informed about the decision and the applicant receives the loan amount earliest within 2 weeks, but definitely within a maximum period of 12 weeks.

Micro-credit Monitoring

In Sonali MFI, micro-credit monitoring is done quarterly. If it is found that a beneficiary is not making any repayments of the loan for the last three months, then a notice is sent to the Area Collector/Agent through whom the loan process was initiated. The Area Collector investigates about the matter and asks the beneficiary to pay the monthly instalments within 15 days. When the 15 days' time period is over, then the Loan Officer again makes 2 to 3 visits and asks the beneficiary to pay the instalments. Even after this, if the payment is not made, then the Area Collector sends the Executive Group comprising of women members of the SHGs and pressurizes the beneficiary for the repayment of the loan.

The micro-credit monitoring agent of the MASK is called "Animator". Every month one Animator looks after 20 SHGs. At present MASK has 8 Animators for monitoring the loans that are given to the beneficiaries. The Animator plays a vital role in opening bank account, conflict management among the SHG members, Cash Book handling and preparation of Ledger and Trial Balances. Animator prepares the monthly supervision and monitoring report of the SHGs. Every Saturday staff meeting is held for regular and effective micro-credit monitoring. Generally, the meeting of the Presidents and Secretaries of all SHG is conducted twice in a year. There is a system of cross-checking of the performance of Animators. In Area Coordinators' Meeting, an assessment of the Animators is also done. From 2005, MASK has no record of any default loans till May 2009.

GRAMIN (Microfinance) regularly monitors the present status of all its loans to different categories of beneficiaries by conducting a weekly meeting. GRAMIN is really dynamic in micro-credit monitoring in the sense that all the key officials starting from Zonal Manager, Operation Manager, HR Manager, Finance & Accounts Officer and the Chairman-cum-CEO meets every week for better and effective micro-credit monitoring of the loans disbursed; and they also critically analyse the repayment schedule of the beneficiaries. Besides this weekly meeting, the Branch Managers from all the Zones meet once every month in the Head Office and discuss the various problematic loan issues. The Branch Manager monitors the loan repayment regularly. In case of any non payment of weekly or monthly loan instalments, he discusses and tries to find out the reason of non-payment with the beneficiary.

Repayment Rates

It is the repayment rate of MFIs that has attracted the attention of everyone in the world related to the financial system. When the professionally managed commercial banking system carries huge amount of non performing assets (NPA) around the world, the MFIs of Bangladesh showed a repayment rate of 98-100%. The repayment rates of the beneficiaries of the MFIs are most important criteria to measure the efficiency of the entire microfinance system. Repayment rate helps in understanding the behaviour of clients and performance of the institution for a particular on-going period. So far as India is concerned, only 46.5% of the banks has a recovery rate of more than 95% which is evident from Table 2.

TABLE 2

Recovery Performance of Indian Banks

Agency	Total no. of Banks reported recovery	No. of banks based on percentage distribution of recovery perfomance of bank loans to SHRs as on 31 March 2008			
		95%	80-94%	50-79%	less than
Commercial Banks (Public Sector)	25	11	5	8	–
Comercial Banks (Private Section)	8	7	–	1	–
Regional Rural Banks (RRBs)	70	22	25	17	6
Co-operative Banks	726	113	39	51	23
TOTAL	329	153	70	77	29
Percentage of Banks		46.5	21.3	23.4	8.8

Source: NABARD Report 2007-2008

TABLE 3

Repayment Rates of the SONALI, MASK and GRAMIN

Period	Sonali MFI	MASK	GRAMIN
2007-08	98 %	100 %	81 %
2006-07	95 %	100 %	80 %
2005-06	100 %	100 %	79 %

Thus we see the repayment rates of the beneficiaries of the three MFIs are substantially high. Sonali and MASK has an average repayment rate for three years as 97.67% and 100%, whereas GRAMIN—though it is more professionally managed—has got a lower repayment rate of 80%. Thus we can say that the repayment behaviour of the clients of these MFIs are regular and positive and this, in turn, reveals that the loans were utilized for the purpose it was taken and has promoted economic productivity in the concerned places. One advantage of the MFIs over the banks is that they know their beneficiaries more closely compared to the bank knowing their clients. The constant monitoring and peer group pressure are also likely to have contributed regular repayment of loans.

Overall Status of MFIs

The overall status of the MFIs can be had from the (next page) Table 4.

Relationship Building of MFIs

The success of these MFIs has become possible because of their strong contacts and links with other institutions and government machineries. All members regularly visit the block office of the local government for information and have a good rapport with the Block Development Officer. They regularly visit the DRDA and local NGOs. Seeing their interest, various government agencies and NGOs conducted training programmes on goat-raising, piggery, fishery, duckery, horticulture, pisciculture, dairy farming, Golden Grass cultivation and processing. In most meetings, the Block Development Officer, Asst. Agriculture Officer and other govt. bureaucrats/technocrats along with NGOs participated. These NGO-MFIs have established a good relationship with the developmental funding agencies. For example SONALI MFI has a regular contact with DRDA, MASK receives assistance from NABARD in micro-credit monitoring and assessment and GRAMIN (Microfinance) has also established a good relationship with SIDBI, ICICI and APEX Bank. GRAMIN has taken a loan of Rs.1.25 Cr, Rs. 2.5 Cr. and Rs. 0.5 Cr. from APEX Bank, ICICI Bank and SIDBI, respectively.

MFI Capacity Building for Sustainability

The MFIs feel that participation and interaction with external bodies and agencies would reduce the inequalities in their social system. Consequently, they keep good contacts with DRDA, Block Offices, local NGOs and NABARD. In turn, these agencies provided training in pisciculture, piggery, goat-raising, duckery, horticulture, dairy farm management, cultivation, squash and pickle-making.

Conclusion

Thus the above analysis reveals that the innovation of MFIs aims not only to facilitate the promotion and protection of livelihood by providing a range of customized financial products to rural residents but also to include them in the financial system and promote entrepreneurial skills. To fulfil this aim,

TABLE 4

Summary Information of SONALI, MASK and GRAMIN

Particulars	SONALI	MASK	GRAMIN
Date of Initiation	February 2005	February 2006	October 2005
Members (in Nos.)	1,800	1,500	12
Total No. of Staff (in Nos.)	20	8	24
Total No. of Agents (in Nos.)	315	NIL	NIL
Yearly Interest Rate (in %)	24	6	18-24
Total Borrowers (in Nos.)	15,000	300	7,229
No of Women Borrowers (in Nos.)	12,000	210	4,340
No of Male Borrowers (in Nos.)	3,000	90	2,889
Corpus Fund (in INR)	NIL	71,051	15,50,800
Member Contribution (in INR)	16,860	10,950	59,98,141
Grant Received (in INR)	NIL	10,000	12,87,345
Cash in Bank (in INR)	2,49,885	179,194	33,77,239
Cash in Hand (in INR)	1,44,096	134,489	1,38,066
Principal Loan Recovery (in INR)	3,640,429	251,700	1,91,63,423
Bank Loan Received (in INR)	NIL	NIL	1,12,41,353
Total Loan Distribution (in INR)	57,41,250	1,14,000	8,803,500
Principal Loan Repaid to the Bank (in INR)	NIL	NIL	1,55,59,318
Loan Portfolio Outstanding (in INR)	86,56,147	115,501	2,12,43,563
Bank Interest Received (in INR)	64,901	1,823	2,60,108
Interest & Fee Expenses (in INR)	8,095	2809	1,51,317
Loan Processing Fees (in INR)	55,785	72,029	2,57,957
Insurance Premium (in INR)	NIL	NIL	70,063
Administrative Expenses (in INR)	1,15,554	62,208	10,18,345
Fixed Assets (in INR)	4,40,969	5,57,284	6,17,270
Net Income (in INR)527,870	94,579	8,41,556	
Current Asset (in INR)	94,10,879	NA	57,73,042
Current Liability (in INR)	1,00,37,316	NA	7,14,045
Staff Salary (in INR)	6,12,385	49,000	1,24,200

microfinance was strategically channelized through self-help groups. The MFIs are clearly different in nature and they significantly differ in their way to reach poor and maintain sustainability. The micro-credit assessment, micro-credit delivery and micro-credit monitoring system is different for all the MFIs under study. Sonali and MASK works closely with the beneficiaries and is more related with the SHGs than GRAMIN which is more professionally managed group. Sonali, on the other hand, is following a different model, offering recurring deposits and fixed deposits and financially more self-reliant successfully working without any subsidies. Self-help groups (SHGs) are used extensively as an effective tool for poverty alleviation, empowerment and livelihood options and have become a fast-developing commercially viable business proposition.

Bibliography

1. Asian Development Bank (2000), Finance for the Poor: Microfinance Development Strategy. Asian Development Bank.
2. Chua, Ronald T. and Gilberto M. Llanto (1997), Assessing the Efficiency and Outreach of Microfinance Schemes, Enterprise and Cooperative Development Department, International Labour Office.
3. Ghate P., (2008), Microfinance in India—a state of the sector report, 2007, Microfinance India.
4. Gutierrez-Nieto, B., Serrano-Cinca, C., and Mar Molinero, C. (2005), Microfinance Institutions and Efficiency. The International Journal of Management Science. Article in Press.
5. Hudon, M. (2006). Subsidies and financial performances of the microfinance institutions: Does management matter? Universit Libre de Bruxelles (ULB).
6. NABARD Report: Microfinance in India 2007-2008.
7. Robinson, Marguerite S, (1998), Microfinance: the Paradigm Shift From Credit Delivery to Sustainable Financial Intermediation, in Strategic Issues in Microfinance, Ashgate Publishing: Aldershot.
8. Sanjay, S. and Sinha, F. (2002). Sustainability and Development Evaluating the Performance of Indian Microfinance. Beyond Micro-Credit: Putting Development Bank into Microfinance (pp. 263). New Delhi: Vistaar Puplication.
9. Temu, A. E. and G. P. Hill (1994). "Some Lessons from Informal Financial Practices in Rural Tanzania." African Review of Money Finance and Banking (1/2): pp. 141-165.

17

Microfinance Institutions in India: An Overview

Gino A Sangma

Abstract: *The conventional financial institutions seldom lend down-market to serve the needs of low-income families and women-headed households. They are very often denied access to credit for any purpose, making the discussion of the level of interest rate and other terms of finance irrelevant. The lack of access to credit for the poor is attributable to practical difficulties arising from the discrepancy between the mode of operation followed by financial institutions and the economic characteristics and financing needs of low-income households. However, the income of many self-employed households is not stable, regardless of its size. A large number of small loans are needed to serve the poor, but lenders prefer dealing with large loans in small numbers to minimize administration costs. The paper is an exploration on microfinance institutions viz, "Mainstream" and "Alternative" Microfinance Institutions, formal institutions and semi-formal institutions.*

Introduction

Micro Finance is defined as the "provision of thrift, credit and other financial services such as money transfer and micro-insurance products for the poor in rural, semi urban or urban areas, to enable them to raise their income levels and improve living standards". Microfinance refers to the entire range of financial services such as small savings, money transfers, insurance services, production and investment credit extended to socially and economically disadvantaged segments of society and also includes the need for skill upgradation and entrepreneurial development that would enable them to overcome poverty. Microfinance provides credit support in small doses along with training and other related services to people who are able to undertake economic activities.

Microfinance rests on the following principles:

- Self-employment/enterprise formation is a viable means for poverty alleviation.

- Lack of access to capital assets/credit is a constraint for existing and potential micro-enterprises.
- The poor are able to save despite their low-level and sporadic incomes.

In the Indian context terms like "small and marginal farmers", "rural artisans" and "economically weaker sections" have been used to broadly define microfinance customers. At present, a large part of micro finance activity is confined to credit only. Women constitute a vast majority of users of micro-credit and savings services.

For several decades, many economies—including the Indian—experimented with subsidized credit for the poor. But the only tangible outcome perhaps was the increase in Non-Performing Assets (NPA), and then came the realization that the core issue for the poor was access to credit rather than the cost of credit. In fact, one of the contributions of microfinance can possibly be the 'end of interest rate debate'.

Microfinance has proved time and again that it is the access and not interest rates that are a constraint for the poor. Another discovery followed—the poor can and will save, and can indeed use a wide range of financial services such as remittances facilities and insurance products. The most well-known and cited international example of a micro-credit institution is the Grameen Bank in Bangladesh. But there are numerous others. Even during the Asian financial crisis, Bank Rayat Indonesia not only survived but also thrived; as did BancoSol in Bolivia.

Microfinance and Poverty Alleviation

Financial services enable the poor to leverage their initiative, accelerating the process of building incomes, assets and economic security, as most of the poor people manage to mobilize resources to develop their enterprises and their dwellings slowly over time. However, conventional finance institutions seldom lend down-market to serve the needs of low-income families and women-headed households. They are very often denied access to credit for any purpose, making the discussion of the level of interest rate and other terms of finance irrelevant. Therefore the fundamental problem is not so much of unaffordable terms of loan as the lack of access to credit itself *(Kim, 1995)*.The lack of access to credit for the poor is attributable to practical difficulties arising from the discrepancy between the mode of operation followed by financial institutions and the economic characteristics and financing needs of low-income households. However, the income of many self-employed households is not stable, regardless of its size. A large number of small loans are needed to serve the poor, but lenders prefer dealing with large loans in small numbers to minimize administration costs. They also look for collateral with a clear title—which many low-income households do not have. In addition bankers tend to consider low income households a bad risk imposing exceedingly high information monitoring costs on operation.

Over the last ten years, however, successful experiences in providing finance to small entrepreneur and producers demonstrate that poor people, when given access to responsive and timely financial services at market rates, repay their loans and use the proceeds to increase their income and assets. This is not surprising since the only realistic alternative for them is to borrow from informal market at an interest much higher than market rates. Community banks, NGOs and grassroots savings and credit groups around the world have shown that these micro-enterprise loans can be profitable for borrowers and for the lenders, making microfinance one of the most effective poverty reducing strategies. To the extent that microfinance institutions become financially viable, self-sustaining, and integral to the communities in which they operate, they have the potential to attract more resources and expand services to clients. Despite the success of microfinance institutions, only about 2% of world's roughly 500 million small entrepreneurs are estimated to have access to financial services (Barry et al, 1996). Although there is demand for credit by poor and women at market interest rates, the volume of financial transaction of microfinance institution must reach a certain level before their financial operation becomes self sustaining. In other words, although microfinance offers a promising institutional structure to provide access to credit to the poor, the scale problem needs to be resolved so that it can reach the vast majority of potential customers who demand access to credit at market rates. The question then is how micro-enterprise lending geared to providing short term capital to small businesses in the informal sector can be sustained as an integral part of the financial sector and how their financial services can be further expanded using the principles, standards and modalities that have proven to be effective.

To be successful, financial intermediaries that provide services and generate domestic resources must have the capacity to meet high performance standards. They must achieve excellent repayments and provide access to clients. And they must build toward operating and financial self-sufficiency and expanding client reach. In order to do so, microfinance institutions need to find ways to cut down on their administrative costs and also to broaden their resource base. Cost reductions can be achieved through simplified and decentralized loan application, approval and collection processes, for instance, through group loans which give borrowers responsibilities for much of the loan application process, allow the loan officers to handle many more clients and hence reduce costs (Otero et al, 1994).

Microfinance institutions can broaden their resource base by mobilizing savings, accessing capital markets, loan funds and effective institutional development support. A logical way to tap capital market is securitization through a corporation that purchases loans made by micro-enterprise institutions with the funds raised through the bonds issuance on the capital market. Savings facilities make large scale lending operations possible. On the other hand, studies also show that the poor operating in the informal sector do save, although not in financial assets, and, hence, value access to client-friendly savings service at least as much access to credit. Savings mobilization also makes financial institutions accountable to local shareholders. Therefore, adequate savings facilities both serve the demand for financial services by the customers and fulfil an important requirement of financial sustainability to the lenders. Microfinance institutions can either provide savings services directly through deposit taking or make arrangements with other financial institutions to provide savings facilities to tap small savings in a flexible manner (Barry 1995).

Governments should provide an enabling legal and regulatory framework which encourages the development of a range of institutions and allows them to operate as recognized financial intermediaries subject to simple supervisory and reporting requirements. Usury laws should be repelled or relaxed and microfinance institutions should be given freedom of setting interest rates and fees in order to cover operating and finance costs from interest revenues within a reasonable amount of time. Government could also facilitate the process of transition to a sustainable level of operation by providing support to the lending institutions in their early stage of development through credit enhancement mechanisms or subsidies.

One way of expanding the successful operation of microfinance institutions in the informal sector is through strengthened linkages with their formal sector counterparts. A mutually beneficial partnership should be based on comparative strengths of each sector. Informal sector microfinance institutions have comparative advantage in terms of small transaction costs achieved through adaptability and flexibility of operations (Ghate et al, 1992). They are better equipped to deal with credit assessment of the urban poor and, hence, to absorb the transaction costs associated with loan processing. On the other hand, formal sector institutions have access to broader resource-base and high leverage through deposit mobilization (Christen et al, 1994). Therefore, formal sector finance institutions could form a joint venture with informal sector institutions in which the former provide funds in the form of equity and the later extends savings and loan facilities to the urban poor. Another form of partnership can involve the formal sector institutions refinancing loans made by the informal sector lenders. Under these settings, the informal sector institutions are able to tap additional resources as well as having an incentive to exercise greater financial discipline in their management.

Microfinance institutions could also serve as intermediaries between borrowers and the formal financial sector and on-lend funds backed by a public sector guarantee (Phelps, 1995). Business-like NGOs can offer commercial banks ways of funding micro-entrepreneurs at low cost and risk, for example, through leveraged bank-NGO-client credit lines. Under this arrangement, banks make one bulk loan to NGOs and the NGOs packages it into large number of small loans at market rates and recover them (Women's World Banking, 1994). There are many ongoing researches on this line but context specific research is needed to identify the most appropriate model. With this in mind we discuss various possible alternatives of formal-informal sector linkages in India. In this context, following strategic, institutional and connectivity issues related to microfinance arise.

Strategic Issues

- Is there a prevailing paradigm for microfinance?
- Are there clearly visible patterns across the country?
- Is there a clearly defined foundation building block such as organizing principles, gender preferences and operational imperatives?
- What are the methodological issues?

Institutional Issues

- Is there a need for a new institution?
- Should it operate all India or in a state?
- Where should it be located?
- Who can lead an institution of this sort?
- What will its contextual interconnections be?
- Who will be its beneficiaries?

Connectivity Issues

- How should the Corporate Financial Sector be involved?
- What is the role of donor agencies?
- How should communities be involved?
- Are there political issues that should be explicitly considered?
- Are there government policy issues?

MFIs in India

Microfinance has emerged as an important sector in many countries for providing financial services. Microfinance has become a global phenomenon. Government initiatives, central banks, donors, practitioners and other developing agencies that are promoting microfinance and also increasingly involving in developing suitable policy initiatives for meeting local needs. In India, a range of institutions in the public sector as well as the private sector, offers microfinance service. These can be broadly categorized into two categories namely, formal institutions and semi-formal institutions. The formal category comprises apex development financial institutions, commercial banks, regional rural banks, and cooperative banks that provide microfinance services in addition to their general banking activities and are referred to as microfinance service providers. On the other hand semi-formal category is those institutions that undertake microfinance as their main activity and are generally referred to as microfinance institutions (MFIs). While both private and public ownership are found in the case of formal financial institutions offering microfinance services, the MFIs are mainly in the private sector.

Microfinance Institutional Structure

Different organizations in this field can be classified as "Mainstream" and "Alternative" Microfinance Institutions (MFI).

Mainstream Microfinance Institutions

National Agricultural Bank for Rural Development (NABARD), Small Industries Development Bank of India (SIDBI), Housing Development Finance Corporation (HDFC), Commercial Banks, Regional Rural Banks (RRBs), the credit co-operative societies etc are some of the mainstream financial institutions involved in extending microfinance.

Problems Associated with Mainstream MFIs

To enable the reach of microfinance services to the needy, the problems associated with the legal, regulatory, organisational systems and the attitudes should be addressed to and the desired changes brought in these, to make them more effective.

The mainstream financial institutions are flush with funds and have access to enormous amounts of low cost savings deposits. Indeed, poorer the region, the lower the credit deposit ratio – most of the eastern Uttar Pradesh, Bihar, Orissa and the North-East India have Credit Deposit ratios of 20-30 percent. Thus while banks are physically present in rural areas and offer concessional interest rates, rural producers are not able to access, with the result that the rest of the deposits are finding their way into the financial sector.

Some of the main reasons for the above are:

1. **Borrower Unfriendly Products and Procedures**: With a majority of the customers being illiterate, and a majority of them needing consumption loans and a majority of them requiring high documentation and collateral security, the products are not reaching the rural poor.
2. **Inflexibility and Delay**: The rigid systems and procedures result in lot of time delay for the borrowers and de-motivate them to take further loans.
3. **High Transaction Costs, both Legitimate and Illegal**: Although the interest rate offered to the borrowers is regulated, the transaction costs in terms of the number of trips to be made, the documents to be furnished

etc. plus the illegal charges to be paid results in increasing the cost of borrowing, thus making it less attractive to the borrowers.

4. **Social Obligation and not a Business Opportunity**: Microfinance has historically been seen as a social obligation rather than a potential business opportunity.

5. **Financing to Alternative MFIs**: NABARD Act does not permit them to refinance any private sector Financial Institutions and do any direct financing (NABARD's direct lending to microfinance NGOs so far has been out of donor funds), similarly SIDBI Act restricts it from extending loans to the agricultural and allied sectors, whereas many of the members of the self-help groups are engaged in such activities.

6. **Legal and Regulatory Framework**

- The policymakers feel that farmers and poor people need low interest and subsidized credit. Thereby we have regulated interest regime for the loans up to Rs 25,000 and Rs 2,00,000/- with an interest cap of 12 percent and 13.5 percent, respectively. They believe that the poor cannot save, they are unwilling to repay the loans, and the administrative costs of servicing them are high.
- Also small loans have been used as a tool for disbursing political patronage, undermining the norm that loans must be repaid. Thus the mainstream institutions feel that these loans are risky, difficult to serve and have a low or negative net spread.
- The Regional Rural Banks Act does not permit any private share holding in any RRBs, and the Cooperative Act of all States do not permit district level cooperative banks to be set up except by the State government. The result of these two laws together is that rural credit has been a monopoly of State owned institutions.

Alternative Microfinance Institutions

These are the institutions which have come up to fill the gap between the demand and supply for microfinance. MFIs were recently defined by the Task Force as "those which provide thrift, credit and other financial services and products of very small amounts, mainly to the poor, in rural, semi-urban or urban areas for enabling them to raise their income level and improve living standards."

The MFIs can broadly be classified as:

- NGOs, which are mainly engaged in promoting self-help groups (SHGs) and their federations at a cluster level, and linking SHGs with banks, under the NABARD scheme.
- NGOs directly lending to borrowers, who are either organised into SHGs or into Grameen Bank style groups and centres. These NGOs borrow bulk funds from Rashtriya Mahila Kosh (RMK), SIDBI, Friends of Women's World Banking (FWWB) and various donors.

- MFIs which are specifically organised as cooperatives, such as the Self Employed Women's Association (SEWA) Bank and various Mutually Aided Cooperative Thrift and Credit Societies (MACTS) in AP.
- MFIs, which are organised as non-banking finance companies, such as BASIX, CFTS, Mirzapur and SHARE Microfin Ltd.

Some of the leading alternative microfinance institutions in this segment are SEWA Bank in Gujarat, which also runs federations of SHGs in nine districts; Association for Sarva Sena Farms (ASSEFA) and its Sarva Jana Seva Kosh Ltd, and Association for Social Advancement (ASA) in Tamil Nadu: SHARE, BASIX, CARE and MACTs in AP promoted among others by the Cooperative Development Foundation (CDF); MYRADA in Karnataka, which has promoted Sanghamitra, a company of its village savings and credit sanghas; PRADAN which has established a large number of SHGs and federated them under Damodar in Bihar, Sakhi Samiti in Rajasthan and the Kalanjiams in Tamil Nadu (the last now run by DHAN Foundation); ADITHI in Bihar has established Nari Nidhi, a federation of women's groups; PREM in Orissa has done the same through the Utkal Mahila Sanchay O Bikas; the Rashtriya Gramin Vikas Nidhi which runs credit and savings programs in Assam and Orissa, on the lines of the Grameen Bank, Bangladesh, as does SHARE in AP, ASA in Tamil Nadu and RDO in Manipur.

Problems for Alternative Microfinance Institutions

The main aim with which the alternative MFIs have come up is to bridge the increasing gap between the demand and supply. A vast majority of them set up as NGOs for getting access to funds as the existing practices of mainstream financing institutions such as SIDBI and NABARD and even of the institutions specially funding alternatives, such RMK and FWWB, is to fund only NGOs, or NGO promoted SHGs. As a result, the largest incentive to enter such services remains through the nonprofit route. The alternative finance institutions also have not been fully successful in reaching the needy. There are many reasons for this:

1. **Inappropriate Legal Forms:** Financial problems leading to setting up of inappropriate legal structures; NGOs invented microfinance but NGOs are not the best type of agencies to carry out microfinance on a long-term sustainable basis. If an MFI opts to become an NGO, it has the following problems:
   - The major sources of funds of NGOs are grants, which are very limited.
   - If the NGOs earn a substantial part of their income from lending activity, they violate section 11 (4) of the Income Tax Act and can lose their charitable status under Section 12.

- Moreover, NGOs do not have the appropriate financial structure for carrying out micro finance activities. NGOs being registered as societies or trusts do not have any equity capital and can never be "capital adequate".

  The other alternative for an MFI is to become a cooperative or a company. As in the long run, the primary source of lending funds for MFIs is deposits, till that stage, the MFI has to rely on borrowings. To be able to attract borrowings, the MFI has to have equity capital. Thus, it is only possible to establish a financially sustainable MFI either as a cooperative or as a company. In most States, with exception of Andhra Pradesh, Maharashtra, and Gujarat, cooperatives are politicized and state controlled and thus not an appropriate form of incorporation for an MFI. That leaves an MFI with the choice to be incorporated as a company and then become an NBFC or a Bank. The latter requires a license and a minimum start up equity of Rs. 100 crores, which is very difficult for an MFI to mobilize. The concept of Local Area Bank, with a lower start up capital of Rs. 5 crores, has not yet been operationalized by the government.

If an MFI opts to become an NBFC, it has the following problems:

- The minimum entry-level capital requirement is Rs 2 crores, wef April 1999.
- It is difficult to mobilise any borrowings from Indian Financial Institutions due to the negative image of NBFCs in general. Further, even deposit mobilisation is not possible at least for the first three years, till a satisfactory credit rating is obtained.
- That leaves the option of borrowing from foreign institutions, which is difficult in the first place, due to RBI's requirement of at least two credit ratings. Further, very few foreign institutions are willing to give rupee denominated loans. Thus the MFI taking foreign currency loans are subject to exchange risks, which they cannot handle.

2. **Lack of Commercial Orientation:** Striving to make the customers credit available at low cost with subsidies and grants, most of the alternate MFIs achieve a lot of success in their programs in the initial period, but they fail to maintain the same record in the long run because of lack of commercial orientation thus making it unsustainable.

3. **Lack of Proper Governance and Accountability**: Governance and accountability are limited in case of non-profits and need to be improved. Their boards must be made aware of their financial liabilities in case of failure. The lenders should be more stringent and insist on nominating a few directors.

4. **Isolated and Scattered**: The alternate MFIs are isolated and scattered. There is no proper coordination among them and also there is lack of information dissemination.

Conclusion

Most of the issues stated above are being tackled at various levels and the initiatives if successful, could substantially remove these hurdles. Over the last few years, the Government of India has been encouraging microfinance as an alternative to IRDP type of poverty alleviation programs because of the sustainability of microfinance activities. The issue of inappropriate legal form for MFIs is being addressed by a Task Force setup by the Reserve Bank of India, which among other things is looking into the regulatory and legal issues concerning microfinance in India. An increasing number of MFIs have begun to address the issue of financial sustainability of their programs and have started taking effective steps towards achieving sustainability. Many of them have increased their interest rates, at least to cover their costs. Some of them have taken steps to convert themselves into for-profit corporations and have sought commercial investors to invest in them. These will not only make microfinance more commercially oriented but will also increase the quality of governance. Another welcome development in the Indian microfinance sector in recent years has been the establishment of networks of microfinance practitioners. These networks not only help in creating awareness but also help in formation, experience sharing etc. These could also develop into a Self-Regulatory Organization of microfinance institutions.

After the pioneering efforts of the last ten years, the microfinance scene in India has reached a takeoff point. With some effort substantial progress can be made in taking MFIs to the next orbit of significance and sustainability. This needs innovative and forward-looking policies, based on the ground realities of successful MFIs. This, combined with a commercial approach from the MFIs in making microfinance financially sustainable, will make this sector vibrant and help achieve its single-minded mission of providing financial services to the poor.

References

1. Barry, N. (1995), "The Missing Links: Financial System that Works for the Majority," Women's World Banking, New York.
2. Barry, Nancy, Armacost, Nicola and Kawas Celina (1996) "Putting Poor people's Economics at the Center of Urban Strategies," Women's World Banking, New York.
3. Chriseten, R. Peck Rhyne, Elisabeth and Vogel, Robert C (1994) "Maximizing the Outreach of Microenterprise Finance: The Emerging Lessons of Successful Programs," September IMCC, Arlington, Virginia.
4. Ghate, P. et al (1992) Informal Finance: Some Findings from Asia, Oxford University Press, Hong Kong.
5. http://www.basixindia.com/micro_finance_in_india.htm
6. http://www.databank.nedfi.com

7. http://www.nedfi.com
8. http://www.nerdatabank.nic.in
9. Karmakar, K. G. (2008) Micro Finance Revisited, Karmakar, K.G (Ed) Micro Finance in India, Sage Publication Pvt Ltd, New Delhi, pp. 33-54.
10. Kim Kyung-Hwan (1995) "Access to Credit, Term of Housing Finance and Affordability of Housing," Housing Finance International 9(4), June 22-27.
11. Ledgerwood, J. (1998): Microfinance Handbook: An Institutional and Financial Perspective, World Bank Publications.
12. Micro Finance in India, 2007-08, NABARD, http://www.nabard.org
13. Mizoram Rural Bank, 25th Annual Report 2007-08, Aizawl, Mizoram.
14. Otero, M. and Rhyne, E.(1994) The New World of Micro-enterprise Finance -Building Healthy Financial Institutions for the Poor, Kumarian Press, West Harford, Connecticut.
15. Rajasekhar, D. (1999): Micro-Finance, Poverty Alleviation and Empowerment of Women, ISEC publications, Bangalore.
16. Robinson, M. (1998): Strategic Issues in Microfinance, Ashgate Publishing: Aldershot.
17. Robinson, M. (2001): The Microfinance Revolution: Sustainable Finance for the Poor, World Bank Publications.
18. Satish P. (2005): Mainstreaming Indian Micro Finance, Economic and Political Weekly, Vol. 40 No. 17 April 23 - April 29.
19. Schreiner, M., Colombet, H.H. (2001): Building or Repairing Institutions: Microcredits in Argentina, Vol-48, Springer Netherlands.
20. Umdor, S. (2007): Micro Finance in North East India, http://www.northeasterner.in
21. Women's World Banking (1994) "United Nations Expert Group on Women and Finance," New York.
22. World Bank, (1997): Sustainable Banking with the Poor: An Inventory of Microfinance Institutions in Latin America and the Caribbean. World Bank Publication, Washington, DC.

18

Common Pool Resource Management and Microfinance Mechanism: A Study of WGHCRMS, Meghalaya

K. C. Kabra

ABSTRACT: *Common Pool Resources (CPRs) significantly contribute to livelihood of people, despite their rapid depletion and decline in the physical productivity. The institutional arrangements play an important role in the management of natural resources, in general, and CPRs in particular, under any property right regime. Recognizing the importance of CPRs management and poor economic conditions of people inhibiting Garo Hills, the Government of India, through International Fund for Agricultural Development (IFAD) initiated "West Garo Hills Community Resource Management Society" (WGHCRMS) as a model demonstration project covering 7070 households out of 35,350 populations from 192 villages. In this line the paper is an attempt to analyse the activities of WGHCRMS including microfinance mechanism.*

Introduction

Common Pool Resources (CPRs) of land, water, forests, fisheries, wildlife and agriculture constitute an important component of community assets in India, and they significantly contribute to livelihood of people, despite their rapid depletion and decline in the physical productivity. Institutional arrangements play an important role in the management of natural resources, in general and CPRs in particular, under any property right regime. In the context of CPRs, institutions may be defined as "collective action in control, liberation and expansion of individual action". An institution is an organized system of social relationship which embodies certain common values and procedures and meets certain needs of the society. It is relatively permanent structure of social patterns of roles and relations that people enact certain sanctioned and unified ways for the purpose of satisfying basic social needs. Thus, institutions express the value system of a society and enforce it in the form of working rules. In other words, institutions are 'working rules' to order relationship among individuals within a society, and structure incentives in human exchange, whether social, economic or political. The institutions (property rights) are part of the 'cultural capital' by which resource user communities convert the 'natural capital' (resources and ecological services) into 'man-made capital'. The importance of community property rights and reconciling the system of common knowledge of indigenous communities with modern fast track science to confer dignity and enhance the utility of the slow track indigenous knowledge that could serve as a useful tool. Full benefits of such integration would, of course, flow only when supported by the systems of open, public participation in the management of natural resources and a just sharing of benefits flowing from relevant commercial applications.

With this in view, over the years, several innovative institutional initiatives by NGOs, cooperatives and user groups for sustainable management of CPRs in India have taken place such as—

- National Tree Growers Cooperative Federation working successfully in several states, Participatory Watershed Development Program, The Gambhira Cooperative Farming Society in Gujarat, Ubeshwar Vikas Mandal (UVM) in Rajasthan, Chakriya Vikas Pranali (CVP) in Bihar, Collective action in salt-affected and waterlogged soils, etc. in the field of Grazing, *panchayat* revenue and wasteland management.
- Joint Forest Management in most of the states, Social Security Plantation and Forest Farming for Rural Poor Programs in several states, Forest Protection Committees in West Bengal, Village Development Committees in Himachal Pradesh, Hill Resource Management Societies in Haryana, Tribal Hamlet Committees in Orissa, etc. in the field of Protected and reserved degraded forest land.
- Tarun Bharat Sangh, NM Sadguru Water and Development Foundation, Rajiv Gandhi Watershed Development Mission and other NGOs working in tribal regions of Rajasthan, Gujarat, MP, Chhattisgarh, Jharkhand, Maharashtra, Orissa and West Bengal in the field of Integrated management of land and water resources.
- Participatory Irrigation Management of Madhya Pradesh and Chhattisgarh, Mohini Water Cooperative Society in Gujarat, Water Users Associations of Andhra Pradesh, Tamil Nadu, Karnataka, Madhya Pradesh, Rajasthan, Orissa, West Bengal and Chhattisgarh in the field of Canal/lift irrigation for surface irrigation.
- PRADAN and other NGOs have been working for tank rehabilitation through collective action in Tamil Nadu, Karnataka, Andhra Pradesh, Madhya Pradesh, Rajasthan, Orissa, West Bengal and Chhattisgarh in the field of Irrigation tanks.

- Pani Panchayats (Gram Gaurav Pratishthan, Maharashtra), Tubewell Cooperatives and Irrigation Companies of Kheda and Mehsana in Gujarat in the field of Groundwater management.
- Tagore Society for Rural Development in the establishment of Multi-purpose village ponds for village population, livestock, and fresh water aquaculture.
- Madhya Pradesh Minor Forest Products Cooperative Society Model for development of Non-timber forest products.
- The Pong Dam Reservoir Cooperative Management Society in Himachal Pradesh, Captain Bhery Fishermen's Cooperative Society in West Bengal, The Marine Fishermen's Cooperative Societies in West Bengal and Kerala, Marine Fisheries Cooperative Societies Karnataka in the field of conserving Inland and marine fisheries.
- Very effective participatory community-based conservation of protected area institutions for management of sacred groves in Rajasthan, Maharashtra, Karnataka, Kerala, Tamil Nadu, West Bengal, Bihar, Jharkand, Madhya Pradesh, Chhattisgarh, Andhra Pradesh, Orissa, Uttaranchal, Uttar Pradesh, Meghalaya, Sikkim and other north eastern States. Village-level institutions for traditional medicinal system, and aromatic plants. National Biodiversity Strategy and Action Plan at state level duly incorporated with traditional/indigenous knowledge of tribal and local communities in the field of managing Traditional ecological Common knowledge and Biodiversity conservation.

Common Pool Resource Management in Garo Hills

Coming to Meghalaya, the *Garo* hills is bestowed by nature with good amount of annual rainfall (3000 mm) and fertile soil suitable for diverse crops; vast forests fields of which more than 90% owned and managed by community, untapped benefits of scientific and commercial forest management; untapped river system of the Brahmaputra, Barak, Subansiri catchments; untapped marketing and packaging of organic produce, traditional handicrafts and handlooms; untapped processing and marketing of bamboo, cane and medicinal herbs.

The Government of India recognized that the socio-cultural framework of the indigenous communities in the upland and mid-hill villages of West *Garo* Hills (1504 villages spread over 3677 sq. km. of which 699 villages electrified divided in 8 Community Development Blocks) with a population of 5.15 lakhs of which 46 % (Census, 1991) were below poverty line (BPL) presents a unique set of constraints and challenges. For example, till recently, most of the *Garo* villages lack safe drinking water facilities as the scarcity of water persisted. Further, it was a sad fact that stagnation in rural economy persisted aggravated by the increasingly lower productivity in *jhum* cultivation as a consequence of shortening *jhum* cycles, and the declining fertility due to continued encroachment on the forest cover and resources and has led to progressive land degradation. The shifting cultivation is no longer recognized as a standalone sustainable livelihood system by the communities practicing it. They lack the opportunity, appropriate technology, vision, credit support and conviction to adopt alternative options and the means to take them because of low literacy percentage due to poverty, poor community participation; absence of village level institutions (e.g. Gram Sabha/Gram Panchayat); lack of transparency, accountability, and monitoring of rural works; lack of entrepreneurship, market information network and infrastructure; low participation of women in decision making, governance & income generation; difficult terrain and lack of adequate infrastructure for connectivity. Planning Commission in 2002 has acknowledged that "the credit needs of the rural poor are at present only partially met by formal credit agencies and a majority of rural poor continues to depend on the informal sources of credit".

It is found from the study conducted by Price Waterhouse Coopers that the overall share of organised sector in credit flow to rural poor is around 16% for the following reasons:

- Non-availability of credit for consumption needs from the organised sector.
- Very high transaction cost to the borrowers from the organised sector.
- Rigidity of terms and conditions for a loan from the organised sector.
- Delay in sanction of loans by the organised sector.
- Very high rate of defaults under the Government sponsored has led to the reluctance on the part of the banks to extend credit to rural poor.

West Garo Hills Community Resource Management Society

In 1999, on recognizing the importance of CPRs management and poor economic conditions of people inhibiting *Garo* Hills, the Government of India, through International Fund for Agricultural Development (IFAD), initiated "West *Garo* Hills Community Resource Management Society" (WGHCRMS) as a model demonstration project covering 7,070 households out of 35,350 population from 192 villages (Table 1) not for quick outputs but for slow, patient process of group formation and sensitization to gain trust and encourage participation at the community level.

At the launch of the project 'WGHCRMS' in 1999—though intended to give a coverage to 7,070 households—it took off from 868 households picking from 17 villages with 3 self-help groups (SHGs). Diagram 1 on wealth ranking status of beneficiaries at induction date depicts that of the households surveyed to be included in the project as its beneficiaries, 4,148 households were poorest, 2,305 were poorer and 431 were poor and none was from better category. However, the rest of the households (2.49 %) were belonging to middle-off category.

Objectives of West Garo Hills Community Resource Management Society

The idea has been to facilitate a new approach to development focusing on interventions, which are technically appropriate, culturally sensitive and institutionally effective and sustainable beyond project life. Recognizing indigenous knowledge and capabilities, its strategy was community demand driven and farmer oriented with full emphasis on transparency and accountability. The project was expected to cause impact on creation and strengthening village based institutions which are self-sustaining and capable of meeting their own requirements. In the light of the above, WGHCRMS's specific objectives may be outlined:

- To enhance the livelihood of vulnerable groups in a sustainable manner through improved resource base management in a way that protects and restore the environment.
- To promote a more sensitive approach to the design and implementation of development intervention.
- To enhance the capability of local people to manage technologies and institutions at the village level.
- To increase incomes through the development of more sustainable farming system and promote non-farm entrepreneurship.
- To make people more aware of the need to preserve and regenerate natural resources from forest and bio-diversity.
- To establish effective and appropriate delivery systems for inputs say credit, extension, etc. and for maintenance of assets and resources.
- To increase the participation of women in local institutions and in decision-making process within the community.
- To enhance saving capacity and establish the habit of thrift.
- To increase access to basic services and infrastructural facilities.

Strategies of West Garo Hills Community Resource Management Society

In order to achieve the aforesaid objectives, it has chosen to adopt to form 25 Apex District Federation (Table 2) covering 590 out of total 852 SHGs divided into 29 clusters and 257 natural resource management groups (NaRM-Gs) (Table 1) and one Confederation of all capacity building organizations (CBOs) into a single consolidated institution with a purpose of meeting, deliberating, planning and operating monthly basis; form SHGs to cover all persons above 18 years; register SHGs into working clusters; arrange direct loans from banks to the SHGs; form cluster organizations with assigned duty of liaising with District Society, conducting DST supported trainings, marketing of produce and purchase of inputs, conducting self-assessment, audit and continuous periodic reviews; establish cluster specific enterprises in all villages, transport networks; phasing out of NGO activities and services through cluster organizations;

optimize *jhum* cultivation plots commensurate with the size of family labour, intensify family labour closer to the homestead by integrating and consolidating all production systems; initiate one year para professional trainings duly formulated with departments like health, agriculture, horticulture, and veterinary, etc.

Table 3 reveals that the project took 2 years' time in picking up its activities, perhaps it required some time in mobilizing (convincing) people and ensuring community participation and started functioning normally from 2001-02 when it added 1,486 households as its beneficiaries. Then, it preferred waiting for the results on pilot basis. On seeing encouraging results, it received increased participation from people and community which resulted in expansion of its ambit by further addition of 4,185 households from 126 villages which were organized into 297 SHGs and 146 NaRM-Gs. In order to motivate NaRM-Gs and SHGs to perform better, to compete among others and to set new heights for them to achieve in future, in December 2002, NaRM-Gs'/SHGs' grading system was introduced using NABARD norms which has even paved way for them to have strengths, weaknesses, opportunities and threats (SWOT) analysis. Table 3 (A and B) shows the changes in NaRM-Gs/SHGs performance over the years. In early stage, most of them were in B and C grade only, but by building their capacity in the weak areas now by the end of March 31, 2007, most of them have reached A, and B grade leaving zero in D grade. This grading system has proved to be useful.

Achievements of West Garo Hills Community Resource Management Society

Diagram 2 on wealth ranking status of beneficiaries reveals that all the activities of the project over last 10 years has resulted into significant achievement that below poverty line (BPL) households reduced to 997 (14.10 %) only at the end of March 31, 2008. The better off households have increased from zero to 823 (11.64 %) and similarly middle off households reached to 1,867 (26.40 %), whereas above poverty line (APL) category households have jumped to 3,383 (47.85 %)

The first breakthrough amongst the major achievements of the project was the consolidation of all the CBOs during October 2006 by forming the Apex Body Confederation in the form of NERCROMP Institute of Micro Finance Banking Institution and Learning Centre of Excellent for Holistic Aspiration of Mothers (NIM – BILCHAM) which resulted in combined corpus of Rs.1.05 crores received from 852 SHGs to be used as the revolving fund for the women's bank. The second breakthrough of the project which was for the first time in the history of Meghalaya that the convergence with the State Government could be established whereby its NaRM-G model was replicated in the form of Village Employment Councils (VEC) in each of the 1,502 villages covering districts like South *Garo* Hills, *Ri-Bhoi* and *Jaintia* Hills. Thus the IFAD model was repeated several times.

During 2006-07, the major focus was on Capacity and Institution Building (CIB) wherein besides infrastructure development (in the form of setting up of one micro hydel unit, electrification of 29 rural villages, construction of 54 culverts, 12 bridges, 6 foot-bridges, and new road making 145 km and improvement of existing roads 107 km) Human Resource Development received major thrust among all the sectors. This was not possible without the empowerment of the local community based organizations of which the Self Help Groups (SHGs) were the fundamental components. Of course, at higher levels the SHG Federation capacity was well promoted from Cluster Associations and Para professionals in different streams. Though the approach has registered minimal tangible 'progress' during early years, still the project's activities may be assigned with very high potential for sustainability at least for groups. This exercise of the project has resulted into the following:

1. Emergence of the class of Community Organizers' (COs) who have shown much progress on the set norms of NABARD. They now attend all the cluster meetings almost without fail and have replaced the NGOs with their role, services and activities by serving as a linkage between the Cluster and the village.
2. For Community Coordinators and Cluster leaders programmes like entrepreneurship development and capacity building were undertaken at IIE, Guwahati, which made possible that around 22 out of total 29 clusters started functioning on their own with little or marginal support from NGOs for running day-to-day affairs. The services which were earlier rendered by the NGOs have been replaced by the Cluster Coordinators (CCs) who are in fact from community volunteers' cadre. They are now able to provide services like trainings on book-keeping, and aspects of monitoring, etc. to about 386 households from 2 different clusters (Rongsak & Bandri) which are functioning fully independently without the involvement of NGOs right from their inception. It has been observed that these clusters are even performing better than the other NGOs assisted clusters. These CCs have been remunerated by cluster village households for their services in the form of very small or nominal monetary sacrifice on monthly basis (say Rs. 5/- per month each household). This is an example of increased community participation. On social front, during last 10 years, 45 drinking water systems, 2,644 low cost sanitary latrines, 30 community halls, 101 garbage disposal units, 19 playgrounds, 6 community groups run schools with buildings were set up. Besides, 27 healthcare training programmes, 12 adult literacy programmes and 45 literacy and sanitation campaign programmes were also organized.

3. As a part of strategy SHG federations were formed which are not only running their own business but also, at the same time, of course on payment basis rendering much needed services to the society in the form of maintaining 4 English medium schools from their own contributions.. About 326 SHGs have been benefited in the form of direct loans from Banks. Owing to good track record of repayment in past, some federations have even received 5th or 6th bank loan from NeDFi and State Bank of India to the tune of Rs.2.5 to 3 lakhs. Finally, 69 lakhs has been made available by formal financing sector, i.e., State Bank of India in the form of 163 loans to SHGs and NaRM-Gs for developing transport system in Garo Hills.

4. Agricultural farmers, horticultural volunteers and para professionals were given training at RRTC, Umran, for seasonal vegetable growing alongwith patchouli plantation, establishment of nurseries, maintenance and harvesting and processing up to dry leaf stage in all cluster villages. This has immediately resulted into setting up of 8 nurseries for medicinal and aromatic plants in their respective villages where patchouli, stevis, Alovera saplings are being grown for sale and multiplication. Farmer to farmer exchange training and exposure programme from cluster to cluster for improved *jhum* practices, multi-cropping and crop diversification at cluster level villages were undertaken. Besides, soil and water conservation measures not only for *jhum*, terraces, orchards and catchment areas but also for drinking water sources in the entire project belt were undertaken. To assess the potential for Agar production a survey was conducted in Mahadeo area of South *Garo* Hills.

5. Training was arranged at RRTC, Umran for Veterinary and Livestock Volunteers for rearing kurioler and vana raja birds and cattle, and because of this, some clusters could obtained loans under various schemes like RSVY and IDDP and received technical assistance from DRDA & Veterinary department for setting up milk chain cooperatives. Similarly, one week training was arranged at RRTC, Umran for Fishery Volunteers who were instrumental in increasing the fish production. The Rombagre Fish Sanctuary had crossed the target of fish production to 5 MT in 2006-07 as against 4 MT in 2005-06. The Natural Resource Management Groups (NaRM-Gs) have partially achieved a sustainable production of bio-mass and restoration of ecological balance in some areas of *Garo* Hills and improved the standard of livelihood of the people. All these efforts resulted in an increased land use over 10 years such as 53 fishery ponds, 819 livestock rearing adoption of improved farming and multiple cropping practices over 53 hectares, farming of medicinal and aromatic plants over 30 hectares, conservation of soil and water over 118 hectares, and provision of minor irrigation facilities over 217 hectares.

6. SHG federations and NaRM-Gs federation were mobilized on participatory planning and development of small-scale industries and processing of existing agro products. Self Employed Business Agents (SEBAs) have been specifically trained in the field of business transactions and now they are allowed to run their own/group business enterprise independently. In a major attempt during 2006-07, efforts were made to market ginger collectively to Kolkata and Hyderabad. Though the initial transactions resulted into a loss of Rs. 1.5 lakhs, the Rengsanggre cluster sold 11 trucks of ginger to Kolkata and 3 trucks of ginger to Hyderabad where the farmers ultimately received encouraging results (A total of 48 MT of ginger was sold with a net profit of Rs. 96,000). The group's self-realization was that the procurement has to be supported by value addition so as to face the competition in the market. Besides, they sold other products like bamboo (20 trucks), tamarind (2 MT), orange juice, etc. with substantial profit. Finally, they learned value addition and have managed to sell 1 MT ginger duly washed and packed at Rs.20/- per kg against local market price of Rs.4/- to Rs.6/- per kg only. The lesson learnt by the group was that the tremendous scope exists for collective procurement, stocking and selling of value added/processed products at lucrative prices. To encourage the group further for adopting a business approach, special emphasis was being given during training on group Enterprise aspects. Towards this end, the DST has conducted a Livelihood Enhancement Action Planning (LEAP) programme where exposure to trade-in and trade-out exercises and value chain exercises were given. To compliment the aforesaid task, credit linkage awareness and aspects of credit management were revealed to participants. All these efforts ultimately resulted in setting up of 68 weaving and tailoring units, 53 grocery shops, 8 cane and bamboo units, 71 vegetable shops, 4 carpentry units, 11 transport operating units, 1 fruit and vegetable processing unit, 2 areca nut processing units, 1 cashew nut processing unit, 1 patchouli, bay leaf distillation unit, 2 broom grass collection units, and 3 bamboo processing units.

Conclusions

This project West Garo Hills Community Resource Management Society has registered a significant progress not only in the field of social and infrastructure development in remote areas but also has marked a significant progress in bringing smile on the face of households by way of arranging credit though microfinance mechanism (e.g. BILCHAM), promoting livelihood activities by imparting group business approach alongwith necessary skills through training. Yet it needs to achieve a lot in the field of promoting eco-tourism, value adding skills in respect of agro-horticultue species and non-timber forest products, collective enterprise marketing, and joint forests management, etc.

References

1. Materials obtained from branch office, IFAD, Tura.
2. Report on West *Garo* Hills Community Resource Management Society (WGHCRMS), Tura, March 2007.
3. Document, Planning Commission, 2002.
4. Report on Study, Price Water House Cooper, 2002.

Table 1

Profile of WGHCRMS

(As on 1April 2006)

Sl. No.	Name	House hold	NaRM-G	Cluster	Village	SHG	Gra-ded	Not Graded
1	AWS	1,584	52	5	38	90	57	15
2	BYACID	1,337	50	2	33	150	126	24
3	NRMC	1,048	34	6	28	100	79	24
4	AEA	812	32	4	31	60	56	4
5	SEWS	808	31	4	27	62	61	1
6	Bethany	580	19	4	17	86	68	18
7	WEDS	556	18	2	14	36	36	0
8	Non-NGO	345	21	2	4	243	143	100
	Grand Total	**7,070**	**257**	**29**	**192**	**852**	**626**	**186**

**84 SHGs, which are below 6 month, are not graded*

Table 2

Status of SHGs Federations

(As on March 31, 2007)

Sl. No.	Name of SHGs Federation	No. of SHGs Participating	Whether SHGs Federation Registered/Under Process
1	Chibra Songma Waldura SHG Federation	18	Registered
2	Durama SHG Federation	26	Registeded
3	Rongbretgre Chibasal SHG Federation	15	Under Process
4	Bibragre SHG Federation	20	Under Process
5	Chinabat Simsang SHG Federation	37	Under Process
	BYACID Area		
6	Kucholson SHG Federation	150	Registered
7	Dilsan SHG Federation	26	Under Process

Contd.

Sl. No.	Name of SHGs Federation	No. of SHGs Participating	Whether SHGs Federation Registered/Under Process
	AEA Area		
8	Ranggira Tangsim SHG Federation	23	Registered
9	Galwangchonggre SHG Federation	21	Registered
10	Nokatgre SHG Federation	20	Under Process
	NRMC Area		
11	Gisiksan SHG Federation	48	Registered
12	Waram Asim SHG Federation	12	Registered
13	Niksengchi SHG Federation	26	Registered
14	Chandime SHG Federation	14	Registered
	SEWS Area		
15	Ribokdokatchi SHG Federation	12	Under Process
16	Chuangka SHG Federation	18	Under Process
17	Tengkam SHG Federation	20	Under Process
18	Nawaldare SHG Federation	12	Under Process
	WEDS Area		
19	Pattanggre Chanang SHG Federation	16	Under Process
20	Akinpara Nikseng SHG Federation	15	Under Process
	Bethany Society Area		
21	Agindarenggre SHG Federation	18	Registered
22	Asim SHG Federation	12	Registered
23	Bakrime Womens' SHG Federation	10	Under Process
24	Chondon Nokat SHG Federation	10	Under process
25	Shaliram SHG Federation	12	Under process
	Total	**590**	

TABLE 3

Profile of the NaRM-G and SHGs (from April 1, 1999 to April 1, 2007)

Sl. No.	Year	No. of NGO involved	Total No. of Villages	Total Nos. of NaRM-Gs formed	Total Nos. of SHGs formed	Total No. Households
1	1999-2000	2	17	17	3	868
2	2000-2001	-	-	3	22	0
3	2001-2002	3	43	69	109	1,486
4	2002-2003	0	0	8	30	26
5	2003-2004	0	126	146	297	4,185
6	2004-2005	2	6	9	59	505
7	2005-2006	0	0	5	89	0
8	2006-2007	0	0	5	243	0
	G. Total	**7**	**192**	**257**	**852**	**7,070**

TABLE 3(A)

Summary report of SHG Grading (from April 1, 2001 to March 31, 2007)

Sl. No.	Year	Total Nos. of SHGs						
		Total 1	SHGs Graded	Grade A	Grade B	Grade C	Grade D	Ungraded
1	2001-02	134	71	8	45	15	3	63
2	2002-03	164	144	12	97	23	12	20
3	2003-04	223	151	43	82	17	10	72
4	2004-05	520	302	144	110	48	0	218
5	2005-06	609	525	176	265	85	0	84
6	2006-07	852	665	317	265	85	0	185

TABLE 3(B)

Summary report of NaRM-G Grading (from April 1, 2001 to March 31, 2007)

Sl. No.	Year	Total Nos. of NaRM-Gs						
		Total	Graded	Grade A	Grade B	Grade C	Grade D	Ungraded
1	2001-02	89	54	2	26	14	12	35
2	2002-03	97	71	8	33	26	4	28
3	2003-04	106	84	14	28	32	10	22
4	2004-05	106	93	23	39	28	3	13
5	2005-06	257	257	41	130	60	0	0
6	2006-07	257	257	137	100	20	0	0

DIAGRAM 1

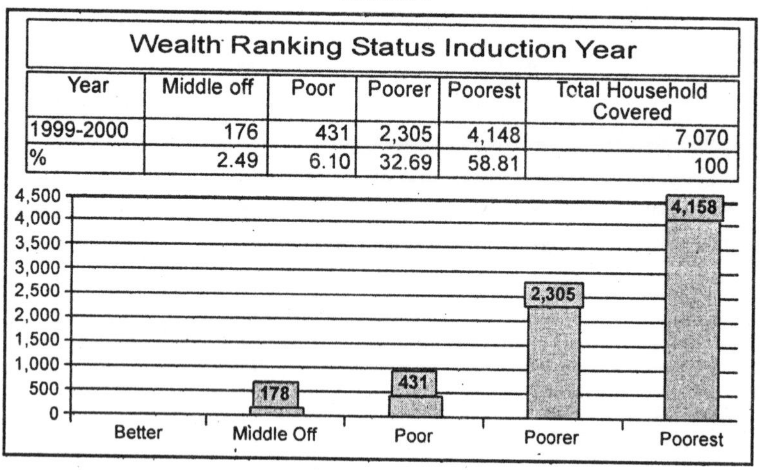

DIAGRAM 2

Wealth Ranking Status After Project as on March '08

Year	Total HH	Better off	Middle off	APL	BPL
31st March 2008	7,070	823	1,867	3,383	997
Perecentage	100	11.64	25.40	47.85	14.10

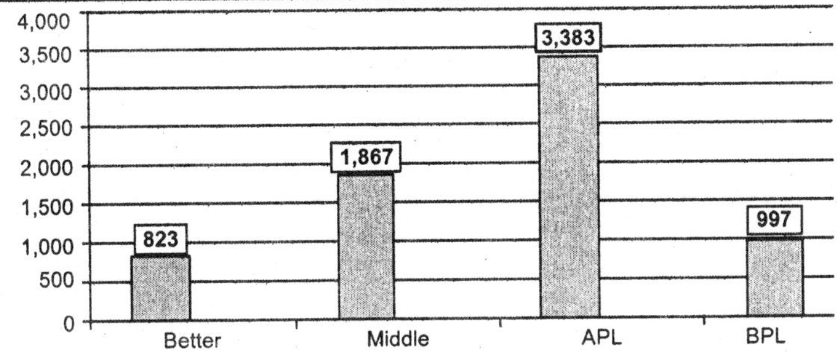

19

BILCHAM—The Torch Bearer: A Women's MFI in Garo Hills, Meghalaya

Sitaram Prasad Sah

Abstract: *West Garo Hills district is one of the seven districts of the State of Meghalaya, bounded in the north by Goalpara district of Assam, in the east by East Garo Hills and South Garo Hills, in the south, by Bangladesh, and in the west by Dhubri District of Assam and Bangladesh. It covers a total area of 3,714 sq. km having major area with hills and stretch of plains is crisscrossed by a large number of rivers and streams. The WGHCRMS (West Garo Hills Community Resource Management Society)—IFAD functions and operates in 233 villages including non project villages through 7 partner NGOs, 257 NaRM-Gs, 1,115 project SHGs and 165, non-project SHGs, 29 cluster associations and 26 SHG federations covering more than 7,070 households. In the West Garo Hills district SHG movement has been accelerated by West Garo Hills Community Resource Management Society. The WGHCRMS-IFAD is an established apex confederation of SHGs, NaRM-Gs, Cluster associations and SHG federations. The BILCHAM is being registered under the Meghalaya Society Act. Currently, they are running their office with two permanent staff and two temporary staff.*

Introduction

For realizing the value of self-dependency, cooperation, socio-culture, socio-economic and small micro-credit business through the SHGs in Garo Hills and to enhance saving capacity and establish the habit of thrift to uplift the living standard of the communities, specially of the women by the united cooperation, without bias towards caste and creed an apex of self-help groups federations called as BILCHAM APEX SHG FEDERATION in short BILCHAM (Banking Institute of Learning Centre of Excellence for Holistic Aspiration of Mothers), was formed on the 25th Oct. 2006 under the Societies Registration Act, 1983.

This Federation was created by West Garo Hills Community Resource Management Society, NERCORMP-IFAD Project, under DONER/NEC,

Government of India, and having realized the need of sustainability of the rural community, the concept of forming an Apex Federation at the district level was evolved after experiencing the success of the project in the areas of livelihood improvement and credit facilities for the women folks in particular by taking the entire communities of Garo Hills covering the 3 districts.

Thus, the women of 1,115 Self Help Groups' 267 NaRM-Gs under 29 Clusters and 26 SHG Federations covering 45,000 population approx. in West Garo Hills, Meghalaya, clubbed together in one Apex Federation at the district level with its HQ at Tura, P.O. Tura, West Garo Hills, Meghalaya.

Name, Area of Operation, Address, Symbol and Motto

1. **Name:** The Name of the Self Help Group is BILCHAM Apex SHG Federation and in short BILCHAM. The abbreviation of BILCHAM is Banking Institute and Learning Centre of Excellence for Holistic Aspirations of Mothers.
2. **Area:** The BILCHAM Apex SHG Federation operates in the areas of West, East and South Garo Hills and other adjoining areas with its HQ at Tura.
3. **Address:** The Office address is Dakopgre, Opposite Office of Commissioner Garo Hills Divisions, P.O. New Tura, Dist, West Garo Hills, Meghalaya 794 002.
4. **Symbol**: Its symbol is the "Burning Torch with Borang/Tree House".
5. **Motto:** "Empowerment of Women through Self-Reliance and Micro-finance and Building on Nature".

Aims and Objectives of BILCHAM: The aim and objectives of BILCHAM are:

1. To maintain the unity and close understanding among the members in particular and the society in general.
2. To promote a faculty of maintaining and encouraging the traditional culture and literature.
3. To facilitate self-economic development through SHG movement by way of enhancing savings capacity and establish the habit of thrift.
4. To provide opportunity and promote women empowerment both in private and public life through SHG movement and thus to inculcate a democratic culture.
5. To promote mutual benefit activities by mobilizing resources both financial, human resource and material resources.
6. To provide small production and investment credit to the poor for their economic development.
7. To help each other through common efforts for bringing economic and social inclusion of the poor/needy and destitute people.

8. To promote a culture of insurance including insurance of life, property and loans, programme, etc.
9. To help in forming new groups in support of the existing groups leaders and provide a forum for collective learning/training to the groups on financial and other management skills.
10. To act as a bridge to link with other institutions such as banks, government/private agencies and thereby to foster an entrepreneurial culture.
11. To create a monetary corpus of the SHG confederations which shall be generated/derived from the self-contributions/capital subscription/ members fee of SHGs/Federations and from the Govt. grants/loans and other sources.
12. To contribute, undertake social welfare activities towards members of the SHGs/Federation in time of natural calamities to the poorest victims and shall act to control the anti-social elements that pollute the image of the Societies.
13. To establish and carry out the microfinance support to people's organizations like Self Help Groups (SHGs), Natural Resource Management Groups (NaRM-Gs), SHGs Federations and NaRM-Gs Cluster Associations, AECs and VECs. etc.
14. To enhance capabilities of the communities to arrange and manage fund.
15. To encourage and collaborate with people and institutions with similar objectives.
16. To collaborate with government and non-government organizations to bring about changes in public policies and practices in favor of the poor and the deprived, particularly in the areas of economic, fiscal, and social administration.
17. To organize communities and build their capabilities to take responsibility for the management of their development through credit venture.
18. In order to achieve the above, to establish and operate the microfinance institute namely BILCHAM in a professional manner by a professional team, to function under its authorized body namely Board of Directors of BILCHAM.
19. To operate under established financial management, proprieties, appropriate software and other mechanisms required to have in place a robust system and an Institute.
20. To gradually increase its corpus by way of additional contribution, interest earned and also bulk borrowings from credible Financial Institutions.
21. To consider for outreaching to all villages at an appropriate stage and time, when the BILCHAM is assured that the broad needs of its members

are well catered and has the necessary capacity and confidence to reach out to others.

22. While all needed operational and decision powers will be provided to the Institute, it shall function under the overall supervision and control of the Board of Directors (BoD), for which an appropriate Memorandum of Understanding (MoU) will be constituted. In turn, the BoD shall have an appropriate relationship and responsibility towards the General Body in adherence to MoU entered which may also be suitably amended from time to time.

23. After a stage when the needs of the groups are broadly met, the BoD may even consider loaning to reliable people's organization, which will also have to fulfil the different requirements and adhere to all disciplines required. The BoD also can resort to safeguard measures like collaterals as they are in a way individual units and not groups, which in effect mean absence of peer pressure unlike the groups mentioned above.

Functions of BILCHAM

For pursuing these objects, the society has taken following functions:

1. To establish and maintain Sub-Units of the Society or Institute, if necessary.
2. To accept loan, grants, gifts, donation and subscriptions whether in cash or securities and of any property either movable or immovable in furtherance of the objects of the Society.
3. To maintain an endowment fund and a separate operating account or accounts and to utilize a part or whole of the fund and/or account towards capital and recurring expenditure of the Society, to make appropriate investment or to deal with the fund in any other way which the Society may deem fit. Expenditure towards capital and recurring expenditure will be from initial support provided for this purpose and may utilize from interests earned. Later on, however, this expenditure will not infringe into the corpus fund or any loan obtained from financial institution.
4. To provide loan to the people's organizations/CBOs like Self Help Groups (SHGs), Natural Resource Management Groups (NaRM-G), SHG Federations, and NaRM-G Associations which are willing to enter into Memorandum of Understanding for taking up various activities according to the guidelines given by the Society. In all these cases the BoD should fully satisfy itself on the credibility of the groups seeking to become a part of it.
5. To purchase, take on lease, or otherwise acquire any land or building wherever situated in India, which may be necessary for the Society.
6. To sell, lease, exchange and otherwise transfer all or any properties of the Society which subject to approval of the General Body (GB) of the Society.

The GB may authorize the BoD to take decision in this regard up to certain specific ceilings delegated by the GB.

7. To undertake and accept the management of any endowment fund, trust fund or revolving fund having objects similar to the objects of the Society.
8. To create administrative, technical, ministerial and other posts under the Society and to make appointment thereto in accordance with the rules of the Society. The ceiling in terms of the number of staffs, position and salary is subject to the approval of the GB.
9. To make rules and bye laws for the conduct of the affairs of the Society and to add, to amend, vary to rescind them from time to time. However, if such amendment is in contrary to the main objectives of the Society, the same should be put up to Society.
10. To create and maintain infrastructural facilities for the smooth and effective functioning of the Society.
11. To cooperate with other institutions in and outside the country having objectives similar to, or relevant for achieving the objectives of the Society by exchange of experts, literature, information, and by collaboration on various relevant areas.
12. To organize, survey and investigations for assessing the scope and expansion of existing agricultural sector, rural industries, handloom & handicraft industries, marketing and further establishment of the same for the benefit of communities and groups.
13. To do all such lawful things as the Society may deem fit for the attainment of all or any of its objectives.

Conclusion and Discussion

This flagship project NERCORMP-IFAD Project of DONER/NEC, Govt. of India recognizes that the socio-cultural framework of the indigenous communities in the upland and mid-hill villages of West Garo Hills represents a unique set of constraints and challenges. It is a sad fact that stagnation in rural economy persists aggravated by the increasingly lower productivity in jhum cultivation as a consequence of shortening jhum cycles, and the declining fertility due to continued encroachment on the forest cover and resources and has led to progressive land degradation. The shifting cultivation is no longer recognized as a stand alone sustainable livelihood system by the communities practicing it, yet they lack the opportunity, appropriate technology, vision, credit support and conviction to adopt alternative options and the means to take them. The guiding note of the project is sustainability beyond project life where the project has ended on the 30th September 2008.

After seeing the success and experiencing the critical gaps of credit requirements of the community, this has been addressed through the creation of BILCHAM for the sustainability of institutions created through NERCORMP - IFAD project. The BILCHAM is functioning satisfactory for the last 36 months. The following numbers of groups are registered under BILCHAM viz. 1,115 SHGs, 267 NaRM-Gs, and 26 Federations and 29 NaRM-Gs Cluster Associations.

BILCHAM is now a strong women independent organization catering to the livelihood and credit for the poorest of the poor who were earlier devoid of all these facilities. BILCHAM is giving services to the entire West Garo Hills and some parts of East and South Garo Hills independently through the SHGs Federations who are also members of the Board and responsible for scrutinizing, sanctioning and recovery of the loans.

With the passing of time, the popularity and recognition of this institute has gained tremendous confidence among the rural poor due to easy access of credit and a feeling of ownership resulting in positive response from all quarters. However, BILCHAM has not been able to provide all the required amount of credit due to shortage of funds at its disposal. The source of fund generated for BILCHAM can be listed as:

- Registration fee @ Rs.500/- for 1,115 SHGs, 257 NaRM-Gs, 28 Cluster Associations and 26 SHGs Federations Rs.2,62,000/-
- SHGs, NaRM-Gs/Cluster Associations and SHGs Federations contribution of Rs.83,20,814/-
- WGHCRMS (NERCORMS – IFAD) contribution of Rs.67,17,186/-
- Total corpus as on Rs.1.62 crores (31st March 2010)
- Loan recovery rate is 94%.

References

1. Anonymous, 2007. *Status Report of the West Garo Hills Community Resource Management Society* (WGHCRMS/Tura) under North Eastern Region Community Resource Management project (NECORMP/ Shillong).
2. Anonymous, 2008. *Status Report of the West Garo Hills Community Resource Management Society* (WGHCRMS/Tura) under North Eastern Region Community Resource Management project (NECORMP/ Shillong).
3. Anonymous, 2009. *Status Report of the West Garo Hills Community Resource Management Society* (WGHCRMS/Tura) under North Eastern Region Community Resource Management project (NECORMP/ Shillong).
4. Bhagat, D. 2009. *"Building of grassroot level rural institutions and its influence on horticulture based agribusiness development: A study in West Garo Hills district of Meghalaya"* paper presented at "4th World Congress on Conservation Agriculture" organized by Indian Council of Agricultural Research, and National Academy of Agricultural Sciences in New Delhi during 4- 7 February 2009.

SECTION V

MICROFINANCE AND MICRO-ENTERPRISES

20

Role of Cooperatives for Promoting Microfinance through Self-Help Groups (SHGs)

Pranay Jyoti Goswami

ABSTRACT: *The cooperative societies in India are playing multi-functional roles both in rural and urban areas. On the basis of the recommendations of an Expert Group constituted by the Government of India in 1990 the Central Government enacted the Multi State Cooperative Societies Act, 2002, which provided for democratic and autonomous working of the Cooperatives, which came into force with effect from August 19, 2002. The main objective of the present paper is to discuss the needs and importance of linkages of SHGs with cooperatives for providing microfinance in order to improve the socio-economic condition of the poor and underprivileged group of population of the country. The article also highlights the performance of cooperatives for the country as a whole as well as NER, Assam and Cachhar district in particular. For the sake of presentation, the present paper is divided into three sections. Section I covers concepts and definition. Section II covers the performance of cooperatives; findings and suggestions are included in section III.*

Introduction

The International Cooperative Alliance (ICA, 1995) has defined 'Cooperation as autonomous association of persons united voluntarily to meet their economic, social and cultural needs and aspirations through a jointly owned and democratically controlled enterprise'. The ICA emphasizes the values of Cooperation such as self-help, self-responsibility, democracy, equality and solidarity. The cooperative organizations operate on the concept of "Cooperation". The term 'Cooperation' comes from the Latin word "*Cooperari*" which has two words '*Co*' means with and '*Operari*' relates to 'to work'. In other words, in its popular sense, 'Cooperation' means 'working together with others for a genuine common purpose'. To be very specific, cooperation discusses the system in which people associate themselves voluntarily to wok together on equal terms and conditions to eliminate their economic exploitation and/or to accomplish their any economic needs common to all of them.

Cooperation has been adopted as an important medium of rejuvenation of socio-economic lifeline of the country. Rural development through Cooperatives promotes regional development of the areas neglected so far by the urban capitalists and industrialists at the same time. Cooperatives also minimize disparities in income and employment as the resultant gains are not pocketed by a few but enjoyed by a large number of people.

In India, cooperatives were legally set up during the British rule. Nicholson, a British Officer in India, suggested introducing Raiffersen model of German agricultural credit Cooperatives in India. As a follow-up of that recommendation, the first Cooperative Society Act of 1904 was enacted to enable formation of "agricultural credit cooperatives" in villages in India under Government sponsorship. With the enactment of 1904 Act, Cooperatives were to get a direct legal identity as every agricultural Cooperative was to be registered under that Act only. The 1904 Cooperative Societies Act was repealed by 1912 Cooperative Societies Act which provided formation of Cooperative societies other than credit. Under 1919 Administrative Reforms Act, Cooperatives were made a provincial subject making each province responsible for Cooperative development. In 1942, the British Government enacted the Multi-Unit Cooperative Societies Act, 1942, with an object to cover societies whose operations are extended to more than one state. The impulses of the Indian freedom movement gave birth to many initiatives and institutions in the post-independence era in India and armed with an experience of 42 years in the working of Multi-Unit Cooperative Societies under the Multi-Unit Cooperative Societies Act, 1942. In 1984, the Central Government enacted a compre-hensive Act known as Multi State Cooperative Societies Act,1984,repealing the Multi-Unit Cooperative Societies Act, 1942. The cooperative credit system of India has the largest network in the world and cooperatives have advanced more credit in the Indian agricultural sector than commercial banks. The village cooperative societies provide strategic inputs for the agricultural sector, consumer societies meet their consumption requirements at concessional rates; marketing societies help the farmer to get remunerative prices and cooperative processing units help in value additions to the raw products etc. In addition, cooperative societies are helping in building up of storage godowns including cold storages, rural roads and in providing facilities like irrigation, electricity, transport, and health.

Thus the cooperative societies in India in fact are playing multi-functional roles both in rural and urban areas. On the basis of the recommendations of an Expert Group constituted by the Government of India in 1990 the Central Government enacted the Multi State Cooperative Societies Act, 2002, which provided for democratic and autonomous working of the Cooperatives, which came into force with effect from August 19, 2002.

In spite of the advantages of cooperatives, that the Cooperative Organizations fail to serve their purpose adequately is noteworthy. Therefore, in the late 1990s it was thought necessary to launch microfinance through SHGs. At the beginning of the programme, as per the policy of the NABARD, bank played a dominant role. The linkage of SHGs and Cooperatives came later. Since, SHGs have special features similar to Cooperative **organization's** philosophy/values, cooperatives can combine SHGs (and start own small groups) to work together for the socio-economic development of their members and society.

In this context, the main objectives of the present paper are to discuss the needs and importance of linkages of SHGs with cooperatives for providing microfinance in order to improve the socio-economic condition of the poor and underprivileged group of population of the country. The article also highlights the performance of cooperatives for the country as a whole as well as NER, Assam and Cachhar district in particular. For the sake of simplicity, the present paper is divided in three sections. Section I covers concepts and definition. Section II covers the performance of cooperatives; findings and suggestions are included in Section III.

Section I

Micro Finance: Micro Finance (MF) is a financial service of small quantity provided by financial institutions (FI) to the poor. These financial services may include savings, credit, insurance, leasing, money transfer, equity, transaction, etc., that is, any type of financial service, provided to customers to meet their normal financial needs, life cycle, economic opportunity, and emergency [Dasgupta and Rao 2003] with the only qualification that (i) transaction value is small and (ii) customers are poor. As per the definition of International Labour Organization (ILO) , Microfinance is an economic development approach that involves providing financial services through institutions to low income clients. The Microfinance sector has grown rapidly over the last decade in India. However, this has not been an unqualified success. There are two main models of Microfinance in India (a) the SHG model under the SHG-Bank Linkage Programme (SHG-BLP) and (b) the Microfinance Institution (MFI) model.

Self-Help Group: SHG is a small voluntary association of 10-20 poor people from the same socio-economic background who come together for the purpose of solving their socio-economic problems through Self-help and mutual help. They collect small savings (thrift) on regular basis. They use their pooled resources to make small interest bearing loans to their members. The process helps them to imbibe the essentials of financial intermediation including prioritization of needs, setting terms and conditions and account keeping.

This gradually builds financial discipline in all of them. They open the savings account in the bank. Once the groups show mature financial behaviour, banks are encouraged to make loans to the SHG in certain multiples of the accumulated savings of the SHG. The bank loans are against group dynamics without any collateral and at market interest rates. The groups continue to decide the terms of loans to their own members. Since the group's own accumulated savings are part and parcel of the aggregate loans made by the groups to their members, peer pressure ensures timely repayment [Gupta, M.S. 2008].

Many MFIs claim that they work through groups. But the essential difference between these groups and SHGs is that, in the SHG model, the loan is a single loan to the group as a whole whereas the MFI tracks loans in the name of individual borrower

Self-Help Promoting Institutions: The role of Self-Help Promoting Institutions (SHPIs) in the entire process under the microfinance programme is very crucial . SHPIs like NGOs, credit cooperative, non-banking financial companies etc. have come together and are engaged in the task of promoting, nurturing and extending credit to the poor through SHGs.

The general approach adopted by SHPIs is to interact with poor families especially women and to identify small homogeneous affinity groups. The groups meet frequently and collect small savings from members. They are taught simple accounting methods to maintain their own accounts. As the pooled thrift increases, the group is eligible to receive external fund in multiples of its own savings. The funds come from SHPIs, banks or donors. The funding facilitates them to provide large loans to members for income generating activities. Decisions to sanction loans and their terms, are taken during the group meetings. Members take loans for various purposes including consumption, health care and other needs. At the same time, they also ensure that they earn adequately to meet repayment obligations timely. The group dynamics, building confidence, creating thrift habit and decision making are the main strengths of the SHGs. In fact SHG has been conceived as 'microbank' meeting both saving and credit needs of its members on their own terms.

NABARD, by way of grant assistance, continued to support NGOs, RRBs, DCCBs, Farmers' Clubs and Individual Rural Volunteers (IRVs) for promoting and nurturing of quality SHGs. It continued to direct its efforts towards roping in the services of new Self-Help Promoting Institutions (SHPIs) while continuing to support the existing ones. During 2007-08, grant assistance of Rs.1,369.77 lakh was sanctioned to various agencies for promoting 52,877 groups, taking the cumulative assistance sanctioned to Rs.6,119.37 lakh for 3.62 lakh groups as at end-March 2008 (Table 2).

Special Features of SHGs Similar to Cooperative Organizations

SHGs have special features similar to Cooperative organizations 'philosophy/ values: hence, cooperatives can combine SHGs (and start own small groups) to work together for the socio-economic development of their members and society.

These similar features can be mentioned as Small groups, homogeneity among members, regular attendance, set of bye-laws, democratic approach, no discrimination, equity, solidarity, saving first, credit letter, thrift and use of savings and funds received for loaning to the members.

SECTION II

It would seem obvious, therefore, that when the SHG initiative was launched to link poorer people with formal financial services, they should look to cooperatives to provide them microfinancial services. There are over 93,000 Primary Agricultural Credit Societies (PACS) in India providing an unrivalled rural network. The Societies are themselves served by 367 districts Cooperative Banks with 12,000 branches, with a further tier of state level apex banks to support them. In spite of these obvious qualifications, PACS and the Cooperative banks have thus far only played a small role in the programmes of linking SHGs to formal financial institutions, as evident from Tables 1 and 2

TABLE 1

Agency wise SHG Credit Linkage

Agency	2007	2008
Commercial Banks	5,71,636 (52)	3,12,359 (42)
Regional Rural Banks	3,81,199 (34)	2,40,596 (33)
Cooperative Banks	1,52,914 (14)	1,86,920 (25)
Total	**11,05,749 (100)**	**7,39,875(100)**

Source: Annual Report of NABARD, 2006-07, 2007-08

The objectives of Cooperative Credit Societies Act, 1904, made it clear that Cooperative movement was basically initiated to reach out to those who were otherwise excluded by the formal financial system such as farmers, artisans, and other people of limited resources. It is interesting to note that now the SHGs have come into existence in a big way in various business operations at local/ community levels. Many people from every corner have applauded its growth and development globally. Cooperatives are the latecomer in SHG linkage Programme. SHG linkage was first promoted solely with commercial banks and RRBs as a result of NABARD's own policy. Even in 2001, cooperative provided only 5.71 percent of total SHG loan supplied by different organizations.

The economic condition of the Cooperatives are far from satisfactory. Many are defunct and totally inoperative, while others are operative only on a part time basis being ineligible for NABARD refinance and are able to lend only from current recoveries. Out of the 367 DCCBs, 332 were capital inadequate according to the generally accepted norm of 8 percent in March 1999. In December 2000, 142 DCCBs failed to comply with the Banking Regulation Act,

TABLE 2

Share of Cooperatives in SHG's Credit Linkage programme

Year	Number of cooperative banks involved	SHGs linked to cooperative	Percent of cooperative linked SHGs in All	SHG Loans Disbursed from cooperative	As a percent of Total SHG Loan
2001	94	12,773	4.84	274.51	5.71
2002	209	38,666	8.38	794.88	7.75
2003	264	78,959	11.01	1,719.88	8.40
2007	369	1,86,920	NA	NA	NA

Source: EPW, April 23, 2005, page 1720, Annual Report, NABARD, 2007-08

1949. The advantages and disadvantages of SHG—Cooperative Linkage are given:

Cooperatives—Advantages for SHGs and their members

1. More locations—convenient and closer to home.
2. PACS can also supply farm inputs or consumer goods.
3. PACs can counter seasonal business.
4. These are owned and controlled by the local community.
5. SHG members can participate in management.
6. PACS or Cooperative banks can deposit savings, substantially.
7. Cooperatives can make clients more representative.
8. It is possible to introduce women—a new client group.

Disadvantages of cooperative-SHGs linkage

1. Strength of cooperatives is doubtful.
2. SHG members have given second class status.
3. These are in many cases politically manipulated.
4. Service hours are irregular.
5. There is high transaction cost.
6. Governance of cooperatives reflects status quo.
7. They require staff to acquire new skills.

SECTION III

Development Scenario and Cooperative Organizations in N.E.R

The North Eastern Region (which consists of Assam, Arunachal Pradesh, Manipur, Meghalaya, Mizoram, Nagaland and Tripura known as 'seven sisters' and lately inclusion of Sikkim as eighth and youngest sister) Cooperative's achievements story is different from other parts of the country. This is because of firstly, man-made demarcation of natural boundary which not only snapped social and family links, but more importantly, the traditional trade links as well as throwing the economy of the bordering states. Assam, Meghalaya, Mizoram and Tripura into haywire. Secondly, the decades of insurgency has also put the clock of progress backward and push the investment curve downward. As a result, the region has largely remained indifferent to modern waves of development. In spite of many attempts made by successive state governments and central, this region is yet to take off the process of development.

Numerically different kinds of organizations were initiated in this region over the years but the functioning and services of the most of them are not up to the mark. Specially the Primary Agricultural Cooperative Societies (PACS) and District Agricultural Credit Societies (DACS) remained unsuccessful due to over-dues and managerial incompetency. In 1973 at Gaon Panchayat Level Samabay Samities (GPLSS) were also formed but most of them have been sponsored by the respective state government (with around ¾th of paid up share capital).

The main problems and difficulties of Cooperatives in this region can be mentioned as:

These are lack of foresightedness, managerial incompetence, lack of commitment, absence of professional approach, political interference, excessive overdues, absence of public-participation, untrained manpower, lack of Co-operative spirit, rampant corruption and absence of periodic audit and supervision at different levels, etc.

To get rid off above said problems and difficulties of Cooperative societies, now it is well established fact that SHGs have great role in development of the people. If the existing Cooperatives start operating as microfinancing institution(s) by organizing, promoting, financial (and adopting) SHGs then it can pave to the way to the economic development of the rural poor by empowering them through social mobilization and economic activation. At the same time, Cooperative can get sizeable profits from its operations.

From the statistical facts and figures, it appears that the performance of cooperative Banks in the SHGs credit lending programme in India is poor. It is poorer in North-Eastern India in spite of Special Package for North-Eastern Region as announced by NABARD. NABARD has given different types of relaxation and concessions to the different types of agencies implementing SHG linkage programme. For the hill districts of North-East, minimum number of members to form SHG have been reduced from 10 to 5 in 2007-08. In this year, NABARD extended refinance of Rs. 1,615.50 crore. In the North East, out of 31 State Cooperative Banks (SCBs), 5 were running in losses and out of 369 District Credit Cooperatives Banks (DCCBs), 97 were loss making banks. The North-Eastern Council (NEC), Shillong, parked a fund of Rs.50 lakh with NABARD during the year for facilitating miscellaneous training programmes involving government/bank officials, NGOs, SHGs from States in the NER and Sikkim. The programme aims at linking savings and credit of SHGs to banks, focussing on improving the quality and viability of financial services under SHG-linkage banking.

Though SHG-Cooperative Linkage started late, more and more SHGs going to be linked with cooperatives recently, Out of 181 reporting banks, 131 co-operative banks reported recovery over 80% in 2007-08.

Activities of Assam Cooperative Apex Bank Ltd., Cachar District

In Assam, there exists two tier Cooperative—in the village level PACS and in the state level Assam State Cooperative Apex Bank Ltd. There are 69 branches of this bank in Assam. But in the Cachhar District, there is only one branch at Silchar. In Hailakandi District, there are two branches—one is located at Lala and another at Hailakandi. In Karimganj District there are three branches—Badarpur, Karimganj, and Ram Krishna Nagar. Thus, in the Barak Valley, the number of branches is 6 and 63 branches are located in Brahmaputra Valley and Hill Districts taken together.

In Cachhar District, the Linkage of Cooperative with SHG came very late and their performance is also very much unsatisfactory. In 2007-08, only one SHG was financed by Cooperative Bank at the amount of Rs. 15,000 only. In 2008-09, that number has increased to 11 and the amount of loan sanctioned was 205 lakhs only. In this context plans are to be formulated so that a lion's share of credit needs of the rural people are satisfied by cooperatives and post offices more particularly in the unbanked and underbanked rural areas.

Suggestions

SHGs can be used and aligned as an instrument for the economic development of the Cooperatives and their members in following manners:

1. In unbanked and underbanked rural areas more credit should be given to the SHGS by the cooperatives on easy terms and conditions.
2. Sustainability of SHGs depends on demand for goods and services produced by the SHGs. So, frequent SWOT analysis is necessary.
3. There must be the minimum level of managerial competency of the group members .Through specific and relevant training programs, it is possible to improve the managerial competency of the group members.
4. Socio-cultural climate must be conducive for the growth and development of the venture promoted by SHGs. By organizing awareness program, it is possible to create proper attitude of the people.

Inline, it can be concluded that the sustainability of any venture promoted by the SHGs depends on the positive attitude and will of the group members. Finance, subsidy can nurture or assists the members of the groups. But real development is a state of mind, People can improve their socio-economic condition only when the group members have farsightedness, strong will, and determination. That is why the business of certain groups, according to their own perception is sustainable, to others, it is not sustainable.

References

1. Alderman, Harold (1987), Cooperative Dairy Development in Karnataka, India.
2. Chopra , S. (2004) : Cooperatives, Kurukshetra, Vol. 52 No . 12.
3. *Das Banishree & Palai Nirod Kumar*, "Problems and Prospects of the cooperative movement in India under the Globalization Regime", collected from Net.
4. Dasgupta, R. (2005): Microfinance in India—Empirical Evidence, Alternative Models and Policy Imperatives; Economic and Political weekly; March 19-25, '2005; Vol. 40, No. 12.
5. Fernandez, A. P. (2007): A Microfinance Institution with a Difference, EPW, March 31.
6. Gupta, M.S. (2008): Microfinance through Self-Help Groups: An Emerging Horizon for Rural Development, The Indian Journal of Commerce, Vol. 61, No. 3, July–September, pp. 36-47.
7. Goswami, Pranay Jyoti. "Microfinance through SHG-Cooperative linkage Programme in SAMABAYIKA, AUETCCS Ltd., Assam University, Silchar. Vol. 1 , No. 1 , 2009.
8. Goswami, Pranay Jyoti and Acharjee P.R. (Ed) "Cooperative Movement in Assam—Problems And Prospects" 2004.
9. Goswami, Pranay Jyoti and Chakraborty, Amalendu. (Ed) "Cooperative Movement in North-East India—Problems And Prospects". AUT and C CO-OP society Ltd, Silchar, 2008.
10. Hermes, W, Lensink, R (2007), "Impact of Microfinance—A Critical Survey "EPW, Vol. 42, No. 46 pp. 462-465.
11. Kanungo, R. N. (1998): Entrepreneurship and Innovation–Models for development, New Delhi: Sage Publications.
12. Khandelwal, A.K. (2007): "Microfinance Development Strategy for India "EPW, Vol. 42, No. 13, pp. 1127-1135.
13. Khandker et al (2005), "Microfinance and Poverty: Evidence using panel Data from Bangladesh", World Bank Economic Review Vol. 19, No. 2, pp. 263-286.
14. Kumar, M. (2007): Rural Cooperative credit, Yojana, September 2007, Vol. 51.
15. M. Selvakumar and R. Sundar (2007), SWARNAJAYANTI Gram Swarozgar Yojana (SGSY) – Tool for Poverty Eradication, Kurukshetra, Dec.
16. Meher Shibalal (2007): Impact of Microfinance on Poverty: A study of Self-Help Groups in Orissa: Journal of Rural Development Vol. 26, No. (3) pp. 315-333, NIRD, Hyderabad.

17. Mishra, J. C. and R. K. Jhanvi (2004): Indian Banking System and Microfinance, Kurukshetra, Feb., 12-15.
18. Mishra, Gopalji. "Microfinance through Self Help Groups: An alternative strategy for Cooperative organization". in SAMABAYIKA, AUETCCS Ltd., Assam University, Silchar. Vol. 1, No. 1, 2009.
19. NABARD (2000): 'Summary and Recommendations, report by the task force on supportive policy and regulatory framework for microfinance in India, available at Eleanor, Margaret Hough, K. Madhava Das (1967), Cooperative Movement in India(Ed): Oxford University Press, p. 506.
20. NABARD (2001): 'Executive Summary and Core Recommendations', report by the expert committee on rural credit available at www.nabard.org/whats/whats. htm.
21. NABARD (2006): Annual Report 2005-06, 2007-08 available at www.nabard.org.
22. NABARD, (2000) Statistical Statements Relating to Cooperative Movement in India – 1997-98—Part I and Part II, Delhi.
23. Nagaya, N. (2000): Microfinance through Self Help Groups, Kurukshetra, August' 2000, Vol. 48, No. 11.
24. Nainta, R. P. (1998): Cooperation—The Need of the Hours, The Corporator, Vol. XXXV, No. 10, New Delhi: NCUI.
25. Puhazhendhi, V and K.J.S Satyasai (2000), Microfinance for poor: An Impact Evaluation, NABARD, Mumbai, India.
26. Samantaray, P. C. (2004), Hundred Years of Cooperative Movement: Emerging Issues and Challenges, Orissa Review. Singh Gurusharan K. (1998), India's Rural Cooperatives/edited, Vedam Books, Delhi, pp. 456.
27. Satish , P. (2005) "Mainstreaming of Microfinance" EPW, April 23, pp. 1731-39.
28. Sing, Rajmoni (2008) "Microfinance for micro-enterprise development—A panacea to poverty alleviation" in DGCCS'S journal of Commerce, Vol. V, No. 1.
29. Sinha, F (2005): "Access , use and contribution of Microfinance in India: Findings from a National Study", EPW, Vol. 40, No. 10, pp. 1714-171
30. Yojana (January 2008): Special Issue on Microfinance, 'Vol. 52.
31. Yojana (Jan. 2008) Special issues on Microfinance.

21

Microfinance Impact on Enterprise Performance and Job Creation: An Assessment

Nazimuddin Khadem

Abstract: *The development and growth of micro-enterprises is globally appreciated because of its stellar role in enhancing economic growth. Obviously, the growth of micro-enterprises depends largely on the financial services they need and how better they gain access to the sources of finance. Such enterprises require modest doses of capital to gear up their production level, exports, technical innovations, revenue and to generate employment opportunities. This paper examines the impact of microfinance on enterprise performance and job creation, using the primary data obtained from a sample of 45 micro-entrepreneurs of 5 different sectors located in Aizawl city of Mizoram. The enterprise performance has been captured in terms of sales revenue of the micro-enterprise units. The cross-sectional data for the financial year 2007-08 have been fitted to the specified regression models and the results have been judged by statistical test techniques for the purpose of impact assessment. The study realizes that microfinance efforts have significant potential to contribute to the revenue generation and job creation of the micro-enterprises.*

Introduction

The development and growth of micro-enterprises is globally appreciated because of its vital role in enhancing economic growth. This very fact is reflected in the form of their rising strength in overall product manufacturing, employment, exports and entrepreneurial skills. Obviously, the growth of micro-enterprises depends largely on the financial services they need and how better they gain access to the sources of finance. Such enterprises require modest doses of capital to gear up their production level, exports, technical innovations, revenue and to generate employment opportunities. Being a perfect opportunity for self-help development, micro-enterprise development is the need of the time, for which adequate supply of micro-enterprise credit through SHGs play crucial part. Micro-enterprise development and particularly microfinance grew to become a key anti-poverty strategy across the world with the success of the experiment done by Muhammad Yunus on the Grameen Bank in Bangladesh (Eversole, 2008).

Conceptually, microfinance is the provision of financial services which generally includes savings and credit services, as well as insurance and payment services for the poor self-employed people. According to Schreiner and Colombet, microfinance is the attempt to improve accessibility of poor households neglected by banks to small deposits and small loans (Rajagopalan-Parikh, 2007). Hence, it involves the provision of savings, loans and insurance services to the self-employed poor people irrespective of urban and rural settings, who are not emphasized by the formal financial sector. This very definition of microfinance clarifies that the concept of microfinance is different from that of micro-credit. While micro-credit refers to small loans, microfinance includes small loans as well as supplementing those loans with other financial services such as savings, insurance etc. It is asserted that microfinance involves providing both credit and non-credit financial services, e.g., savings, insurance, pensions and payment services, whereas micro-credit is a component of microfinance (Rajagopalan-Parikh, 2007). The concept of microfinance is relatively new in the field of development first emerged in 1970s (Robinson 2001). Earlier, throughout the period from 1950s to 1970s, the provision of financial services was basically in the form of subsidized rural credit programmes by governments, which often resulted in high loan defaults, high losses and non-reach to the beneficiaries (Robinson, 2001).

According to International Labour Organization: "Micro-enterprises are those entrepreneurial activities which engage ten or less than ten workers including the owner, and paid and unpaid family workers" (Krishna, 2008). Many of Indian writers use working definition as "those enterprises which employ less than ten workers fall under the category of micro-enterprises" (Singh-Joshi-Mehta, 2004). Shetty in his study realizes that the future of rural micro-enterprises relies on quality and stability in the production, extension of markets, and capacity building to the entrepreneurs. Provision of microfinance and other support services to micro-enterprises has large potential to facilitate income and employment generation and thereby socio-economic development (Shetty, 2008). Another study signifies that despite the rural populace are trained in various technologies some of them could not start their own enterprises due to hindrances like marketing problems, financial crisis, limited scope of farming, seasonal availability of raw-materials, lack of medication in broiler farming and difficulty in getting license (Khadem-Rashid, 2008).

The decade 1980s earmarked in the history of microfinance when Micro-finance Institutions (MFIs) such as Grameen Bank and BRI could be able to provide small loans and savings services to the poor preferably on a huge scale. The 1990s again registered tremendous growth in the number of MFIs and turned microfinance into an industry realizing that the poor had a demand for such financial services. The contribution of Nobel Laureate Prof. Mohd Yunus in the field of microfinance development through his Grameen Bank Model in Bangladesh is worth mentioning here. The importance of microfinance was again reinforced with the launch of the Micro-credit Summit in 1997, aiming to reach credit and other financial services to 175 million of the world's poorest families, especially the women, by 2015 (Rajagopalan-Parikh, 2007).

In this perspective, it is pertinent here to assess the impact of microfinance on employment and poverty which can better be judged through the contribution of micro-enterprises to employment generation. Notwithstanding, the contribution to employment generation by micro-enterprises depends largely on their business performance which can be expressed in terms of revenue generation. As the enterprise's business income increases, it has a spread effect beyond the household through employment and contribution to local economy. It thus helps a poor family to increase their income, which has an instant and lasting impact on quality of life, i.e. the ability to offer food, shelter, education and healthcare, and, in turn, it helps in raising their employability. It is very obvious that the growth of micro-enterprises relies on the financial services they need and accessibility to the sources of finance. Access to finance is often reduced to access to credit on the assumption that job creation depends on investment which requires finance from external services. Reference to this, microfinance here will mean access of micro-enterprises to micro-loans or micro-credit services for investment purposes. Generally, the investment in new production technology and innovation is considered to be the precondition for job creation. In fact, Hulme and Mosley observe that, with limited technological innovation labor productivity increased as a result of micro-loans (Hulme-Mosley, 1996).

Objectives and Hypotheses

The basic objectives of the study are:

- To assess the impact of microfinance on the business performance of the micro-enterprises in Aizawl.
- To examine the effect of microfinance on job creation by the micro-enterprises in Aizawl.

The null hypotheses framed for the study are:

- H0: No relationship between the level of micro-loans and the sales revenue of the micro-enterprises.
- H0: No association between the level of micro-loans and the job created in micro-enterprises.

Research Methodology

The Aizawl district of Mizoram has been selected for the purpose of the study featuring a hilly and geographically isolated area. Micro-enterprise sectors, viz.,

Food Processing, Livestock, Forestry, Hotels and Lodges, Manufacturing, Repairing, Trade and Services, etc. have been operating in large-scale across the district territory. The sampling design of the study is two-stage stratified random sampling, considering the selection of micro-enterprise sectors at the first stage. The second stage of sampling is the selection of Micro-enterprise Units under each chosen Sector. The sample size covers around 20 percent of the total micro-enterprise units spread over different micro-enterprise sectors across the district. To achieve the objectives and to test the hypotheses the study bases mainly on primary data obtained from the field survey with the help of sampling designed mentioned above. Primary data have been obtained from a sample of 45 micro-entrepreneurs of 5 different sectors located in Aizawl city of Mizoram. Direct Personal Interview method has been adopted to collect primary information from micro-enterprise owners spread over the entire district through Well-devised Questionnaire.

Empirical Analysis and Main findings

As the micro-loans are used to enlarge the working capital of a micro-enterprise it has definite repercussions on revenue and employment. The impact of micro-loans and other financial services depends on the use made of financial resources by the entrepreneurs. How effectively credit use translates into job creation is determined by enterprise business performance. In order to assess this, a comprehensive survey has been conducted on the enterprise revenue, employment and micro-loans from external sources in Aizawl district of Mizoram, following the methodology designed. Majority of the micro-enterprises in Aizawl are run by low income people who mostly depend on local based MFIs for their capital needs. The percentage share of capital supplied by MFIs to these micro-enterprises has certain repercussions on their business performance and job creation. The business performance of enterprises is captured by their sales revenue in terms of market value, while job creation is measured by the number of persons employed in micro-enterprises including self-employed and wage-employed persons. Reference to the foregone explanation, it is presumed that higher the share of microfinance to the capital of a micro-enterprise sector, larger is the revenue generation and job creation. The average amount of outsourced finance received by an enterprise sector is being converted into the percentage share of total capital volume of that particular sector. The sales revenue volume of a sector is divided by the number of selected enterprise units under that sector and being presented in terms of mean value. Similarly, the mean values have been computed for the proportions of the micro-loans as well as employment, according to different sectors of the micro-enterprises. The processed data is presented in the following Tables 1 and 2.

TABLE 1

Sector wise Distribution of Micro-loans, Employment and Sales Revenue

Code	Enterprise Sectors	Sales Revenue (in Lac rupees)	Employment (in Numbers)	Micro Loans (in peresent total investment)
A	Food Processing	403.2	56.7	356.4
B	Livestock312.3	44.1	166.5	
C	Hotels and Lodges	525.6	153	487.8
D	Trade and Services	341.1	73.8	288
E	Manufacturing	452.7	99	412.2

Source: *Field Survey, Aizawl, 2007-08*

1. Nine micro-enterprise owners have been interviewed from each of the selected Sector.
2. The above figures are the total values of all the micro-enterprise units in a Sector.

TABLE 2

Sector-wise Enterprise Performance, Employment and Microfinance
(Mean Values)

Code	Enterprise Sectors	Sales Revenue (in Lac rupees)	Employment (in Numbers)	Micro Loans (in peresent total investment)
A	Food Processing	44.8	6.3	39.6
B	Livestock	34.7	4.9	18.5
C	Hotels and Lodges	58.4	17	54.2
D	Trade and Services	37.9	8.2	32
E	Manufacturing	50.3	11	45.8

Source: Field Survey, Aizawl, 2007-08

The tables delineate that micro-enterprise sector of hotels and lodges secured the highest position in generating sales revenue to the extent of Rs. 58.4 thousand in average of all units in that sector under study. In case of employment the sector also exhibits the highest level of employment showing 17 persons in average. This can be substantiated by the fact that the proportion of capital from external sources accessed by hotels and lodges touches the highest constituting 54.2 percent. This indicates that the said sector gained better access to microfinance which has positive impact upon its revenue generation and the consequent employment. The same positive relationships between micro-loans and sales revenue as well as micro-loans and employment are revealed in case of manufacturing and livestock sectors. However, it is observed that though the food processing and the trade and services sectors experience an increasing level of their sales revenues with an increasing proportion of their access to micro-loans, their employment figures are not in the same trend. Because, as per the ranking of the sectors in terms of revenue generation and micro-loans, food processing and trade and services secure third rank and fourth rank, respectively, in ascending order of magnitude. But the same rankings are not possible in case of employment. The reason being that food processing sector achieves Rs. 44.8 thousand sales revenue and 6.3 level of employment in it, with micro-loans of 39.6 percent. As against this, trade and services sector achieves Rs. 37.9 thousand of revenue and 8.2 level of employment coupled with the proportion of micro-loans of 32 percent. Here the figures of employment put trade and services sector in third rank and food processing sector in fourth rank which is just opposite to their rankings in sales revenue and employment. Notwithstanding, the processed data (Table 1) depicts that there exists an overall positive associations between revenue generation and micro-loans, as well as employment and micro-loans, with respect to micro-enterprise sectors.

In order to substantiate the tabular results the study follows econometric analysis using the bi-variate regression models and t-test of significance for testing the null hypotheses framed for the study. Based on the presumption that sales revenue of micro-enterprise sectors depends on the improved access to microfinance, ceteris paribus, the following regression equation has been estimated by fitting the cross-sectional enterprise data for the year 2007-08. In this case the null hypothesis of no relationship between sales revenue and micro-loans has been tested. The estimated equation and the regression results are given inTable 3.

$$SR = -0.564 + 0.752ML^{*}$$

TABLE 3

Regression Results—I

Particulars	Value
R-square	0.565
Standard Error of the Estimate	3.64
Intercept	–0.564
β Co-efficient	0.752
t-statistic	1.976
Critical Value	1.96
Level of Significance	5%

*Significance at 5% level

The estimated equation reveals that the magnitude of relationship between sales revenue and micro-loans is to the extent of 0.565. This implies that around 57 percent of the variation in enterprise sales revenue is explained by the change in the proportion of micro-loans. Since the coefficient value is positive showing 0.752, it indicates that micro-loans have positive impact on enterprise business performance. The negative intercept value of 0.564 implies that micro-enterprises cannot generate revenue at no financial services. The marginal propensity to sales revenue with respect to micro-loans is 0.752. That is, with every increase in the level of micro-loans to the enterprises sales revenue increased by 75 percent. This positive relationship is found to be statistically significant judged by t-statistic at 5% significance level. Since t-vaule (1.976) is greater than its critical value (1.96) the null hypothesis is rejected at 95% confidence interval. We, therefore, conclude that microfinance has positive and significant impact on business performance of the micro-enterprises. This can be substantiated by the fact that micro-enterprises in Aizawl are operating with inadequate capital– both fixed and working, and so any of their improvement in access to microfinance leads them to generate higher volume of revenue with adoption of modern and innovative methods of production.

Again, it is assumed that employment level in micro-enterprise sectors depends on the improved access to microfinance on the condition that other things remain the same. The following bi-variate regression equation has been estimated by fitting the cross-sectional enterprise data for the year 2007-08. The null hypothesis in this case has been framed as no relationship between micro-loans and employment. The following are the estimated equation and the regression results:

$$EM = -9.354 + 0.830ML^{**}$$

TABLE 4

Regression Results—II

Particulars	Value
R-square	0.689
Standard Error of the Estimate	3.08
Intercept	–9.354
® Co-efficient	0.830
t-statistic	2.580
Critical Value	2.58
Level of Significance	1%

**Significance at 1% level

The results say that the magnitude of association between job creation and micro-loans is to the extent of 0.689, implying that about 69 percent of the variation in employment is due to the variation in the proportion of micro-loans to the enterprises. The positive regression coefficient value of 0.830 indicates that micro-loans have positive impact on job creation in the micro-enterprises. The intercept value is negative implying that micro-enterprises cannot employ hard labour in the absence of financial services and so cannot generate any employment opportunities. The marginal propensity to job creation with respect to micro-loans is 0.830. It means with every increase in the level of micro-loans to the enterprises, employment increased by 83 percent. This positive association is found to be statistically significant confirmed by t-statistic at 1% significance level. The value of t-statistic is 2.58, and the null hypothesis is rejected at critical value of 2.58 at 99% confidence interval. Thus it is clear that microfinance has positive and statistically significant impact on job creation in the micro-enterprises. The reason being that, in the emerging markets due to globalization, micro-enterprises in Aizawl need more and more financial services to capture the market through innovation and skilled manpower. It is, therefore, any improvement of micro-enterprises in access to microfinance results in generating more employment opportunities within the enterprise structure.

Conclusion

We, therefore, conclude that microfinance has positive and significant impact on business performance of the micro-enterprises and job creation. This can be substantiated by the fact that micro-enterprises in Aizawl are very informal in nature—having lack of capital both in terms of fixed and working capital. With such inadequate capital facilities the entrepreneurs are unable to adopt modern and innovative production techniques and to hire skilled manpower, and, hence, they have no choice but to rely mostly upon unskilled labor force including the non-paid family members equipped by poor and labor-intensive techniques. With this status they cannot cope up with competitive market in the face of globalization and, hence, remain unable to reap the benefits of globalization.

In such a situation any improvement in the access to capital, from the sources of microfinance institutions, naturally dictates the conscious entrepreneurs to adopt modern tools and product innovation techniques coupled with hiring of skilled laborers, with a view to generate higher volume of revenues amidst competition. The present findings of the study justify that micro-entrepreneurs in Aizawl are very sensitive, and if proper and adequate financial services could be provided this sector would play special role in the economic development of Mizoram. All these lead us to conclude that MFIs have crucial role to play in the improvement of business performance of the micro-enterprises which can create more employment opportunities in the area. For this reason MFIs should be restructured considering the need of the enterprises so that they can provide better financial services at subsidized rates, which is possible by government and NGO initiatives. In this regard, entrepreneurs should be ensured with easy and direct access to the microfinance services through constant monitoring of the services by the government. Besides, the entrepreneurs should make the best possible use of the financial resources in order to optimize their business performance and employment outcomes.

In view of this the MFIs should be supported by the government to bring the client to produce the optimal employment effect of financial services through strengthening SHG bank linkages. In addition, it is the need of the time to support the MFIs in offering parallel non-financial services, information and guidance to optimize enterprise business performance and employment.

References

1. Dunn, Elizabeth and Arbuckle, Gordon (2001): 'Microcredit and Micro enterprise Development Performance: Impact Evidence from Peru', SED, Vol.. 12, No. 4, December.
2. Eversole, Robyn (2008): 'Solving Poverty for Yourself: Micro-Enterprise Development, Microfinance and Migration', in Micro-enterprises–Perspectives and Experiences ed by Sridhar Krishna, The Icfai University Press, Punjagutta, Hyderabad.
3. Hulme, David and Mosley, Paul (1996): 'Finance against Poverty: Effective Institutions for Lending to Small Farmers and Micro-enterprises in Developing Countries', Vol. 2, London: Routledge
4. Hulme, D. (2000): 'Impact Assessment Methodologies for Microfinance: Theory, Experience and Better Practice', World Development, Vol. 28, No.1. Schreiner, M (2002): 'Aspects of Outreach: A Framework for the Discussion of the Social Benefits of Microfinance', Journal of International Development, Vol. 14, pp. 1-13.
5. Krishna, Sridhar (2008): Micro-enterprises – Perspectives and Experiences, The Icfai University Press, Punjagutta, Hyderabad.
6. Khadem, N U, and A Rashid (2008): 'Hindrances Faced by Rural Entrepreneurs: A Case Study', Accepted for publication in the edited volume Development Perspective of Northeast, Unpublished.
7. Kalran, Dean (2001): 'Microfinance Impact Assessments: The Perils of Using New Members as a Control Group', Journal of Microfinance, Vol. 3, No. 2, pp. 76-85.
8. Khandker, Shahidur, Samad, Hussain and Khan, Zahed (1998): 'Income and Employment Effects of Micro-credit Programmes: Village-level Evidence from Bangladesh', Journal of Development Studies, Vol.35, No.2, December, pp. 96-124.
9. Morduch, J and Haley, B (2002): 'Analysis of the Effects of Microfinance on Poverty Reduction', Wagner Working Paper 1014, June, New York University.
10. Puhazhendi V and Satyasai KJS (2001): 'Economic and Social Empowerment of Rural Poor through SHGs', Indian Journal of Agricultural Economics, Vol.56, No.3.
11. Robinson, M (2001): 'The Microfinance Revolution: Sustainable Finance for the Poor', World Bank, Washington.

12. Rahman A (1999): 'Microcredit Initiatives for Equitable and Sustainable Development: Who Pays?' World Development, Vol. 27, No. 1.
13. Rajagopalan, S. and Parikh, N. (2007): Microfinance: Impacts and insights, The Icfai University Press, Hyderabad.
14. Singh, A K, Ashutosh Joshi and G S Mehta (2004): 'Employment Structure, Conditions and Productivity in Micro and Small Enterprises: Findings of a Field Survey in Uttar Pradesh', The Indian Journal of Labour Economics, Vol. 47, No. 4.
15. Shetty, Naveen Kumar (2008): 'Microfinance: An Integrated Approach for Micro-Enterprise Development in India', in Micro-Enterprises–Perspectives and Experiences, ed by Sridhar Krishna, The Icfai University Press, Punjagutta, Hyderabad.
16. Yunus, M. (1994): 'Credit for Self Employment: A Fundamental Human Right', in D. Gibbons (ed), The Grameen Reader, Dhaka.

22

Microfinance for Micro-enterprise Development with Special Reference to Nagaon District of Assam

Balin Hazarika and G. Singaiah

ABSTRACT: *Of all the problems faced by the micro-enterprise in the district of Nagaon, non-availability of sufficient finance seems to be one of the major hurdles. Wherever for the country as a whole, institutional finance played a vital role in the process of industrial development. The position of Assam is far from satisfactory. The flow of institutional finance in the state is still at very low ebb. The micro-credit facilities in the district which consists of a series of schemes have not been able to create much spurt in the growth of industries. In recent years, there is a marked increase in the amount of financial assistance flowing to the district from the banks and financial institutions, but still all the areas in the district are not able to get full support from the financial institutions. Generally, banks don't take practical or pragmatic view and they are more security conscious. Though the banks have mobilized substantial amount of deposits from the region, the same are transferred to the neighbouring region. Therefore the credit-deposit ratio of the banks in the region is low. Besides these financial problems, some other problems involved in micro-enterprise in the district have been identified.*

Introduction

Microfinance include micro-credit and savings which is sometimes called 'social loan' and common objective is that it is improving living standard of the poor, by strengthening their ability to gain food, medical, housing facilities and creating jobs. NABARD task force on supportive and regulatory framework for microfinance (1999) define, microfinance as "provision of thrift credit and other financial service and products of very small amount to the poor in rural, semi-urban and urban areas for enabling them to raise their income and improvement of the standard of living."

Since the word "micro" represents small, the MSMED Act, 2006 defines that the enterprise engagement in the manufacturing or production of goods, investment in plant and machinery does not exceed twenty five lakh rupees, and enterprise engage in providing or rendering of services, the investment in equipment does not exceed ten lakh rupees.

Significance of micro-enterprise: In India majority of the people are living in rural areas, and, again, majority of them are poor, living below the poverty line. For alleviation of poverty and solving the unemployment problems, micro-enterprise proved great help. But for starting a micro-enterprise finance is the most important factor. In India, many small enterprises are primarily of micro-enterprise. If we accept investment as criterion for small enterprises having investment in the plant and machinery up to Rs. 2 lakhs, then 82.8 percent of small enterprise in small scale sector can be considered as micro-enterprise (second all-India census 1990). Therefore sufficient micro-credit is very essential

TABLE 1

Growth of Small Scale Enterprises in Assam as on 2005

Year	No. of units Employment	Nos. of units	Production in Lakhs	Fixed Investment (Rs. in Lakhs)
1995-1996	29,617	120,568	60,020	57,968
	(10.14)	(19.92)	(36.28)	(9.23)
1996-1997	32,084	131,049	81,752	60,022
	(15.00)	(10.00)	(17.51)	(9.23)
1997-1998	34,241	141,636	89,265	75,045
	(11.65)	(13.35)	(7.16)	(83.39)
1998-1999	36,465	150,957	109,460	87,397
	(9.37)	(9.88)	(14.56)	(6.33)
1999-2000	38,286	158,064	147,021	91,335
	(10.14)	(9.29)	(10.40)	(4.43)
2000-01	40,402	168,324	163,034	96,627
	(8.20)	(8.08)	(14.57)	(3.34)
2001-02	42,930	179,863	179,411	101,693
	(6.50)	(8.08)	(11.45)	(25.02)
2002-03	45,270	190,977	198,375	106,561
	(6.90)	(6.58)	(9.19)	(16.46)
2003-04	47,624	202,746	218,072	113,753
	(5.00)	(4.71)	(22.62)	(4.51)
2004-05	49,691	212,142	147,021	120,873
	(4.99)	(6.49)	(34.31)	(5.80)

Note: Both SIDO and Non-SIDO units as on 31st March of the respective year and figures in brackets refer percentage over previous year.

Sources: Directorate of Industries, Assam

TABLE 2

SSI Registered in Nagaon District with Assam up to 31st March, 2005

Year	No. of Smalls Scale Industries				%
	Nagaon	Total	Assam	Total	
Up to 2001	1,817	1,817	29,537	29,537	6.15
2001–2002	69	1,886	2,528	32,065	2.72
2002–2003	138	2,024	2,246	34,311	6.14
2003–2004	118	2,142	2,348	36,659	5.02

Source: Directorate of Industries, Assam, with 3rd All India Census

for development of micro-enterprise. But it is unfortunate that direct institutional finance is still not able to provide-sufficient finance to this system.

Statement of problem: In India financial institutions have spread their network in every nook and corner of the country (nearly 1.25 lakhs rural credit outlets). But still a vast majority of the rural poor have little access to formal banking system. Micro-credit Summit-World Report observed that 2 percent of micro-enterprise of developing countries has access today to financial services. The All India Debt and Investment Survey Reports (1991), that approximately 24 percent of rural household debt are either from formal or informal sources. Out of this, 36 percent had to still depend on informal credit viz, moneylender, shopkeepers and relatives etc.

Need of the study: Micro-enterprise plays a important role for alleviation of poverty and creating employment—especially among the poor. Though we have lots of financial institutions, the credit scenario is not satisfactory in Assam in general and Nagoan district in particular. In the district almost all branches of financial institutions are situated but still in the district is 3.35 thousand BPL families and about 1 lakh job seekers. So, the present study attempts to observe the micro-credit aspects of financial institutions for alleviation of poverty and creating employment generation through promotion of micro-enterprise in the district.

Objective of the paper: The main objective of the paper is to analysis the lending pattern and performance of financial institutions regarding micro-credit for promotion of micro-enterprise in the Nagaon district of Assam.

Present micro-credit delivery system in the district: In India different types of credit delivery systems prevail which are followed by Nagaon district of Assam. This can be classified in five groups:

(i) Individual credit delivery model: Credit given directly to the individual by the FI for starting the micro-enterprise to the unemployed, weaker section of society with collateral security or fixed deposit. These systems are predominant mainly in priority sector banks, especially the regional rural banks and cooperative banks.

(ii) People voluntarily form small groups of five people to provide mutual, morally binding guarantees in lieu of the collateral required by commercial banks. In this system only two members of a group are allowed for loan. Depending on their performance repayment, the next two borrowers can then apply and subsequently the fifth member as well. It has been adopted in many countries with modification to suit local condition and culture.

(iii) This model is to an extent on expansion of the group approach where the basic necessities of the poor, especially the women, are met through the community banking system. The community or village banks are organized with 30-50 members.

(iv) Cooperative credit society provides credit and other financial services to their members from the deposits of members according to their requirements.

(v) The SHG model is considered as the basic micro-credit model in India. SHG is a novel strategy developed and promoted by NABARD. It has started SHGs programmed in order to eliminate unemployment and create more number of self-employed people to alleviate poverty in the country. The SHGs open a formal bank account in the name of groups. The groups meet often and use the pooled thrift to provide small loan to members to help meet their small emergent needs.

Performance of Financial Institution in Nagaon District

Table 3—Commercial Banks are the major financial institutions that provide credit to this district. RBI Guideline states that 40% of the total lending should be given to the priority sector, but overall credit deposit ratio in this district is not satisfactory or below the standard of RBI Guideline.

TABLE 3

SSIs Registered in Nagaon District with Assam up to 31st March 2005

Bank Group	No. of Branch	Deposits (Rs. in lakhs)	Advances (Rs. in lakhs)	CD Ratio %
Commercial Bank	56	76,347.45	27,424.39	36
Regional Rural Bank	31	10,227.19	4,010.00	33
Cooperative Bank	4	3,742.93	1,110.76	24
Total	**91**	**90,317.57**	**32,561.15**	**36**

Source: *Lead Bank , UBI, Nagaon*

TABLE 4

Loan Outstanding

Bank Group	No. of Branch	2001-02 (Lakhs)	2002-03 (Lakhs)	2003-04 (Lakhs)	% share on 31.03.2004
Commercial Bank	57	13,858.00	14,603.00	17,858.00	82
Regional Rural Bank	30	1,666.00	2,033.00	2,919.00	13
State Cooperative Bank	4	920.00	972.00	1,005.00	5
Total	**91**	**16,444.00**	**17,608.00**	**21,782.00**	**100**

Source: *Potential Link Credit Plan, NABARD*

Table 1.4—it is observed that the outstanding of all banks has increases to Rs. 21,782 Lakhs as on 31.03.2004 from Rs. 17.608 Lakhs, registering a growth rate of 23.70%. While reviewing the agency-wise growth rate under loan and advances it was observed that RRB had done excellent growth rate with 44% followed by Commercial Banks 22% . The State Co-operative Bank had growth only 3%.

TABLE 5

Recovery Position (2003-04)

Agency	Disbursed	Recovery	% of Recovery
CBs	2,233.60	769.40	34
RRBs	421.81	223.85	53
SCBs	395.37	38.07	10
Total	**3,050.78**	**1,031.32**	

Source : *Lead Bank , UBI, Nagaon, Assam*

The overall recovery position of the district was 34% in 2003-04. Agency-wise analysis of the data reveals that RRB had better recovery with 53% while the State Cooperative Bank had very poor recovery position with only 10%. Efforts should make for recovery of loan for better recycling of funds.

For improving of economic condition of the BPL families, the Govt. of India had launched the scheme of Integrated Rural Development programme (IRDP) from October 1976 and then switched over to new scheme known as Swarnajayanti Gram Swarojgar Yojana (SGSY) from April 1999. In Nagaon district there are 3.35 lakh BPL families according to the district rural development agency (DRDA) of the Government of Assam. SGSY is a holistic programme of micro-enterprise; it covers all aspects of self-employment viz. promotion of self-help groups among the rural poor. SGSY scheme is implemented by the DRDA through the panchayt samities and with the active is involvement of other panchayati raj institutions—Banks and the NGOs. Under SGSY, more emphasis has been given for active cluster and group finance. Some activities are identified/approved by the block level/district level SGSY committee's viz. chira, muri making, cane and bamboo product, poultry and chital patti.

TABLE 6

Performance of SGSY Schemes

Year	Phy (No.)	FA	Phy (No.)	FA
2001-02	Group = 256 Individual = 756	453.56	Group = 138 Individual = 608	Group = 247.48 Individual=133.89 Total = 381.37
2002-03	Group = 188 Individual =213	405.43 53.25 458.68	Group = 138	Group = 273.19 Individual = 120 Individual =26.08 Total = 299.27
2003-04	Group = 312 Individual = 92	650.73 23.00 673.73	Group = 359 Individual = 95	Group = 586.11 Individual =19.00 Total = 605.11

Sources: *DRDA, Nagaon District, Assam*

From Table 6, it is shows that the performance of SGSY programme is very satisfactory. In terms of economic activities with the help of SHG, the achievement was 115%, while in financial terms the achievement was 90% of the target. Again, the repayment of loan under SGSY group was above 85%.

Conclusions and suggestions

A number of constraints have been responsible for the slow pace of industrial development in the state. Of all the problems faced by the micro-enterprise in the district, non-availability of sufficient Finance seems to be one of the major hurdles. Wherever for the country as a whole, institutional finance played a vital role in the process of industrial development. The position of Assam is far from satisfactory. The flow of institutional finance in the state is still at very low ebb. The micro-credit facilities in the district which consists of a series of schemes have not been able to create much spurt in the growth of industries. In recent years, there is a marked increase in the amount of financial assistance flowing to the districts from the banks and financial institutions, but still all the areas in the district are not able to get full support from the financial institutions. Generally, banks don't take practical or pragmatic view and they are more security conscious. Though the banks have mobilized substantial amount of deposits from the region, the same are transferred to the neighbouring region. Therefore the credit deposits ratio of the banks in the region is low. Besides these financial problems, some other problems are involved in micro-enterprise in the district have been identified. These are location, labour, marketing, power, raw materials, and infrastructural problems.

In such a scenario the only ray of hope is the MEs sector for labour surplus economy like ours. Within the SSE sector the development of the MEs will hold the finest promise for tackling the unemployment problems.

The credit dispensation in case of MEs will undergo the following six steps:

(i) Identification of the project.

(ii) Appraisal of the project.

(iii) Assessment of the loan requirement.

(iv) Disbursal of loans.

(v) Monitoring the projects, and

(vi) Recovery of loan.

With the help of above-mentioned credit mechanism, bank and financial institutions should deliver credit either through the NGO or through SHG. The linkage between the NGO and the SHG with the commercial banking set up should be established in order to smoothen the flow of credit. The bank should be asked to open ME development wings in every district for proper monitoring and guidance. A fixed percentage of the priority sector credit should be earmarked for financing the MEs and freed from all kinds of state and local taxes for enhancing the cost competitiveness. The financial institutions should play a role more of a development nature rather than being merely credit institutions. Mobile banking facilities should be introduced so that the poor and remote people can get finance.

23

Microfinance Assisted Micro-enterprises in Meghalaya and their Position of Sustainability

S. Rajbongshi and M. Chakraborty

ABSTRACT: *The analysis of this study is done on the financial position of business operation of different micro-enterprises (MEs) in Meghalaya state carried out by micro-entrepreneurs. The study is limited to non-crop economic activities which includes the group as well as individual MEs established by the SHGs themselves collectively and the members of SHGs individually. The financial performance of group micro-enterprises (GMEs) and individual micro-enterprises (IMEs) are analyzed by considering several parameters. The sustainability of their operation is highlighted through several ratios such as profitability, solvency, financial self-sufficiency, etc. The main objective of this study is to examine the sustainability of MEs that have been developed with micro-credit under the microfinance programme.*

Introduction

Under the microfinance programme, a newly established micro-enterprise can face problems from different angles, such as shortage of capital, accessibility to formal credit markets, social factors and economic catastrophe that impede the growth and development of MEs in the long-term. The accessibility to formal credit—which was the prime obstacle for micro-entrepreneurs—has been removed largely by the proliferation of microfinance programme in many parts of the country. Evidences around the world suggest that the programme has been very successful in providing a sustainable source of income through the promotion of micro-enterprises and creating more job opportunities for the poor and unemployed people. From the studies that are carried out on the sustainability of microfinance by the programmers and practitioners, they have come to agree that financial sustainability is a sine qua non for the breadth and depth of outreach in a longer term. According to the viewpoint of programme, the sustainability of participants is the end result if the participants reach the level of income generating status and employment. But this is not for micro-enterprises because the main accountability of sustainability for micro-enterprises starts after the establishment of enterprises.

Sustainability is not an end in itself but rather a means to the end of improved social welfare. 'Sustainability is traditionally measured in terms of 'self-sufficiency'. *Self-sufficiency indicators are cost recovery measures that compare income to expense.* The 'operational self-sufficiency' measures the degree to which cash inflows of current income cover current expenses, excluding depreciation and other adjustments' (P Satish, 2005 p.1734). The institutions that cannot cover these costs require periodic injections of outside funds in order to keep running. Successful MFIs have to be operationally efficient (Rhyne, 1998). This sustainability measurement for MFI is also applicable for micro-enterprises since the main motive of micro-entrepreneurs is to earn profit i.e. profit motive. Therefore, the self-sufficiency indicators are the comparative measurement of trend of income and expenses to justify the sustainability of micro-enterprises in the long term. The programmers and donors do the measurement of sustainability after providing available opportunities and it depends on the different degrees or parameters that affect on the participants. But in case of microfinance institutions most of the discussions regarding sustainability in many countries have been taken to mean for full cost recovery or profit making and it is associated with the aim of building microfinance institutions that can last into the future without continued reliance on government subsidies or on donor funds (Conning, 1999).

Microfinance started with the objective that it might have brought an opportunity for poor people to access to credit with which poor households can establish an enterprise to manage family needs and hunger. Community banks, NGOs, grassroots savings, and credit groups around the world have shown that these micro-enterprising loans can be profitable for borrowers and for the lenders, making microfinance one of the most effective poverty reducing strategies (Barry et al, 1996) in the world. However, the microfinance programmes carry some limitations, which create the problems of sustainability. Therefore, the question arises how far are the micro-enterprises sustainable that can solve unemployment problems and poverty alleviation at the same time. Therefore, in this paper the main target is to analyze the problems of sustainability of micro-enterprises in the state that limit the development of micro-enterprises in the long-run.

Methodological Design: Sample Data and Its Classification

The analysis of this paper is based on the primary data. The primary data are collected with the help of preset questionnaire asked to the owners of micro-enterprises. All the SHGs linked with the bank branches of Meghalaya are considered as population for the primary survey. The growth and development parameters like number of units, output, revenue, etc., are identified with the help of primary survey. For this purpose, 200 sample units of micro-enterprises from the state of Meghalaya, which are linked to the commercial banks and have taken loan for at least three years, have been considered for our study. In the actual sample data 204 SHGs are considered from 5 districts except East Garo Hills and South Garo Hills because these two districts do not have many SHGs which fit to the study parameters. After doing a scrutiny of 300 randomly collected SHGs' data and more than 3,000 individuals' data, we have arrived at the final set of 204 cases of non-crop activity micro-enterprises and they are selected as sample in this analysis.

TABLE 1

Sample Classifications

Activity-wise Classification of Sample Data	No.	% of Shares
Group Farm Activity Micro-enterprise (GFAME)	43	21.1
Group Non-farm Activity Micro-enterprise (GNFAME)	58	28.4
Individual Farm Activity Micro-enterprise (IFAME)	51	25.0
Individual Non-farm Activity Micro-enterprise (INFAME)	52	25.5
Total Farm Activity Micro-enterprise (FAME)	94	46.1
Total Non-farm Activity Micro-enterprise (NFAME)	110	53.9
Group Activity Micro-enterprise (GME = GFAME + GNFAME)	101	49.5
Individual Activity Micro-enterprise (IME = IFAME + INFAME)	103	50.5
Total Sample Data (GFAME + GNFAME + IFAME + INFAME)	**204**	**100.0**

Source: *Field Survey*

Out of those SHGs or members of SHGs who have established economic activities such as farm or non-farm micro-enterprises with the bank credit have been randomly selected. Out of the 204 sample SHGs, 101 are involved in group economic activities i.e. group micro-enterprises (GMEs) and 103 groups are individual economic activities, i.e., individual micro-enterprises (IMEs). The detail classification of sample is presented in the Table 1. The different activities carried out by FAME are goatery, piggery and poultry activities for both groups as well as individual micro-enterprises. On the other hand, in case of NFAME three different types of non-farm activities for both group as well as individual micro-enterprises are considered such as 'Business', (which includes betel nut selling, vegetables selling, rice selling and dry and raw fish selling), 'Shops' (which includes grocery shops, fair price shops and small shops) and VMI which means Village Micro Industries (it includes broomstick making, cane and bamboo works, rice mills, transport operator, spice cult, weaving and tailoring).

West Garo Hills is the most SHG populated district from which 154 sample enterprises have been collected followed by East Khasi Hills (31) and West Khasi Hills (12) (Table 2). Out of 101 of GMEs, 43 groups are engaged in farm-activity group businesses, i.e., group farm activity microenterprises (GFAMEs) and 58 groups are in non-farm-activity group microenterprises (GNFAMEs) such as shops at village level and businesses of selling of agricultural products. The remaining numbers i.e., 103, are doing individual activities. These individual members are those members of SHGs who have received loans from groups and have started either farm or non-farm business activities. Around 51 members are doing individual farm-activity micro-enterprises (IFAMEs) and 52 members are doing individual non-farm-activity micro-enterprises (INFAMEs) in our sample.

TABLE 2

Sample Data Classification in Meghalaya

Micro-enterpri-ses (MEs)	Activities	East Khasi Hills	West Khasi Hills	West Garo Hills	Jaintia Hills	Ri-Bhoi	State Total Sample	% of Total Sample
FAME	Goatery	1	8	5	–	1	15	(7)
	Piggery	16	3	45	–	3	67	(33)
	Poultry	–	–	12	–	–	12	(6)
	Total	17 (18)	11 (12)	62 (66)	–	4 (4)	94 (100)	(46)
NFAME	Business	5	1	39	–	–	45	(24)
	Shops	5	–	48	1	–	54	(25)
	VMI	4	–	5	2	–	11	(5)
	Total	14 (13)	1 (1)	92 (84)	3 (3)	–	110 (100)	(100)
Grand Total		**31** (15)	**12** (6)	**154** (75)	**3** (2)	**4** (2)	**204**	(100)

Source: Field survey

Notes: Figures in brackets indicate percentage to total, FAME = Farm Activity Micro-enterprise, NFAME = Non-farm Activity Micro-enterprise

TABLE 3

Gender-wise Sample Classification

Micro-enterprises (MEs)	Gender-Wise Classification	FAMEs				NFAMEs				State Grand Total Sample
		Goatery	Piggery	Poultry	Total	Business	Shops	VMI	Total	
Group	Men	1	6	–	7	–	3	–	3	**10** (9.9)
	Women	8	18	3	29	19	21	6	46	**75** (74.3)
	Mixed	3	4	–	7	3	4	2	9	**16** (15.8)
	Total of GMEs	12 (11.9)	28 (27.7)	3 (3)	43 (45.7)	25 (24.8)	25 (24.8)	8 (7.9)	58 (57.4)	**101** (49.5)
Individual	Men	–	7	–	7	5	–	–	5	**12** (11.7)
	Women	3	32	9	44	18	26	3	47	**91** (88.3)
	Total of IMEs	3 (3)	39 (37.9)	9 (8.7)	51 (54.3)	23 (22.3)	26 (25.2)	3 (3)	52 (50.5)	**103** (50.5)
Grand Total		**15** (16)	**67** (71)	**12** (13)	**94** (100)	**45** (43)	**54** (47)	**11** (10)	**110** (100)	**204** (100)

Source: *Field Survey*

Notes: Figures in brackets indicate percentage to total. GMEs = Group Micro-enterprises; IMEs = Individual Micro-enterprises.

The maximum numbers of sample groups as well as individual micro-enterprises (MEs) are owned by women. Out of 101 GMEs, 74.3 percent are women micro-entrepreneurs followed by mixed 15.8 percent and men micro-entrepreneurs 9.9 percent (Table 3). In case of IME, 88.3 percent are women micro-entrepreneurs and 11.7 percent are men micro-entrepreneurs. Out of the total sample of 204 MEs, 94 are FAME and 110 are NFAME category. Under FAME, there are 71 percent piggery activities, 16 percent goatery activities and 13 percent poultry activities, respectively. Moreover, the classification of FAME into group and individual MEs gives 54.3 percent of IMEs and 45.7 percent of GMEs, respectively. In case of NFAME, however, there are 46 percent of shops, and followed by 44 percent of businesses and 10 percent VMIs have been found in the sample. Again, the group and individual classification under the NFAME gives 57.4 percent of GMEs and 50.5 percent of IMEs, respectively. Out of the total sample, GME is shared 49.5 percent and IME is 50.5 percent according to the total sample classification. The classification of GMEs and IMEs are almost in equal percent so that the data gives an unbiased distribution of sample population for the analysis.

In total, 116 SHGs are linked to all these enterprises. Out of which exclusive group economic activities are undertaken by 86 SHGs (Table 4). Samples are also drawn from SHGs (15) in which group activities as well as individual activities are found. These SHGs are doing a common business for all members and run by two to three members and rest of the members are also doing their individual business with borrowed fund from the group at the individual level. On an average 12 member per SHG are found and out of which 3 to 4 members are involved in individual economic activities and the rest of the members are doing agriculture activities.

TABLE 4

Sample Classification: Types of SHGs and Linkage Status

Categories	Number of SHGs involved in sample	No. of Economic Activities in GMEs	No. of Economic Activities in IMEs	Total Sample MEs
(a) Group Activity SHGs	86(74)	86	–	86
(b) *Mixed SHGs (Group & Indv.)	15(13)	15	58	73
(c) Individual Activity SHGs only	15(13)	–	45	45
Nature-wise SHGs/Members (a+b+c)	**116(100)**	**101**	**103**	**204**
(1) SHGs linked with RRB	22(19)	22	–	22
(2) SHGs linked with SBI	94(81)	79	103	182
Bank-wise SHGs/Members (1 + 2)	**116(100)**	**101**	**103**	**204**
(i) SGSY-SHGs	84(72)	69	57	126
(ii) Non-SGSY-SHGs	32(28)	32	46	78
Category-wise SHGs/Members (i + ii)	**116(100)**	**101**	**103**	**204**

Source: Field survey.

Note: Figures in brackets indicate percentage of Total Number.
*SHGs involved in group as well as individual activitie.

However, some of them are doing nothing except individual household works. Apart from these there are also 15 SHGs from which only individual enterprises are considered. So the sample profile is highly dominated by the group activities. Considering the large presence of SBI in the entire state more than 80 percent of the sample SHGs are linked to this bank and rest are with the lone RRB. Moreover, there is a bias distribution of RRB branches in the state that the entire Garo Hills is cut off from RRB during our survey period.

Since most of the samples are from West Garo Hills and where only SBI operates, this bias is obvious. Further, from the same Table 4 it is also observed the schematic classification of SHGs as they are selected for identifying the micro-enterprises formed under the SGSY and non-SGSY categories.

Sustainability Measurement of MEs

The microfinance programme is the programme to give a sustainable source of income to the rural poor people through the development of micro-enterprises. Nevertheless, their sustainability depends on the sustainability of economic activities carried out by these micro-entrepreneurs or groups. One of the indicators of sustainability is the consistency in its income generation activities. This is analyzed through the coefficient of variations of different business variables.

Another issue with sustainability is how the businesses of micro-enterprises are able to maintain the profitability in the long-run and remain financially viable after meeting various expenditures of their businesses. Therefore, in this study, the evaluation of profitability and self-sufficient positions of micro-enterprises is attempted with the help of important ratios and their trends over the period of three years data.

Consistency Test through Coefficient of Variations

The coefficient of variation (CV) reveals the variability and consistency of various important variables of enterprises that highlights the business status and their changing dynamics. Business parameters which shows higher CV have greater dispersion, thus are highly inconsistent than the one in which it is lower. The CV of the important parameters like sales, total income, total expenditure and

Table 5

Variations in Business Parameters of GMEs and IMEs

Variables	Coefficients of Variations					
	GMEs	GFAME	GNFAME	IMEs	IFAME	INFAME
Sales	19.58	11.00	31.63	51.44	39.23	58.27
Other Inc.	16.13	16.42	16.08	53.41	53.33	69.80
Interest Inc.	23.31	45.17	12.81	—	—	—
Total Inc.	15.44	6.57	26.70	50.73	38.32	57.82
Business Exps.	6.73	18.34	35.84	49.53	38.82	55.84
Operating Exps.	14.08	4.55	23.93	22.66	32.85	16.84
Interest paid	10.93	15.47	7.60	16.49	17.95	15.06
Total Exps.	3.19	14.26	25.04	46.33	36.09	52.54
NP/NL	46.35	59.26	30.92	125.19	125.16	125.31

Source: *Field Survey Note: Inc. = Income, Exps. = Expenses and NP/NL = Net profit/Net loss.*

TABLE 6

LT-wise Variations in Business Parameters of GMEs and IMEs

Variables	Coefficients of Variations						
	GMEs			IMEs			
	1LT	2LT	3LT	1LT	2LT	3LT	4LT
Sales	7.61	25.37	26.81	13.00	56.03	59.67	44.34
Other Inc.	11.99	16.23	46.26	49.94	58.82	66.75	32.60
Interest Inc.	20.53	36.04	6.33	—	—	—	—
Total Inc.	6.99	18.84	24.54	12.46	54.90	59.25	43.59
Business Exps.	8.23	15.50	16.01	13.95	55.05	57.73	41.47
Operating Exps.	16.41	18.30	15.04	18.15	35.47	22.96	11.16
Interest Exps.	26.21	12.08	19.67	33.90	12.21	28.09	21.60
Total Exps.	9.29	9.09	15.20	12.89	51.23	54.68	39.05
NP/NL40.87	46.62	69.42	157.78	109.08	127.26	137.06	

Source: *Field Survey Notes: LT = Times of Loan Taken by the Groups and Individual Members.*

net profit show varying degree of consistency across the categories of MEs (Table 5). In comparison to IMEs, GMEs show a better consistency in their operation. Though the overall variations across the parameters do not reveal any pattern for any concrete inference, the high CV for the net profit indicates inconsistent profitability of MEs.

The variability test in post loan taken situation of different MEs as depicted in Table 6 provides almost similar type of conclusion. IMEs are more inconsistent in their operations. Improved consistency has not been observed in case of MEs —those who have taken loan for more number of times. From these two tables it is very difficult to trace any indication of sustainability of economic activities undertaken by the MEs.

Trend Analysis of Profitability Ratios

The sustainability can be a buzzword but the permanency of micro-enterprises matters to give permanent job opportunities to micro-entreprenuers. Profits protect sustainablity (Schrciner M. J., 1997) and micro-enterprises need to earn profits for their permanency in the different economic and social environments. The permanency matters to regular flow of income to the micro-entrepreneurs to run their enterprise and family equally and also the status of dependancy need to be reduced on subsidised or donors' fund to make themselves self-sustainable. If a micro-enterprise can achieve this position then it would be a successful micro-enterprise through microfinance programme.

The setting up of micro-enterprises through the programme is to give permanent job opportunities to poor people, which is the intention of the governments, programmers and practitioners. Nevertheless, how far the micro-enterprises are sustainable to provide the permanent livelihood to micro-entrepreneurs depend on their income and profit. The profitability ratios are the second level of measures of the performance of the micro-enterprises. It implies positive true profits for the micro-entrepreneurs and favourable ratios indicate the entrepreneurs' ability to meet its business obligations and whereby they can achieve sustainable position without donors fund or subsidy supports from government.

The framework of the profitability ratios is the most common way to judge a micro-enterprise. A micro-enterprise does business primarily for profit. Therefore, its ultimate performance measure is profit. Profitability ratios measure profit in relative terms, with reference to either sales or assets or capital employed. These ratios tell how far a micro-enterprise is able to earn profit for all its capital so employed. Four profitability ratios, namely, operating expenses ratio, interest expenses ratio, net profit ratio and return on capital ratio are used to analyse the sustainability of micro-enterprises. Not all these ratios show the sustainability of micro-enterprises as such, since they provide only the annual picture of an enterprise. In that particular year, the enterprise may earn more or less profits due to certain market condition and under a set of risks. But these ratios cannot consider the cause of other factors of business fluctuations. But if these ratios are analysed over a periods can give an overall idea about the business performance of an entrepreneur and it helps to understand the sustainability of micro-enterprises.

(a) Operating Expenses Ratio (OER) = Operating Expenses / Total Income × 100. Where, Total Income = Total Sales + Other Income + Interest Income

(b) Interest Expenses Ratio (IER) = Total Interest Expenses / Total Income × 100

(c) Net Profits Ratio = Net Profit/ Total Income × 100.
Where, Net profit = Total Income – Total Expenses

(d) Return on Capital Ratio (ROCR) = Net Profit/Capital × 100.
Where, Capital = Average Equity Capital + Average Loan.

One of the major problems in the sustainability of these enterprises is that they spend a lot on maintaining the business. Petty administration, travel, stationery etc. take away a sizable share of the income, which reduces the profit margin for them. The trend of operating expenses to total income ratio for GMEs, presented in Table 7, clearly shows an improvement over the years. Apart from poultry business, all others have been managing their businesses with less expense. The overall ratio hovers around 5 percent for the GMEs, signifying a lesser percentage of income utilized for such expenditure.

Across all the types of activities, a similar trend has been observed for different GMEs. This indicates that over the years they have been able to cut down their expenditure. The share of OER is obviously small in case of IMEs because they do business at a very small scale and most of the labour charges are not paid to any outsider as the entrepreneur does most of the work by own self. The ratio has come down to around 0.75 percent from 2.75 percent (Table 9). This is definitely a better improvement in the management of expenditure, which contributes to overall profitability and which would help them in running the businesses smoothly and their sustainability for a long-run.

TABLE 7

Category-wise Operating Expenses Ratio (OER)

Category of MEs	Operating Expenses Ratio (OER)					
	GMEs			IMEs		
	2004	2005	2006	2005	2006	2007
(a) Piggery	4.53	3.61	3.80	2.77	2.93	0.76
(b) Poultry	32.38	29.92	17.55	3.17	2.93	1.26
(c) Goatery	7.09	9.82	12.07	2.41	2.38	0.41
(i) FAME (a+b+c)	**4.96**	**4.30**	**4.58**	**2.78**	**2.91**	**0.79**
(1) Business	8.19	6.32	12.36	2.75	2.24	0.71
(2) Shops	5.47	3.65	5.39	2.72	2.45	0.76
(3) VMI	13.86	3.81	5.18	2.41	2.06	0.71
(ii) NFAME (1+2+3)	**7.16**	**4.37**	**6.67**	**2.71**	**2.31**	**0.72**
Total (i +ii)	**5.78**	**4.33**	**5.56**	**2.74**	**2.55**	**0.75**

Source: *Field Survey*

Interest is the biggest burden to the microfinance-supported enterprises. Group pays interest almost at the market rate and sometimes more when non-bank intermediaries provide such finance. Similarly, individual members pay simple interest at least at the rate of 24 percent to the groups. In no case, microfinance is a cheap source. However, in Meghalaya, since most of SHGs are financed through commercial banks, the cost of fund remains low for the groups but not for the individuals. As observed from the Table 8 for GMEs the interest expenditure to income ratio has been decreasing over the years, which because of the fact that the income has been increasing at a faster rate than the interest expenses.

An overall decrease in IER is observed in case of both the categories of GMEs and IMEs and also across the activities of different categories. In case of IMEs this ratio also declines to around half of the percentage over the 2005 figures (Table 8). The loan balances decline over the period because of repayment of loan instalment and so the interest payment slides accordingly. The farm activities like poultry, goat rearing and piggery have a larger percentage of interest to their income in comparison to non-farm activities. Therefore, it indicates that the cost of capital in case of non-farm activities is much less than the farm activities though the FAMEs are having better margin of profits than the NFAMEs.

TABLE 8

Category-wise Interest Expenses Ratio (IER)

Category of MEs	Operating Expenses Ratio (OER)					
	GMEs			IMEs		
	2004	2005	2006	2005	2006	2007
(a) Piggery	19.00	17.47	11.28	9.84	6.89	5.81
(b) Poultry	1.68	2.84	2.10	14.54	10.22	13.01
(c) Goatery	33.71	38.89	28.80	8.55	10.18	10.56
(i) FAME (a+b+c)	**20.58**	**19.07**	**12.55**	**10.19**	**7.37**	**6.49**
(1) Business	27.92	16.22	14.97	8.59	6.02	3.28
(2) Shops	17.97	13.79	11.41	8.27	6.25	4.25
(3) VMI	62.23	25.17	20.71	8.57	6.37	6.61
(ii) NFAME (1+2+3)	**25.51**	**16.38**	**13.79**	**8.46**	**6.13**	**3.86**
Total (i +ii)	**22.43**	**17.78**	**13.13**	**9.14**	**6.62**	**4.69**

Source: *Field Survey*

TABLE 10

Category-wise Net Profit Ratio (NPR)

Category of MEs	Net Profit Ratio (NPR)					
	GMEs			IMEs		
	2004	2005	2006	2005	2006	2007
(a) Piggery	06.18	36.98	38.57	5.10	0.81	08.41
(b) Poultry	31.61	–3.75	08.76	–12.29	–4.82	–0.88
(c) Goatery	36.12	22.61	26.78	17.47	–5.71	0.42
(i) FAME (a+b+c)	**09.69**	**35.52**	**37.37**	**04.22**	**–0.04**	**07.48**
(1) Business	42.86	42.70	38.63	6.79	–0.58	14.71
(2) Shops	31.09	23.47	23.71	7.93	2.52	10.36
(3) VMI	-49.58	31.00	36.06	17.45	4.01	12.40
(ii) NFAME (1+2+3)	**26.72**	**29.73**	**28.80**	**08.17**	**0.95**	**13.16**
Total (i+ii)	**16.08**	**32.75**	**33.37**	**6.63**	**0.56**	**11.38**

Source: *Field Survey*

The NP ratios vary inconsistently over the years for both individual and group micro-enterprises (Table 9). This ratio indicates how the enterprises are using the income and how much margin of profits is left for future upgradation of businesses as well as for family expenditure of micro-entrepreneurs. All the activities under GMEs and IMEs have improved their profitability position; however, the margin is quite impressive in case of GMEs. On an average, the margin of profit for GMEs is more than three times than the profit of IMEs, which shows higher profitability of similar activities when undertaken under the aegis of group format. The scale of economies could be the one of the possible reasons of such phenomenon. Another observation from these figures is that profit margin has improved more consistently for GMEs than IMEs. This indicates toward a poor sustainability of the latter.

The ultimate indicator of profitability is the rate of return on the capital employed. The ratio of net profit to total capital indicates the overall efficiency of any entrepreneurial activity. The initial capital of micro-entrepreneur is always the loan provided by MFIs. Subsequently, profit is accumulated which forms the equity capital, known as capital fund. Therefore, capital fund and borrowed capital form the capital base of such enterprises. The ratio between these two is obviously titled towards debt because of the dominance of loan capital. The rate of returns earned by GMEs and IMEs are presented in Table 10. GMEs have shown a consistent increase in ROCR indicating a better sustainability in comparison to IMEs. Under both the group and individual format of enterprises, piggery has been the prime driver of farm activities. Individual enterprises show a very inconsistent trend of profitability because of two apparent reasons. One

TABLE 10

Category-wise Return on Capital Ratio (ROCR)

Category of MEs	Return on Capital Ratio (ROCR)					
	GMEs			IMEs		
	2004	2005	2006	2005	2006	2007
(a) Piggery	4.52	24.85	15.81	10.66	1.73	16.60
(b) Poultry	17.64	-0.19	6.43	-19.91	-9.73	-1.32
(c) Goatery	14.08	4.11	3.83	35.93	-8.16	0.52
(i) FAME (a+b+c)	**6.44**	**18.23**	**13.42**	**8.58**	**-0.08**	**14.19**
(1) Business	20.83	10.53	9.23	13.96	-1.12	32.54
(2) Shops	24.05	11.08	12.01	18.47	5.16	20.92
(3) VMI	-19.57	21.62	16.59	36.31	5.22	24.98
(ii) NFAME (1+2+3)	**16.13**	**11.89**	**11.85**	**17.61**	**1.83**	**28.05**
Total (i+ii)	**10.30**	**14.81**	**12.74**	**13.97**	**1.12**	**23.36**

Source: *Field Survey*

important reason is the lack of knowledge of managing business activities. Secondly, consumption of items for personal use is not accounted for in their businesses.

All the above-discussed ratios are revisited in the context of loan receiving status of the enterprises. After obtaining each of the loan instalments these ratios are calculated to see whether loan infusion do really bring some change in profitability and whether this change is consistent or not. It is found that among the GMEs those who have taken loan for the third time have shown better profitability. They have reduced their operating ratio, improved NP ratio and ROCR. This provides linking towards the possibility of an impact of microcredit on the performance of micro-enterprises. Almost similar trend is observed in case of IMEs also (Table 10).

Analysis of Self-sufficiency

The sustainability of micro-enterprises is basically the self-sustainability of micro-entrepreneurs. Those who are meeting goals now with subsidised funds at the preliminery stage and replace their captial status with market loans (formal credit from banks) for long-term these micro-enterprises need to be taken care of financial self-sustainabilty which is the most important to run a business with a view to maximise the profits and expansion of business in future for their sustainablity. along with the capacity to repay the market loans in time. Although the sustainability requires more than financial self-sufficiency the demand of pity micro-enterpises mostly intended to finance than the other factors of output of the enterprises. Both the operating self-sufficiency and financial sufficiency are crucial to judge the overall sustainability of enterprises.

Operating Self-sufficiency

While the financial self-sufficiency shows the ultimate position, the operating self-sufficiency shows the operating viability of an enterprise. Whether the income generated from the principal activity is sufficient, enough to cover the normal business expenditure of the businesses but it is very crucial with these enterprises. Sometimes business shows profit because of some other income, like interest income in case of group entities, which is not the true income from the operation for which the business is meant. This is captured though the Operating Self-Sufficiency Ratio (OSSR):

Operating Self-Sufficiency Ratio (OSSR) = (Total Sales + Any Other Income)/(Business Expenses + Any other Expenses).

The OSSR is an indication of a micro-enterprise's ability to generate revenue through its usual operating of economic activities to cover operating expenses such as business purchases, operating expenses, interest expenses and any other direct expenses relating to micro-enterprises. The OSSR does not give the complete information about the self-sustainability of micro-entrepreneurs. This ratio is just a part of measuring the self-sustainability. In a micro-enterprise—whether established under the microfinance programme or others—the ratio helps the entrepreneurs and even the analysts to find it out how the enterprise is financially sound and how day-to-day income is generating to operate the businesses well. Therefore, the calculation of OSSR is to understand and justify the business performance of MEs in the state and to give results in quantitative terms. We assume that if the OSSR shows a better position in any category of MEs then the business performance of MEs will be better in terms of operation, margin of profits and contribution to the household expenses of micro-entrepreneurs.

The Table 11 for GMEs and IMEs indicate that almost all the economic activities are operationally viable with the exception of poultry activity under GMEs. Piggery and VMI under GMEs show a much better ratio in comparison to other categories. On the other hand, all the activities under IMEs show almost similar ratios in each year but with an upward trend over the period.

TABLE 11

Category-wise Operating Self-sufficiency Ratios (OSSR)

Category of MEs	Operating Self-sufficiency Ratio (OSSR)					
	GMEs			IMEs		
	2004	2005	2006	2005	2006	2007
(a) Piggery	1.20	2.06	1.85	1.18	1.08	1.17
(b) Poultry	0.94	0.51	0.75	1.02	1.06	1.14
(c) Goatery	1.39	1.89	1.66	1.35	1.05	1.12
(i) FAME (a+b+c)	**1.21**	**2.02**	**1.82**	**1.17**	**1.08**	**1.16**
(1) Business	2.07	1.41	1.14	1.18	1.06	1.22
(2) Shops	1.52	1.35	1.36	1.19	1.10	1.17
(3) VMI	0.95	2.10	2.23	1.35	1.12	1.23
(ii) NFAME (1+2+3)	**1.52**	**1.47**	**1.44**	**1.20**	**1.08**	**1.21**
Total (i+ii)	**1.30**	**1.73**	**1.63**	**1.19**	**1.08**	**1.19**

Source: *Field Survey*

Financial Self-sufficiency

The problems of sustainability for micro-enterprises basically arise from the problems of financial self-sufficiency and it needs a yardstick to measure the financial self-sufficiency of micro-entreprneurs. The financial self-sufficiency of a micro-enterprise is the flow of funds which can come from the output of enterprises that is in term of 'profits'. Availability of profit for servicing the debt obligations (Debt Service Coverage Ratio, i.e. DSCR) is most important among the ratios. Apart from this the debt equity ratio (DER) is also another common indicator which indicates financial solvency position of MEs.

Debt Service Coverage Ratio (DSCR) = Profits available for Credit Servicing/Repayment of Debt installment alongwith Interest.

Where, Profits available for Debt Servicing = Net Profit + Depreciation and other Non-cash charges + Interest on loan (debt). Repayment of Debt instalment along with Interest = Loan Instalment + Interest on Loan.

The problems of sustainability arise how the business of micro-enterprises are able to cover the credit services provided by the financial institutions. The favourable DSCR is a good attraction to lenders, which also indicates the financial soundness of the enterprises. DSCR is calculated considering three years profits and indebted position of both categories of micro-enterprises i.e. group and individual MEs. The higher DSCR is an indicator of better credit rating of the enterprise. The DSCR is also the indicator of the ability of a micro-entrepreneur to pay-off current instalment and interest of loan out of profit. The higher the ratio better is the ability of the micro-entrepreneur to obtain the services of loans or credit. A ratio of equal to one indicates the capacity of the enterprise just to repay the loan amount and if the ratio is more than one it indicates soundness of business position of micro-entrepreneurs. Looking at the fragile nature of financial positions of micro-enterprises a ratio above 1.5 is considered ideal.

TABLE 12

Category-wise Debt Service Coverage Ratio (DSCR)

Category of MEs	Debt Service Coverage Ratio (DSCR)					
	GMEs			IMEs		
	2004	2005	2006	2005	2006	2007
(a) Piggery	1.16	2.14	1.90	0.63	0.51	1.37
(b) Poultry	0.39	-0.02	0.24	0.31	2.49	5.14
(c) Goatery	1.71	0.99	0.75	1.15	0.00	0.00
(i) FAME (a+b+c)	**1.25**	**1.91**	**1.66**	**0.65**	**0.56**	**1.48**
(1) Business	2.99	1.79	0.99	0.69	0.17	1.43
(2) Shops	1.98	1.44	1.30	0.58	0.43	1.22
(3) VMI	0.80	1.93	1.72	1.33	1.52	0.77
(ii) NFAME (1+2+3)	**2.22**	**1.63**	**1.28**	**0.68**	**0.28**	**1.27**
Total (i+ii)	**1.61**	**1.78**	**1.47**	**0.67**	**0.35**	**1.32**

Source: *Field Survey*

The DSCR under various activities of GMEs and IMEs are presented in Table 12. GMEs as a group enterprise show a comfortable ratio over the period of three years. Whereas activities like poultry and goat rearing under farm activities and 'business' category under non-farm activities are below the comfort level and the ratio is sliding year after year. This indicates poor sustainability of this category of activities during the period of our survey. IMEs are the worst performers in this front. Most of the activities are showing a ratio of below one, which is a threat to financial sustainability.

However, in case of IMEs, the trend of DSCR shows an upward trend and it indicates that individual micro-enterprises can reach the level over next few years. The subsidy component loans can be the best support for these types of MEs at the time of adverse DSCR. This (subsidy) can help the MEs at that time and can make credit relationship with financial institutions much better. In this case, the loan component under the SGSY scheme is the most favourable option to sustain their business activities during the period of adverse DSCR.

Debt equity ratio is another indicator, which shows composition of owned fund to outsider's fund. A high ratio obviously warrants more outflows in form of interest and thus reduces the net profit. As micro-enterprises promoted under micro-credit programme are mainly dependent on loan capital there is every possibility they show a high DER. Further, the formation of equity capital is very slow as small entrepreneurs withdraw almost the entire profit for personal consumption. Ploughing back of profit in the business—though considered ideal for any entrepreneurial activity does not so happen at very small scale of activities. Considering the nature of capital and equity of MEs a debt equity ratio is also discussed below and may be taken as an ideal to analyse the financial self-sufficiency position of MEs.

TABLE 13

Category-wise Debt Equity Ratio (DER)

Category of MEs	Debt Service Coverage Ratio (DSCR)					
	GMEs			IMEs		
	2004	2005	2006	2005	2006	2007
(a) Piggery	29.96	4.94	2.96	5.54	2.82	1.97
(b) Poultry	3.68	68.42	4.48	53.75	11.81	4.37
(c) Goatery	12.06	8.19	7.29	2.74	1.54	1.23
(i) FAME (a+b+c)	**22.88**	**5.99**	**3.42**	**5.95**	**3.02**	**2.07**
(1) Business	3.99	5.09	1.96	5.33	3.78	2.34
(2) Shops	3.70	4.56	2.41	4.48	2.67	1.85
(3) VMI	-17.64	80.91	5.28	2.72	1.73	1.64
(ii) NFAME (1+2+3)	**5.01**	**5.38**	**2.50**	**4.65**	**3.04**	**2.09**
Total (i +ii)	**9.94**	**5.65**	**2.97**	**5.11**	**3.03**	**2.08**

Source: *Field Survey*

Debt Equity Ratio (DER) = Average Loan/Average Equity Capital.

Where Average Loan = Opening Balance of Loans + Closing Balance of Loan/2. Average Equity capital = Opening Balance of Equity Capital + Closing Balance of Equity Capital/2.

Table 13 portrays the DER for both GMEs and IMEs, respectively. GMEs have shown improvement in their repayment and thus reduced their debt composition in the total to a large extent. Still, many activities like poultry, goat rearing and VMI have higher ratio than the desirable. IMEs, on the other hand, managed to operate with less loan capital. Their ratios are far low than the GMEs

TABLE 14

Category-wise Debt Equity Ratio (DER)

MEs		No. of Times Loan Taken	Profitability Ratios				Self-Sufficiency Ratios		
			OER	IER	NPR	ROCR	DSCR	OSSR	DER
GMEs	2004	1LT	5.05	21.61	18.74	18.92	1.98	1.40	8.20
		2LT	5.70	24.52	15.62	8.48	1.57	1.28	4.24
		3LT	7.83	17.51	11.26	3.25	1.04	1.14	2.47
	2005	1LT	5.08	14.76	39.80	16.45	2.02	1.86	2.73
		2LT	4.12	19.64	30.45	10.29	1.65	1.74	2.36
		3LT	3.64	17.77	27.11	14.61	1.79	1.52	4.33
	2006	1LT	6.64	11.78	33.53	13.27	1.62	1.57	1.73
		2LT	5.45	13.43	30.28	9.86	1.31	1.57	2.04
		3LT	4.15	14.35	42.40	10.24	1.77	1.99	1.15
IMEs	2005	1LT	2.85	0.00	12.28	28.32	0.68	1.12	6.06
		2LT	2.77	0.49	14.21	32.71	0.58	1.15	5.11
		3LT	2.69	0.28	17.03	36.59	0.77	1.19	4.47
		4LT	2.73	0.00	16.24	36.27	0.61	1.17	4.51
	2006	1LT	2.63	0.15	8.41	13.93	3.08	1.06	3.04
		2LT	3.19	1.98	7.28	14.53	0.54	1.05	2.82
		3LT	2.45	2.24	4.20	8.35	0.22	1.04	2.60
		4LT	1.97	1.74	3.95	7.61	0.36	1.03	2.95
	2007	1LT	1.40	0.00	11.50	17.80	1.03	1.14	1.59
		2LT	0.73	1.32	12.98	27.26	1.07	1.15	2.06
		3LT	0.68	1.51	15.16	31.10	1.41	1.18	1.77
		4LT	0.71	2.98	15.19	28.12	1.56	1.21	2.07

Source: *Field Survey*

and have shown much better improvement by the time they reach the third year of operation. A ratio of 2.08 for the entire IMEs is ideal. Low ratio among IMEs is because of their small loan size, which they repay within the same year.

Self-sufficiency ratios are also calculated as per the loan receiving status of the enterprises. Ratios of operational and financial self-sufficiency in post loan taken situations are presented in Table 14 for GMEs and IMEs, respectively. It is found that among the GMEs those who have taken loan for one time or twice during the study period have not improved either the DSCR or the OSSR ratios. Only DER has shown some improvement. Marked improvement across all the ratios of GMEs are, however, observed in case of three time loan takers.

Findings

Sustainability of MEs depends on the sustainability of economic activities carried out by these micro-entrepreneurs or groups. One of the indicators of sustainability is the consistency in its income generation activities. Another issue with sustainability is how the businesses of micro-enterprises are able to maintain the profitability in the long-run and remain financially viable after meeting various expenditures of the business. The CV of the important parameters like sales, total income, total expenditure and net profit show varying degrees of consistency across the categories of MEs. In comparison to IMEs, GMEs show a better consistency in their operation. The high CV for the net profit indicates inconsistent profitability of MEs. The variability test in post loan taken situation of different MEs provides almost similar type of conclusion. IMEs are more inconsistent in their operations. Improved consistency has not been observed in case of MEs those who have taken loan for more number of times.

One of the major problems in the sustainability of these enterprises is that they spend a lot on maintaining the business. Petty administration, travel, stationary etc takes away a sizable share of the income, which reduces the profit margin for them. The trend of operating expenses to total income ratio for GMEs, shows an improvement over the years. Apart from poultry business, all others have been managing their businesses with less expense. The overall ratio hovers around 5 percent for the GMEs, signifying a lesser percentage of income utilized for such expenditure. Across all the types of activities GMEs have been able to cut down their expenditure. The share of OER is obviously small in case of IMEs, which has come down from 2.74 percent to around 0.75 percent during the year 2007.

Interest is the biggest burden to the microfinance supported enterprises. Group pays interest almost at the market rate and sometimes more when non-bank intermediaries provide such finance and individual members pay simple interest which fluctuates from 12 to 24 percent annually depending upon the decision and rates as charged by the groups. In no case, microfinance is a cheap source. However, in Meghalaya, since most of SHGs are financed through commercial banks, the cost of fund remains low for the groups but not for the individuals. For GMEs the interest expenditure to income ratio has been decreasing over the years, which is because of the fact that the income has been increasing at a faster rate than the interest expenses. In case of IMEs this ratio also declines to around half of the percentage over the 2005 (9.14 percent). The farm activities like poultry, goat rearing and piggery have a larger percentage of interest to their income in comparison to non-farm activities. The share of interest in case of non-farm activities is much less than the farm activities.

The NP ratios vary inconsistently over the years for both individual and group micro-enterprises. All the activities under GMEs and IMEs have improved their profitability position; however, the margin is quite impressive in case of GMEs (37 percent for 2006). On an average, the margin of profit GMEs is three times of IMEs, which show higher profitability of similar activities when undertaken under the aegis of group format. The scale of economies could be the one of the plausible reasons of such phenomenon. Another observation from these figures is that profit margin has improved more consistently for GMEs than IMEs. This indicates toward a poor sustainability of the latter. However, those MEs who have taken loans more than twice have shown an upward trend of NPR and it was 11.26 percent in 2004 and 42.40 percent in 2006, respectively.

It is observed that almost all the economic activities are operationally viable with the exception of poultry activity under GMEs. Piggery and VMI under GMEs show a much better OSSR ratio in comparison to others. On the other hand, all the activities under IMEs show almost similar ratios in each year but with an upward trend over the period. GMEs as a group enterprise show a comfortable ratio over the period of three years. Whereas activities like 'poultry' and 'goat rearing' under farm activities and 'business' under non-farm activities are below the comfort level and the ratios are sliding year after year. This indicates poor sustainability of these activities. IMEs are the worst performers in this front. Most of the activities are showing a ratio of below one, which is a threat to financial sustainability. GMEs have shown improvement in their repayment and have thus reduced their debt composition in the total to a large extent. Still many activities like poultry, goat rearing and VMI have higher DER than desirable. IMEs, on the other hand, managed to operate with less loan capital. Their ratios are far lower than the GMEs and have shown much better improvement by the time they reached the third year of operation. A ratio of 2.08 for the entire IMEs is ideal. Low ratio among IMEs is because of their small loan size, which they repay within the same year and investment in the businesses is also very small, wherefrom they cannot expect a bigger margin of returns.

Conclusion

Though the development of microfinance programme for the benefits of poor people, carries some disadvantage, the overall benefits from the programme is better than the other programmes of rural development. The different sources of flow of micro-credit in the country have the positive effect on the development of poor people but the success is a step behind from the beneficiaries' performance to grasp the benefits of micro-credit. The GMEs and IMEs are totally dependent on credit, so it is the formal credit and the improvement of the microfinance programme to shape the future business status of micro-entrepreneurs in the state. Moreover, the cooperative efforts in regards to financial performance of the existing enterprises need to be satisfied to enhance the linking position to a better stage and also supporters' ability to cooperate with the needs of micro-entrepreneurs in a long-term basis are most important for the success of the programme as well as the sustainability of MEs in the state. Participants should urge to create convenient and permanent mechanism to provide financial services, which can give better performance and good impact of credit on a long-term basis. This will help the groups or individual micro-enterprises to achieve a better shape of sustainability in their businesses and which will also help to develop rural economy in the state.

References

1. Barry, Nancy, Armacost, Nicola and Kawas Celina, (1996): "Putting Poor people's Economics at the Center of Urban Strategies", Women's World Banking, New York.
2. Conning, Jonathan, (1999): "Outreach, sustainability and leverage in monitored and peer-monitored lending", Journal of Development Economics, Vol. 60, Pp. 51-77.
3. Rhyne, E., (1998): "The yin and yang of microfinance: reaching the poor and sustainability", In Christen R.P., McDonald, J. Eds., The Microbanking Bulletin, Vol. II. The Economics Institute, Boulder, 1.
4. Satish, P., (2005): "Mainstreaming of Microfinance", Economic and Political Weekly, 40(17), Pp. 1731-1739.
5. Schreiner, Mark Joseph, (1997): "A Framework for the Analysis of the Performance and Sustainability of Subsidized University, Grameen Bank of Bangladesh," unpublished Ph.D. dissertation, Columbus: The Ohio State Microfinance Organizations with Application to BancoSol of Bolivia.
6. www.microfinance.com

24

The Role of Microfinance in Developing Micro-enterprise in North East India

K. Lalromawia

Abstract: *Microfinance is considered a viable tool for reaching the unreached. It has access to all societies in developmental activities hitherto overlooked because of various reasons. Micro-credit is a part of microfinance, which is the provision of financial services to the very poor, apart from loans; it includes savings, micro-insurance and other financial innovations. The inclusion of the neglected into the mainstream of the society through microfinance initiative has been widely recognized in almost all parts of the world. The paper analyzed how microfinance has helped in nurturing micro-enterprise in north east India and what are the needs for further development. The economic condition of north east was studied and the developmental barrier was found. It also finds out how microfinance would break those barriers.*

Introduction

Microfinance is the extension of very small loans (micro-loans) to the unemployed, to poor entrepreneurs and to other living in poverty that is not bankable. These individuals lack collaterals, steady employment and a verifiable credit history and, therefore, cannot meet even the most minimal qualifications to gain access to traditional credit. Micro-credit is a part of microfinance, which is the provision of financial services to the very poor, apart from loans; it includes savings, micro-insurance and other financial innovations.

"Little drops of water makes a mighty ocean" — the growth and development of micro-enterprises would lead to the development of the whole economy. They outnumber the large one in every corner of the globe. Micro-enterprises have a direct bearing on the operations of the country. From micro-enterprises, entrepreneurs get inspiration to start large units, which have wider impact on the economy as a whole.

The North East India

India's Northeast, also known as the Land of the Seven Sisters, comprises the States of Arunachal Pradesh, Assam, Manipur, Meghalaya, Mizoram, Nagaland and Tripura, which collectively account for about 8 per cent of the country's geographical area and roughly 4 per cent of its population. The region is known for its ethnic, linguistic, cultural, religious and physiographical diversity. On the one hand, the region is diverse and heterogeneous. On the other, it is quite homogeneous; the social stratification found in other parts of the country is not present in the Northeast. The tribal societies in the hill areas are egalitarian. As a result, the type of poverty found in many other parts of India does not exist in most of the hilly States of the region.

Economy of North East India

The main economy of the North-East region is dependent on agriculture and allied activities. Due to under development of industry and service sector, there has not been much change in the main occupancy of the region in last decades. In comparison to the hilly areas the valleys are economically more developed in the region and the Brahmaputra valley—the nerve centre of economic activities. The indigenous people dominate the population composition in four states viz. Meghalaya, Nagaland and Arunachal Pradesh and Mizoram. There are differences among the seven states in the North-East region with respect to their resource endowments, level of industrialization as well as infrastructural facilities. The industrial sector has mainly grown around tea, timber in Assam and mining, sawmills and plywood factories in other parts of the region. The economy of the region is still primarily agrarian but its full potential is yet to be exploited. Since agriculture and industry has not really taken off in spite of the potential in the form of vast unexploited resource base available in the region, the pressure for employment is on the service sector.

Economic Problems Faced by North East India

The region is grossly deficient of infrastructure to tap the available resources and push the economy forward. An examination of the infrastructure index–a composite profile of the availability of physical, social and institutional infrastructure available in the states—revealed that all the states of the region are at the lowest rung of the infrastructure index ladder. It shows that the level of infrastructural development in the region is almost negligible.

Small-scale industries will be the backbone of the future economy of North East India. The distance of the region from the main commercial centres and the difficulties in transportation will inevitably lead to a greater focus on the small scale and cottage industries like agro-industries and handicrafts. Compared to the large-scale industries these are ecologically friendly, easy to set up and invest in and easy to transport. Therefore, for entrepreneurs, it is the small scale and cottage industries which will prove to be a lucrative area for investment. More importantly, focusing on items that are tourist oriented or export oriented will be of great advantage.

It is, therefore, imperative that the small scale and cottage industries provide a boost to the much-needed development of the region. This becomes more significant when one takes into account the future operation of India's "Look East Policy" where the economy of North East India will be integrated with that of the South East Asian Economy. It can thus be aptly described as the "Gateway to the East" where the movement of goods and people across the border will be the main economic development indicators in the future of the region.

Role of Microfinance in Developing Micro-enterprise

As we know, North East India region has to face a number of problems in order to carry out a large scale industry or business due to the diverse culture, landscape, insurgency, political problem, transportation and all type of infrastructure problem. The only way to create employment and to develop the region is harnessing on the micro-enterprise.

Micro-entrepreneurs in North East India

Microfinance is important to rural entrepreneurs for agriculture, but, under conditions of increasing diversification, even more so for non-agricultural enterprises. Microfinance thus comprises all segments of the rural population. In fact, non-agricultural activities often complement agricultural income and labor flows and, hence, help build livelihood stability and growth. It is further argued that rural financial services actually become much better if we take the micro-specificity away and concentrate on sustainable financial services to a wider array of rural households and businesses. This increases institutional viability, reduces unit costs for services to the poorest and helps finance not only other poor but other important rural actors including – truckers, agribusinesses, side businesses, etc. all of which have an important role to play in rural development.

What is the Need of Micro-entrepreneurs?

Quality is of crucial importance. Quality (together with standardization and packaging) is crucial throughout the commodity chain and in the process of adding value. Each commodity has its own range of opportunities for adding value and improving quality. In the case of meat, hides, leather, this starts with the quality of livestock and its veterinary care, which has a bearing on the post-processing of meat and leather. The major needs are training of producers in clean production and processing, quality awareness and quality management, capacity-building, access to finance, accurate information, and essential utilities and services. For a substantial improvement in the processing and marketing of leather, better cooperation between private producers, producer associations, commercial institutions, government agencies and donors is required. Another example is perishable fruits and vegetables. Depending on seasonal and regional variation, many developing countries produce an excess of tomatoes, yet import large quantities of tomato concentrate. There may also be a seasonal abundance of fruit like mangoes, much of which, in the absence of processing facilities, is lost. The drying and processing of fruits and vegetables would offer solutions to these problems. The preservation and processing of fruits and vegetables adds value, generates employment, and improves diet. Key issues are: Is processing worthwhile? And can farmers supply the material on a regular basis? Can economies of scale be achieved? Value creation requires the planning of diversified processing of several fruits and vegetables over the year to maximize plant utilization; intermediate-scale processing through contract farming and the pooling of producers; the use of locally available raw materials and appropriate technologies to minimize capital expenditure and, at the same time, maximize product quality. Success factors are adequate training, the quality of raw material, and market analysis. The history of financing is full of failures. The sector needs experienced micro-entrepreneurs linked to farmers who are willing and able to grow fruits and vegetables, thereby guaranteeing:

- A steady source of supply
- Appropriate risk management, such as spreading production over several fruits and vegetables
- Good linkages between producers and processors
- Financial engineering comprising savings mobilization as a basis for self-financing
- The provision of investment capital
- A balancing of individual and group lending technologies
- A legal framework for sanctions against defaulters.

Strategies for Financial Institution

Focus must be on sustainable financial institutions with sustainable financial services, combining credit with savings as a service to customers and as a source of loanable funds, thus moving away from credit-only provided through projects and programmes. Any MFI, bank or micro-bank striving for sustainability must: mobilize their own resources, apply appropriate lending technologies, provide attractive loan products with appropriate interest rates, have their loans repaid, manage their risks, make a profit, finance the growth of outreach from the growth of savings and profits, and through advocacy strive for a conducive policy and legal environment. Evidence to the contrary in the old world of development finance notwithstanding, sustainable MFIs in the new world of development finance, with appropriate risk management technologies, have demonstrated their ability to lend to the agricultural sector including producers, processors and traders at low default rates and high profits. The number of such institutions has substantially increased in recent years: in all ownership categories, including government-owned banks, private and community-based rural banks, and various types of MFIs. Networks and associations of MFIs and banks have a crucial role to play in disseminating the positive experience and developing support strategies in cooperation with government and donor agencies.

Issues and Recommendations

No single player can take the development of rural enterprise and microfinance fully into his own hands, as coordinated interventions are far more likely to be successful. Single players can sometimes achieve great things; but coordinated interventions are far more likely to be successful. Great care is to be taken that interventions do not do more harm than good. This can be the case with well-meaning interest subsidies which may undermine institutional viability; and grants which may discourage local resource mobilization.

1. ***Local resources mobilization:*** Savings mobilization strengthens the self-reliance and self-financing capacity of rural entrepreneurs, at the same time freeing their credit absorptive capacity for larger loans and investments.
2. ***Equity:*** Domestic resources can be effectively mobilized through equity instead of deposits by shareholder-driven RMFIs. Equity provided by external investors may bridge liquidity shortages and leverage own resources.
3. ***Legal framework for local financial institution:*** A legal framework is important for establishing deposit-taking local financial institutions (micro-banks) as self-reliant institutions which can grow dynamically on the basis of local resource mobilization (savings, equity, retained earnings). Such regulated financial institutions would be fully integrated within the formal financial sector.
4. ***Effective supervision:*** The growth of sustainable RMFIs(Rural Micro-finance Institutions) and sustainable financial services is contingent upon effective supervision. Supervision of RMFIs, whether deposit-taking or equity-driven, is crucial; supervision must be effective, i.e., able and willing to suspend or close non-performing RMFIs.
5. ***MFI-Bank linkages:*** Linkages provide a full range of banking services, including safe-keeping of deposits, access to bank credit, liquidity balancing, equity participation, money transfer, check clearing, payments, monitoring and supervision. Proposal: Support model projects of horizontal networking among non-formal MFIs, including SHGs in remote areas (with incentives-driven upgrading), and vertical linkages with banks.

6. ***Cooperation and co-financing:*** Co-financing of studies and programmes with research funding agencies and international development agencies would not only increase the flow of funds; it would also bridge the gap between basic and applied research; this would lead to more relevant and more systematic research as well as better communication and coordination between the worlds of research and development.

Conclusion

The economic benefits of sustainable micro-entrepreneurship in North East are compelling, and its potential effects on the development process are equally promising. In terms of development and social impact, the microfinance industry allows significant improvements in quality of life for the micro-entrepreneurs of the North East. They can now stabilize the cash flow of their economic activity, bringing security to the enterprise. This allows them to better manage spending, which often generates savings; and this provides better standards of living to their family and dependants in terms of housing, nutrition, health and education. Finally, an access to banking and increased security promotes a sense of entrepreneurship, and thus their self-esteem and reputation increase. Furthermore, estimates indicate that today only 5% of the micro-credit demand is fulfilled, thus, the microfinance industry is expected to grow significantly in the coming years. Despite several challenges ahead, this emerging industry and the process of sustainable micro-entrepreneurship combine to offer a potential alleviation solution to the poverty crisis of the 21st century,—and into a sustainable future.

References

1. World Bank, 2003, "India: Scaling-up Access to Finance for the Rural Poor"
2. Yunus, Muhammad, 1994: Grameen Bank, "Major Uses of Loan Funds", Bangladesh (1994); and Extracts from the keynote address delivered at 85Rotary International Convention help in Taipei, Taiwan, on June 12, 1994
3. Hickson, Robert, 2001, "Financial Services for the Very Poor – Thinking Outside the Box", Small Enterprise Development 12, no. 2 (2001)
4. Micro-enterprise Development and possibilities by ASEED
5. Vatta. K. (2003), "Microfinance and Poverty Allevation". Economic and Political Weekly. 38 (5): 432-433.
6. The World Bank Group, 2001, "Microfinance and Small- and Medium-Sized Enterprises"
7. www.worldbank.org/wbi/banking/microfinance.
8. www.nedfi.com
9. www.dhriiti.com
10. www.syngentafoundation.com

Some exciting gifts are up for grabs with this book!!

MICROFINANCE REVOLUTION IN INDIA

Success and Sustainability

J U Ahmed, D Bhagat and G Singaiah

FREE Gifts Rs. 1000/-

DEAR READERS

By now you must have gone through this book in the entirety. So we invite your assessment on this title with absolute impartiality and candid observations. After all, we publishers blindly depend on your benchmarking. Friends, please fill up the open spaces below with CAPITAL LETTERS. You may add some extra sheets of paper if the space provided is not sufficient for you.

i. What are the important topics of your syllabus which are not adequately covered in this book?

ii. In which chapters and on what topics the treatment of the subject-matter by the author is not satisfactory and why?

iii. Have you come across the typos, factual inaccuracies, inconsistencies, and other forms of mistakes in the book? If yes, then please specify the mistakes and page numbers.

iv. Name top three books on the same subject, which, in your consideration, are better than this book. Could you provide some reasons?

Your 1st Preference: ....

Your 2nd Preference: ....

Your 3rd Preference: ....

v. Any suggestion to improve the quality of illustrations, diagrams etc.?

vi. How did you like the cover design? Any suggestions on colours?

vii. Suggestions for further improvement of production standard:

viii. Who recommended you this book:

☐ Teacher ☐ Friend ☐ Parents ☐ Bookseller ☐ Librarian

ix. Name of the person who has recommended:

Designation: ....

Address: ....

Phone No.: ....

e-mail: ....

x. Name and address of the bookseller from whom you have purchased this book:

....

....

....

xi. Name and address of the library where you would like to find the book:

....

....

xii. Name and address of your institution (Please mention the University or Board):

....

....

xiii. Your name, e-mail, and complete postal address:

....

....

....

xiv. A few other titles published by us that you would like to read:

....

....

The best assessment will be rewarded half-yearly. The award will be in the form of our publications, as decided by the Editorial and Marketing Operations Division, amounting to Rs. 1000/- (Rupees one thousand) only.

....

Please mail the filled up coupon at your earliest to :

Editorial & Marketing Operations Division

NEW CENTRAL BOOK AGENCY (P) LTD

8/1 Chintamoni Das Lane, Kolkata 700 009

West Bengal, INDIA

Ph. No.: 033 + 22418411, 22418573, 22419094

Fax: 033 + 22419573, 22413852

e-mail: ncbapvtltd@eth.net, ncba@cal2.vsnl.net.in

Website: www.centralgroup.com